Enduring
Issues
in
Sociology

Other Books in the Enduring Issues Series:

Criminology
Philosophy
Psychology
Religion

Enduring
Issues
in
Sociology

Lynn Barteck
Karen Mullin

David L. Bender, *Publisher*
Bruno Leone, *Executive Editor*

Bonnie Szumski, *Series Editor*

Lynn Barteck and Karen Mullin, *Book Editors*,
University of Cincinnati

Greenhaven Press, Inc., San Diego, CA 92198-9009

Library of Congress Cataloging-in-Publication Data

Enduring issues in sociology / Lynn Barteck & Karen Mullin, book editors.
    p.   cm.   — (Enduring issues series)
    Includes bibliographical references and index.
    ISBN 1-56510-258-4 (lib. bdg.) — ISBN 1-56510-257-6 (pbk.)
    1. Sociology. I. Barteck, Lynn   . II. Mullin, Karen
. III. Series.
HM51.E54   1995
301—dc20   94-24938
                                               CIP

Copyright © 1995 by Greenhaven Press, Inc.
P.O. Box 289009, San Diego, CA 92198-9009
Printed in the U.S.A.

Contents

Chapter 3: Does Inequality Exist?

Chapter 4: How Do Institutions Work?

Chapter 5: How Do Societies Change?

FOREWORD

"When a thing ceases to be a subject of controversy, it ceases to be a subject of interest."

William Hazlitt

The Enduring Issues Series is based on the concept that certain fundamental disciplines remain interesting and vibrant because they remain controversial, debatable, and mutable. Indeed, it is through controversy that these disciplines were forged, and through debate that they continue to be defined.

Each book in the Enduring Issues Series aims to present the most seminal and thought-provoking issues in the most accessible way—by pitting the founders of each discipline against one another. This running debate style allows readers to compare and contrast major philosophical views, noting the major and minor areas of disagreement. In this way, the chronology of the formation of the discipline itself is traced. As American clergyman Lyman Beecher argued, "No great advance has ever been made in science, politics, or religion, without controversy."

In an effort to collect the most representative opinions of these disciplines, every editor of each book in the Enduring Issues Series has been chosen for his or her expertise in presenting these issues in the classroom. Each editor has chosen the materials for his or her book with these goals in mind: 1) To offer, both to the uninitiated and to the well read, classic questions answered by the leading historical and contemporary proponents. 2) To create and stimulate an interest and excitement in these academic disciplines by revealing that even in the most esoteric areas there are questions and views common to every person's search for life's meaning. 3) To reveal the development of ideas, and, in the process, plant the notion in the reader's mind that truth can only be unearthed in thoughtful examination and reexamination.

The editors of the Enduring Issues Series hope that readers will find in it a launching point to do their own investigation and form their own opinions about the issues raised by these academic disciplines. Because it is in the continued contemplation of these questions that these issues will remain alive.

Introduction

Compared with other sciences, sociology is a relatively new discipline. Early speculation about the operation of society and interpersonal behavior came from philosophy, literature, and religion and produced an idealized view of the way society and relationships *should* operate. Not until the nineteenth century did scholars begin to suggest that society could and should be studied scientifically. Now, sociologists divide the study of society into five main areas: social theory, interpersonal behavior, stratification, institutions, and social change.

Early statements about the nature of society, such as the first three in Chapter 1, helped to define sociology as a legitimate academic field. Karl Marx, Emile Durkheim, and Max Weber made influential and opposing statements that formed a basis for the subsequent three general perspectives in sociology: structural functionalism, conflict theory, and symbolic interaction. Over time, other theorists built on or reacted to these early foundations. Based on Durkheim's theory, Talcott Parsons developed the structural-functional view that society is best studied as a stable system of interdependent and harmoniously functioning parts. Conflict theory, based on Marx and extended by Ralf Dahrendorf, emphasizes class conflict and social change. Symbolic interaction, as defined by George Mead and influenced by Georg Simmel, focuses on development of the self and interpersonal behavior.

Once sociologists established viable alternative ways of thinking about society, they could examine explanations for interpersonal behavior. One explanation maintains that socialization is the most important influence because people learn acceptable social behavior from others. Within this view, some contend that through the family and educational institutions, children are indoctrinated by the next generation. Other sociologists argue that people actively interpret the socializing efforts of others throughout their lives. A second explanation is that people take their cues on how to behave from others who occupy the same social structure as their own. Anthropologist Ralph Linton defined the sociological concepts of status and role to describe these positions and related behavior, and others expanded the concepts to apply to larger units of analysis—families, small groups, organizations, and nations.

A third explanation claims that interaction in small groups—with emphasis on rewards and punishments, conformity, or impression management—best explains social behavior.

Stratification theories about the source and nature of inequality continue to provoke sociological and political debate, even as many people deny that inherent inequality exists. From a traditionally functionalist perspective, inequality benefits society by assuring that all necessary tasks are performed by people best suited to perform them. In opposition, conflict theorists ask "who gets what and why?" and assert that society treats whole categories of people differently based solely on their observable physical characteristics. Taking a third perspective on the issue, Robert Merton considers how prejudicial attitudes and discriminatory actions perpetuate inequality.

Institutions—organized ways of solving ongoing social problems—develop in all societies and sociologists study the institutions from opposing viewpoints that reflect current political debates. In keeping with their stratification arguments, functionalists claim that stable family roles benefit both society and the family itself, while conflict theorists examine whether family structure consistently benefits some members over others. Many sociologists agree with Durkheim's claim that religious beliefs unite society, while others document the divisive religious influences of the past. Especially when united against a common enemy, the religious elements of patriotism (civil religion) produce unification. Much study has been devoted to the economic and political institutions, including the ideas of oligarchy (the tendency for power to become concentrated in the hands of a few people), capitalist control over workers, and elite control over society.

Many of the enduring sociological issues above describe and explain social order and social structure—but sociologists also investigate and develop theory about social change. Most sociologists agree that societies evolve from simpler to more complex forms, but hold opposing viewpoints on identifying the causes of this evolution. One idea is that change in a stable social system must come from outside that system. Others argue for the influence of elements within social systems: collective behavior, a capitalist economy, or technology.

In choosing the issues and viewpoints for this collection, we selected those that represent the core of sociological thought. We hope that readers will join us in marveling that the ones written as long ago as the last century continue to apply to modern life. Social theory has advanced considerably by building on the ideas presented in these viewpoints. Understanding basic sociological viewpoints provides a good foundation for further study and for facing the challenges of living in a complex and rapidly changing society. These viewpoints also help readers develop what C. W. Mills called a "sociological imagination"—a way of connecting individual experience with the history, structure, and influence of the larger society. Development of a sociological imagination characterizes both the focus of sociology and the intent of this book.

How Is Society Possible?

CHAPTER PREFACE

Sociology developed as a science in the nineteenth century. Thomas Hobbes, a nineteenth-century English philosopher, argued that the "natural state" of humanity is a "war of every man, against every man" leading to life that is "solitary, poor, nasty, brutish, and short." This conclusion led Hobbes to ask: How, then, is society possible at all? If individual self-interest perpetually leads to conflict, how do social order and organization occur?

Auguste Comte (1789-1857), who coined the term "sociology," proposed that the new science should study the question, "How is society possible?" by following the pattern established for other sciences. Science begins with empirical observation and discovers laws about structure and change. Comte founded sociology based on the idea that society is composed of individuals in the same way as a line is composed of points. In studying the properties of a line, the focus must be on the collection of points; observations of society must focus on collections of individuals. Even though individuals differ, sociologists study the patterns of organization and social behavior that exist within and across societies. Based on Comte's concept of "social statics," sociologists study stable social structure and organization, and Comte's "social dynamics" led sociologists to study changes in society.

Since Comte's time, sociologists have developed three main ways to investigate answers to the question "How is society possible?": structural-functionalism, conflict theory, and symbolic interaction. Interest in enduring social structure and organization led to the development of the structural-functional perspective: Society is a system of coordinated institutions that solve ongoing social problems. Agreement on shared values and use of socialization to indoctrinate new members make society possible and stable. Structural-functionalists emphasize social order and equilibrium: Any change in one part of society leads to orderly matching change in the other parts.

A second way to answer the question of how society is possible directly contradicts Hobbes's view. Conflict theorists argue that human nature is basically harmonious. As societies develop, competition and power differences override these natural human tendencies and generate conflict. From this viewpoint, society is composed of stratified classes with conflicting values and interests that compete for scarce resources. Economic competition makes society possible, since those with economic power also control dominant values and norms. Conflict theorists focus on the social changes produced by conflict, and study the ways that each social form evolves into the next.

Both the structural-functional and conflict perspectives take the "macro" view of society as a social system. Symbolic interactionists have formulated the third answer to the question of how society is possible using a "micro" perspective to study patterns of interaction between individuals and groups. They study the way people communicate using language and gestures to transmit and share values and ideas. This communication is the basis for society: People interact to develop the shared meaning that makes society possible. Symbolic interactionists try to understand how people define situations and how they interpret their own and others' actions. Interaction with others leads to the development of self—an awareness of individuality within a larger society.

Although each of the three major perspectives answers questions about society differently, each provides a useful social analysis. As an example, why do most people walk on the right side of the sidewalk, even though walking on the sidewalk is not regulated by law? Structural-functionalists would argue that people walk on the right because they have been taught to do so by parents socialized to drive on the right. Conflict theorists would say that pedestrians stay on the right side, especially when sidewalks are crowded, because they fear being jostled (or worse) by someone larger and more powerful (social control). Symbolic interactionists would take the view that pedestrians interactively develop a shared understanding of the meaning of staying to the right. Each explanation offers additional, and not necessarily contradictory, insight.

Discussions of society in this chapter come from some of the founders of sociology: Marx, Durkheim, Weber, Simmel, Mead, Parsons, and Dahrendorf. Although the founders interpreted society somewhat differently, together they establish a basis for all students of society. To study society, we must know about class (Marx), solidarity (Durkheim), beliefs (Weber), interaction (Simmel), the self (Mead), how the social parts fit together (Parsons), and conflict and change (Dahren-dorf). In the process of defining society, these theorists also developed the three perspectives described above. Although the reading may be difficult, remember many of these writings were written in another language (German or French) and in another century. When these authors use the term "man," they mean to indicate all persons.

Most ideas from these viewpoints have survived to form a foundation for current sociological thought. As you read the viewpoints, consider how remarkably applicable they are to modern society. Evidence from current everyday life supports Marx's discussion of alienation from work, Durkheim's observations on social crisis, and Weber's explanation for accumulation of wealth. People still broaden their exposure to others different from themselves through their organizational affiliations as Simmel suggests, and people gain identity through meaning shared by a community as Mead argues. Daily media reports support Dahrendorf's characterization of conflict as a vehicle for social change. Think about which current events each theory can best explain and how the theories could combine to usefully explain current social conditions.

Class Conflict Defines Society

KARL MARX

Karl Marx (1818-1883) studied philosophy and considered himself a political activist, but he also developed many ideas important to sociology. Human nature is basically harmonious, he thought, but is corrupted by the advance of civilization, which leads to human competition and conflict. Marx argued that all societies are based on human physical needs that are satisfied as humans produce what they need to live from the environment. Work satisfies both physical and creative needs. As the technology required to produce sustenance advances, new needs emerge as the former needs are satisfied in a cycle of production and consumption. Because modern production operates through a hierarchical and expanded division of labor, however, owners exploit the working class. As a result, workers become alienated from the products of their labor. Put another way, a worker no longer makes a chair or a pair of shoes in which pride of ownership can be felt and through which creativity can be expressed. Workers own nothing but their own labor power and can no

From Karl Marx and Frederick Engels, *Manifesto of the Communist Party*, authorized English translation. New York: International Publishers, 1948. Copyright 1948 by International Publishers Co., Inc. Reprinted with permission.

longer provide for their own physical needs. They must depend on owners of the means of production for sustenance. Because of this dependence, owners (Marx's "bourgeoisie") can establish the cultural values that workers (Marx's "proletariat") must accept.

By this "real process of production," bourgeoisie values dominate and become the basis for social order. As an example, think about the legitimate authority of employers to regulate the way employees live. For further illustration, think of the well-known axiom "a fair day's work for a fair day's pay" and notice the direction of emphasis. Because they own the means of production, the small bourgeoisie segment forms the dominant class in society, oppressing and exploiting the much larger proletariat working class. Marx said society rests on the foundation of this economic substructure from which all other social institutions arise—government, religion, family, and education.

QUESTIONS

1. One important idea from Marx is that each societal form contains elements of the previous form along with factors leading to its own destruction. What remnants of feudal society does Marx say capitalist society contains?
2. Marx says capitalism leads workers to become alienated from their work. How does he say this happens?
3. According to Marx, how will class consciousness develop and how will it lead to the fall of capitalism? Do you see any evidence of this happening?

The history of all hitherto existing society is the history of class struggles.

Freeman and slave, patrician and plebeian, lord and serf, guildmaster and journeyman, in a word, oppressor and oppressed, stood in constant opposition to one another, carried on an uninterrupted, now hidden, now open fight, a fight that each time ended, either in a revolutionary reconstitution of society at large, or in the common ruin of the contending classes.

In the earlier epochs of history, we find almost everywhere

a complicated arrangement of society into various orders, a manifold gradation of social rank. In ancient Rome we have patricians, knights, plebeians, slaves; in the Middle Ages, feudal lords, vassals, guild-masters, journeymen, apprentices, serfs; in almost all of these classes, again, subordinate gradations.

The modern bourgeois society that has sprouted from the ruins of feudal society, has not done away with class antagonisms. It has but established new classes, new conditions of oppression, new forms of struggle in place of the old ones.

Our epoch, the epoch of the bourgeoisie, possesses, however, this distinctive feature: It has simplified the class antagonisms. Society as a whole is more and more splitting up into two great hostile camps, into two great classes directly facing each other—bourgeoisie and proletariat.

From the serfs of the Middle Ages sprang the chartered burghers of the earliest towns. From these burgesses the first elements of the bourgeoisie were developed.

The discovery of America, the rounding of the Cape, opened up fresh ground for the rising bourgeoisie. The East Indian and Chinese markets, the colonization of America, trade with the colonies, the increase in the means of exchange and in commodities generally, gave to commerce, to navigation, to industry, an impulse never before known, and thereby, to the revolutionary element in the tottering feudal society, a rapid development.

The Industrial Revolution

The feudal system of industry, in which industrial production was monopolized by closed guilds, now no longer sufficed for the growing wants of the new markets. The manufacturing system took its place. The guild-masters were pushed aside by the manufacturing middle class; division of labor between the different corporate guilds vanished in the face of division of labor in each single workshop.

Meantime the markets kept ever growing, the demand ever rising. Even manufacture no longer sufficed. Thereupon, steam and machinery revolutionized industrial production. The place of manufacture was taken by the giant, modern industry, the place of the industrial middle class, by industrial millionaires—the leaders of whole industrial armies, the modern bourgeois.

Modern industry has established the world market, for which the discovery of America paved the way. This market has given an immense development to commerce, to navigation, to communication by land. This development has, in its turn, reacted on the extension of industry; and in proportion as industry, commerce, navigation, railways extended, in the same proportion the bourgeoisie developed, increased its capital, and pushed into the background every class handed down from the Middle Ages.

We see, therefore, how the modern bourgeoisie is itself the product of a long course of development, of a series of revolutions in the modes of production and of exchange.

Each step in the development of the bourgeoisie was accompanied by a corresponding political advance of that class. An oppressed class under the sway of the feudal nobility, it became an armed and self-governing association in the medieval commune; here independent urban republic (as in Italy and Germany), there taxable "third estate" of the monarchy (as in France); afterwards, in the period of manufacture proper, serving either the semi-feudal or the absolute monarchy as a counterpoise against the nobility, and, in fact, cornerstone of the great monarchies in general—the bourgeoisie has at last, since the establishment of modern industry and of the world market, conquered for itself, in the modern representative state, exclusive political sway. The executive of the modern state is but a committee for managing the common affairs of the whole bourgeoisie.

The bourgeoisie has played a most revolutionary role in history.

The bourgeoisie, wherever it has got the upper hand, has put an end to all feudal, patriarchal, idyllic relations. It has pitilessly torn asunder the motley feudal ties that bound man to his "natural superiors," and has left no other bond between man and man than naked self-interest, than callous "cash payment." It has drowned the most heavenly ecstasies of religious fervor, of chivalrous enthusiasm, of philistine sentimentalism, in the icy water of egotistical calculation. It has resolved personal worth into exchange value, and in place of the numberless indefeasible chartered freedoms, has set up that single, unconscionable freedom—Free Trade. In one word, for exploitation, veiled by religious and political illusions, it has substituted naked, shameless, direct, brutal exploitation.

The bourgeoisie has stripped of its halo every occupation hitherto honored and looked up to with reverent awe. It has converted the physician, the lawyer, the priest, the poet, the man of science, into its paid wage-laborers. . . .

The Bourgeoisie Expands and Advances

The bourgeoisie cannot exist without constantly revolutionizing the instruments of production, and thereby the relations of production, and with them the whole relations of society. Conservation of the old modes of production in unaltered form, was on the contrary, the first condition of existence for all earlier industrial classes. Constant revolutionizing of production, uninterrupted disturbance of all social conditions, everlasting uncertainty and agitation distinguish the bourgeois epoch from all earlier ones. All fixed, fast-frozen relations, with their train of ancient and venerable prejudices and opinions, are swept away, all new-formed ones become antiquated before they can ossify. All that is solid melts into air, all that is holy is profaned, and man is at last compelled to face with sober senses his real conditions of life and his relations with his kind.

The need of a constantly expanding market for its products chases the bourgeoisie over the whole surface of the globe. It must nestle everywhere, settle everywhere, establish connections everywhere.

The bourgeoisie has through its exploitation of the world market given a cosmopolitan character to production and consumption in every country. To the great chagrin of reactionaries, it has drawn from under the feet of industry the national ground on which it stood. All old-established national industries have been destroyed or are daily being destroyed. They are dislodged by new industries, whose introduction becomes a life and death question for all civilized nations, by industries that no longer work up indigenous raw material, but raw material drawn from the remotest zones; industries whose products are consumed, not only at home, but in every quarter of the globe. In place of the old wants, satisfied by the production of the country, we find new wants, requiring for their satisfaction the products of distant lands and climes. In place of the old local and national seclusion and self-sufficiency, we have intercourse in every direction, universal inter-dependence of nations. And as in material, so also in intellectual production. The intellectual creations of individual nations become common property. National one-sidedness and narrow-mindedness become more and more impossible, and from the numerous national and local literatures there arises a world literature.

The bourgeoisie, by the rapid improvement of all instruments of production, by the immensely facilitated means of communication, draws all nations, even the most barbarian, into civilization. The cheap prices of its commodities are the heavy artillery with which it batters down all Chinese walls, with which it forces the barbarians' intensely obstinate hatred of foreigners to capitulate. It compels all nations, on pain of extinction, to adopt the bourgeois mode of production; it compels them to introduce what it calls civilization into their midst, i.e., to become bourgeois themselves. In a word, it creates a world after its own image.

The bourgeoisie has subjected the country to the rule of the towns. It has created enormous cities, has greatly increased the urban population as compared with the rural, and has thus rescued a considerable part of the population from the idiocy of rural life. Just as it has made the country dependent on the towns, so it has made barbarian and semi-barbarian countries dependent on the civilized ones, nations of peasants on nations of bourgeois, the East on the West.

More and more the bourgeoisie keeps doing away with the scattered state of the population, of the means of production, and of property. It has agglomerated population, centralized means of production, and has concentrated property in a few hands. The necessary consequence of this was political centralization. Independent, or but loosely connected provinces, with separate interests, laws, governments, and systems of taxation, became lumped together into one nation, with one government, one code of laws, one national class interest, one frontier, and one customs tariff.

The bourgeoisie, during its rule of scarce one hundred years has created more massive and more colossal productive forces than have all preceding generations together. Subjection of nature's forces to man, machinery, application of chemistry to industry and agriculture, steam-navigation, railways, electric telegraphs, clearing of whole continents for cultivation, canalisation of rivers, whole populations conjured out of the ground—what earlier century had even a presentiment that such productive forces slumbered in the lap of social labour?

Economic Change Promotes Social Change

We see then that the means of production and of exchange, which served as the foundation for the growth of the bourgeoisie, were generated in feudal society. At a certain stage in the development of these means of production and of exchange, the conditions under which feudal society produced and exchanged, the feudal organisation of agriculture and manufacturing industry, in a word, the feudal relations of property became no longer compatible with the already developed productive forces; they became so many fetters. They had to be burst asunder; they were burst asunder.

Into their place stepped free competition, accompanied by a social and political constitution adapted to it, and by the economic and political sway of the bourgeois class.

A similar movement is going on before our own eyes. Modern bourgeois society with its relations of production, of exchange and of property, a society that has conjured up such gigantic means of production and of exchange, is like the sorcerer who is no longer able to control the powers of the nether world whom he has called up by his spells. For many a decade past the history of industry and commerce is but the history of the revolt of modern productive forces against modern conditions of production, against the property relations that are the conditions for the existence of the bourgeoisie and of its rule. It is enough to mention the commercial crises that by their periodical return put the existence of the entire bourgeois society on trial, each time more threateningly. In these crises a great part not only of the existing products, but also of the previously created productive forces, are periodically destroyed. In these crises there breaks out an epidemic that, in all earlier epochs, would have seemed an absurdity—the epidemic of over-production. Society suddenly finds itself put back into a state of momentary barbarism; it appears as if a famine, a universal war of devastation had cut off the supply of every means of subsistence; industry and commerce seem to be destroyed. And why? Because there is too much civilization, too much means of subsistence, too much industry, too much commerce. The productive forces at the disposal of society no longer tend to further the development of the conditions of bourgeois property; on the contrary, they have become too powerful for these conditions, by which they are fettered, and no sooner do they overcome these fetters than they bring disorder into the whole of bourgeois society, endanger the existence of bourgeois property. The conditions of bourgeois society are too narrow to comprise the wealth created by them. And how does the bourgeoisie get over these crises? On the one hand, by enforced destruction of a mass of productive forces; on the other, by the conquest of new markets, and by the more thorough exploitation of the old ones. That is to say, by paving the way for more extensive and more destructive crises, and by diminishing the means whereby crises are prevented.

The weapons with which the bourgeoisie felled feudalism to the ground are now turned against the bourgeoisie itself.

Exploitation Produces Alienation

But not only has the bourgeoisie forged the weapons that bring death to itself; it has also called into existence the men who are to wield those weapons—the modern working class—the proletarians.

In proportion as the bourgeoisie, i.e., capital, is developed, in the same proportion is the proletariat, the modern working class developed—a class of laborers, who live only so long as they find work, and who find work only so long as their labor increases capital. These laborers, who must sell themselves piecemeal, are a commodity, like every other article of commerce, and are consequently exposed to all the vicissitudes of competition, to all the fluctuations of the market.

Owing to the extensive use of machinery and to division of labor, the work of the proletarians has lost all individual character, and, consequently, all charm for the workman. He becomes an appendage of the machine, and it is only the most simple, most monotonous, and most easily acquired knack, that is required of him. Hence, the cost of production of a workman is restricted, almost entirely, to the means of subsistence that he requires for his maintenance, and for the propagation of his race. But the price of a commodity, and therefore also of labor, is equal to its cost of production. In proportion, therefore, as the repulsiveness of the work increases, the wage decreases. Nay more, in proportion as the use of machinery and division of labor increases, in the same proportion the burden of toil also increases, whether by prolongation of the working hours, by increase of the work exacted in a given time, or by increased speed of the machinery, etc.

Modern industry has converted the little workshop of the patriarchal master into the great factory of the industrial capitalist. Masses of laborers, crowded into the factory, are organized like soldiers. As privates of the industrial army they are placed under the command of a perfect hierarchy of officers and sergeants. Not only are they slaves of the bourgeois class, and of the bourgeois state; they are daily and hourly enslaved by the machine, by the over-looker, and, above all, by the individual bourgeois manufacturer himself. The more openly this despotism proclaims gain to be its end and aim, the more petty, the more hateful and the more embittering it is.

The less the skill and exertion of strength implied in manual labor, in other words, the more modern industry develops, the more is the labor of men superseded by that of women. Differences of age and sex have no longer any distinctive social validity for the working class. All are instruments of labor, more or less expensive to use, according to their age and sex.

No sooner has the laborer received his wages in cash, for the moment escaping exploitation by the manufacturer, than he is set upon by the other portions of the bourgeoisie, the landlord, the shopkeeper, the pawnbroker, etc. . . .

The social conditions of the old society no longer exist for the proletariat. The proletarian is without property; his relation to his wife and children has no longer anything in common with bourgeois family relations; modern industrial labor, modern subjection to capital, the same in England as in France, in America as in Germany, has stripped him of every trace of national character. Law, morality, religion, are to him so many bourgeois prejudices, behind which lurk in ambush just as many bourgeois interests.

Revolt of the Proletarians

All the preceding classes that got the upper hand, sought to fortify their already acquired status by subjecting society at large to their conditions of appropriation. The proletarians cannot become masters of the productive forces of society, except by abolishing their own previous mode of appropriation, and thereby also every other previous mode of appropriation. They have nothing of their own to secure and to fortify; their mission is to destroy all previous securities for, and insurances of, individual property.

All previous historical movements were movements of minorities, or in the interest of minorities. The proletarian movement is the self-conscious, independent movement of the immense majority, in the interest of the immense majority. The proletariat, the lowest stratum of our present society, cannot stir, cannot raise itself up, without the whole superincumbent strata of official society being sprung into the air.

Though not in substance, yet in form, the struggle of the proletariat with the bourgeoisie is at first a national struggle. The proletariat of each country must, of course, first of all settle matters with its own bourgeoisie.

In depicting the most general phases of the development of the proletariat, we traced the more or less veiled civil war, raging within existing society, up to the point where that war breaks out into open revolution, and where the violent overthrow of the bourgeoisie lays the foundation for the sway of the proletariat.

Hitherto, every form of society has been based, as we have already seen, on the antagonism of oppressing and oppressed classes. But in order to oppress a class, certain conditions must be assured to it under which it can, at least, continue its slavish existence. The serf, in the period of serfdom, raised himself to membership in the commune, just as the petty bourgeois, under the yoke of feudal absolutism, managed to develop into a bourgeois. The modern laborer, on the contrary, instead of rising with the progress of industry, sinks deeper and deeper below the conditions of existence of his own class. He becomes a pauper, and pauperism develops more rapidly than population and wealth. And here it becomes evident, that the bourgeoisie is unfit any longer to be the ruling class in society, and to impose its conditions of existence upon society as an overriding law. It is unfit to rule because it is incompetent to assure an existence to its slave within his slavery, because it cannot help letting him sink into such a state, that it has to feed him, instead of being fed by him. Society can no longer live under this bourgeoisie, in other words, its existence is no longer compatible with society.

The essential condition for the existence and sway of the bourgeois class, is the formation and augmentation of capital; the condition for capital is wage-labor. Wage-labor rests exclusively on competition between the laborers. The advance of industry, whose involuntary promoter is the bourgeoisie, replaces the isolation of the laborers, due to competition, by their revolutionary combination, due to association. The development of modern industry, therefore, cuts from under its feet the very foundation on which the bourgeoisie produces and appropriates products. What the bourgeoisie therefore produces, above all, are its own grave-diggers. Its fall and the victory of the proletariat are equally inevitable.

Social Solidarity Defines Society

EMILE DURKHEIM

Emile Durkheim (1858-1917) said a broad consensus on values keeps order in society. Early agricultural societies had a relatively simple social structure with little division of labor. Most people performed the same kinds of work: farming and the work necessary to provide for the needs of their households. Social solidarity was based on shared norms and values, and Durkheim called this "mechanical" solidarity. In complex modern societies each person does specialized work. Auto mechanics, physicians, plumbers, teachers, and accountants each depend on the others for their particular knowledge. This functional interdependence produces solidarity through differences, what Durkheim called "organic" solidarity.

In this viewpoint, Durkheim uses the term "moral" differently from our current modern usage (like all work translated from another language, subtleties of meaning may change). When we talk about something that is "moral," we refer to judgments about whether something is good or bad. When Durkheim uses the word "moral," he means the extent to which members of society interact and the basis for that interaction. Durkheim claimed that there are two basic and equally valuable reasons for human interaction: shared culture and functional interdependence. In agricultural societies, most households were self-sufficient; each household could and usually did produce everything its members needed— food, clothing, and shelter. Social interaction between households was not strictly required for survival. Such social solidarity as did exist arose from interaction based on shared norms and values. Religious and community social events are examples of this kind of interaction.

In complex modern societies, increased division of labor forces functional interdependence: members must depend on and communicate with others. The basis for interaction changes from the old shared culture to mutual functional need. Members of society become more geographically mobile and autonomous, reducing the impact of the former traditional culture that more tightly controlled those who spent their entire lives in one place. A "moral crisis" occurs when people try to apply traditional values to a society where the division of labor is changing.

In the final section of this viewpoint, Durkheim points out that change in the common culture ("morality") does *not* arise from individual choice or through promotion by liberal academics. Instead, the need for cultural change arises from change in the division of labor. Further, he suggests that the crisis will be resolved when a new morality develops based on the current social reality. Is this work applicable to today's "moral crisis"?

QUESTIONS

1. How does Durkheim describe "social solidarity"?
2. According to Durkheim, how does the "collective conscience" differ in mechanical and organic societies?
3. What reasons does Durkheim give for arguing that "higher societies can maintain themselves in equilibrium only if labor is divided"?

29

If there is one rule of conduct which is incontestable, it is that which orders us to realize in ourselves the essential traits of the collective type. Among lower peoples, this reaches its greatest rigor. There, one's first duty is to resemble everybody else, not to have anything personal about one's beliefs or actions. In more advanced societies, required likenesses are less numerous; the absences of some likenesses, however, is still a sign of moral failure. Of course, crime falls into fewer different categories; but today, as heretofore, if a criminal is the object of reprobation, it is because he is unlike us. Likewise, in lesser degree, acts simply immoral and prohibited as such are those which evince dissemblances less profound but nevertheless considered serious. Is this not the case with the rule which common morality expresses when it orders a man to be a man in every sense of the word, which is to say, to have all the ideas and sentiments which go to make up a human conscience? No doubt, if this formula is taken literally, the man prescribed would be man in general and not one of some particular social species. But, in reality, this human conscience that we must integrally realize is nothing else than the collective conscience of the group of which we are a part. For what can it be composed of, if not the ideas and sentiments to which we are most attached? Where can we find the traits of our model, if not within us and around us? If we believe that this collective ideal is that of all humanity, that is because it has become so abstract and general that it appears fitting for all men indiscriminately. But, really, every people makes for itself some particular conception of this type which pertains to its personal temperament. Each represents it in its own image. Even the moralist who thinks he can, through thought, overcome the influence of transient ideas, cannot do so, for he is impregnated with them, and no matter what he does, he finds these precepts in the body of his deductions. That is why each nation has its own school of moral philosophy conforming to its character.

On the other hand, we have shown that this rule had as its function the prevention of all agitation of the common conscience, and, consequently, of social solidarity, and that it could accomplish this role only by having a moral character. It is impossible for offenses against the most fundamental collective sentiments to be tolerated without the disintegration of society, and it is necessary to combat them with the aid of the particularly energetic reaction which attaches to moral rules.

But the contrary rule, which orders us to specialize, has exactly the same function. It also is necessary for the cohesion of societies, at least at a certain period in their evolution. Of course, its solidarity is different from the preceding, but though it is different, it is no less indispensable. Higher societies can maintain themselves in equilibrium only if labor is divided; the attraction of like for like less and less suffices to produce this result. If, then, the moral character of the first of these rules is necessary to the playing of its role, it is no less necessary to the second. They both correspond to the same social need, but satisfy the need differently, because the conditions of existence in the societies themselves differ. . . .

The Purpose of Laws Describes Societies

Perhaps we can even generalize further in this matter.

The requirements of our subject have obliged us to classify moral rules and to review the principal types. We are thus in a better position than we were in the beginning to see, or at least to conjecture, not only upon the external sign, but also upon the internal character which is common to all of them and which can serve to define them. We have put them into two groups: rules with repressive sanctions, which may be diffuse or organized, and rules with restitutive sanctions. We have seen that the first of these express the conditions of the solidarity, *sui generis*, which comes from resemblances, and to which we have given the name mechanical; the second, the conditions of negative solidarity and organic solidarity. We can thus say that, in general, the characteristic of moral rules is that they enunciate the fundamental conditions of social solidarity. Law and morality are the totality of ties which bind each of us to society, which make a unitary, coherent aggregate of the mass of individuals. Everything which is a source of solidarity is moral, everything which forces man to take account of other men is moral, everything which forces him to regulate his conduct through something other than the striving of his ego is moral, and morality is as solid as these ties are numerous and strong. We can see how inexact it is to define it, as is often done, through liberty. It rather consists in a state of dependence. Far from serving to emancipate the individual, or disengaging him from the environment which surrounds him, it has, on the contrary, the function of making him an integral part of a whole, and, consequently, of depriving him of some liberty of movement. We sometimes, it is true, come across people not without nobility who find the idea of such dependence intolerable. But that is because they do not perceive the source from which their own morality flows, since these sources are very deep. Conscience is a bad judge of what goes on in the depths of a person, because it does not penetrate to them.

Morality Is Group Solidarity

Society is not, then, as has often been thought, a stranger to the moral world, or something which has only secondary repercussions upon it. It is, on the contrary, the necessary condition of its existence. It is not a simple juxtaposition of individuals who bring an intrinsic morality with them, but rather man is a moral being only because he lives in society, since morality consists in being solidary with a group and varying with this solidarity. Let all social life disappear, and moral life will disappear with it, since it would no longer have any objective. The state of nature of the philosophers of the eighteenth century, if not immoral, is, at least, *amoral*. Rousseau himself recognized this. Through this, however, we do not come upon the formula which expresses morality as a function of social interest. To be sure, society cannot exist if its parts are not solidary, but solidarity is only one of its conditions of existence. There are many others which are no less necessary and which are not moral. Moreover, it can happen that, in the system of ties which make up morality, there are some which are not useful in themselves or which have power without any relation to their degree of utility. The idea of utility does not enter as an essential element in our definition.

As for what is called individual morality, if we understand by that a totality of duties of which the individual would, at the same time, be subject and object, and which would link him only to himself, and which would, consequently, exist even if he were solitary,—that is an abstract conception which has no relation to reality. Morality, in all its forms, is never met with except in society. It never varies except in relation to social conditions. To ask what it would be if societies did not exist is thus to depart from facts and enter the domain of gratuitous hypotheses and unverifiable flights of the imagination. The duties of the individual towards himself are, in reality, duties towards society. They correspond to certain collective sentiments which he cannot offend, whether the offended and the offender are one and the same person, or whether they are distinct. . . .

Solidarity and Duty in Organic Societies

But not only does the division of labor present the character by which we have defined morality; it more and more tends to become the essential condition of social solidarity. As we advance in the evolutionary scale, the ties which bind the individual to his family, to his native soil, to traditions which the past has given to him, to collective group usages, become loose. More mobile, he changes his environment more easily, leaves his people to go elsewhere to live a more autonomous existence, to a greater extent forms his own ideas and sentiments. Of course, the whole common conscience does not, on this account, pass out of existence. At least there will always remain this cult of personality, of individual dignity of which we have just been speaking, and which, today, is the rallying-point of so many people. But how little a thing it is when one contemplates the ever increasing extent of social life, and, consequently, of individual consciences! For, as they become more voluminous, as intelligence becomes richer, activity more varied, in order for morality to remain constant, that is to say, in order for the individual to remain attached to the group with a force equal to that of yesterday, the ties which bind him to it must become stronger and more numerous. If, then, he formed no others than those which come from resemblances, the effacement of the segmental type would be accompanied by a systematic debasement of morality. Man would no longer be sufficiently obligated; he would no longer feel about and above him this salutary pressure of society which moderates his egoism and makes him a moral being. This is what gives moral value to the division of labor. Through it, the individual becomes cognizant of his dependence upon society; from it come the forces which keep him in check and restrain him. In short, since the division of labor becomes the chief source of social solidarity, it becomes, at the same time, the foundation of the moral order.

We can then say that, in higher societies, our duty is not to spread our activity over a large surface, but to concentrate and specialize it. We must contract our horizon, choose a definite task and immerse ourselves in it completely, instead of trying to make ourselves a sort of creative masterpiece, quite complete, which contains its worth in itself and not in the services that it renders. Finally, this specialization ought to be pushed as far as the elevation of the social type, without assigning any other limit to it. No doubt, we ought so to work as to realize in ourselves the collective type as it exists. There are common sentiments, common ideas, without which, as has been said, one is not a man. The rule which orders us to specialize remains limited by the contrary rule. Our conclusion is not that it is good to press specialization as far as possible, but as far as necessary. As for the part that is to be played by these two opposing necessities, that is determined by experience and cannot be calculated *a priori*. It is enough for us to have shown that the second is not of a different nature from the first, but that it also is moral, and that, moreover, this duty becomes ever more important and pressing, because the general qualities which are in question suffice less and less to socialize the individual. . . .

The Social Crisis

It has been said with justice that morality—and by that must be understood, not only moral doctrines, but customs—is going through a real crisis. What precedes can help us to understand the nature and causes of this sick condition. Profound changes have been produced in the structure of our societies in a very short time; they have been freed from the segmental type with a rapidity and in proportions such as have never before been seen in history. Accordingly, the morality which corresponds to this social type has regressed, but without another developing quickly enough to fill the ground that the first left vacant in our consciences. Our faith has been troubled; tradition has lost its sway; individual judgment has been freed from collective judgment. But, on the other hand, the functions which have been disrupted in the course of the upheaval have not had the time to adjust themselves to one another; the new life which has emerged so suddenly has not been able to be completely organized, and above all, it has not been organized in a way to satisfy the need for justice which has grown more ardent in our hearts. If this be so, the remedy for the evil is not to seek to re-suscitate traditions and practices which, no longer responding to present conditions of society, can only live an artificial, false existence. What we must do to relieve this anomy is to discover the means for making the organs which are still wasting them-selves in discordant movements harmoniously concur by in-troducing into their relations more justice by more and more extenuating the external inequalities which are the source of the evil. Our illness is not, then, as has often been believed, of an intellectual sort; it has more profound causes. We shall not suffer because we no longer know on what theoretical notion to base the morality we have been practicing, but because, in certain of its paths, this morality is irremediably shattered, and that which is necessary to us is only in process of formation. Our anxiety does not arise because the criticism of scholars has broken down the traditional explanation we use to give to our duties; consequently, it is not a new philosophical system which will relieve the situation. Because certain of our duties are no longer founded in the reality of things, a breakdown has resulted which will be repaired only in so far as a new disci-pline is established and consolidated. In short, our first duty is to make a moral code for ourselves. Such a work cannot be im-provised in the silence of the study; it can arise only through it-self, little by little, under the pressure of internal causes which make it necessary. But the service that thought can and must render is in fixing the goal that we must attain. That is what we have tried to do.

Ideas Define Society

MAX WEBER

Max Weber (1864-1920) was a German professor of law and
economics who said that to understand the way societies
work, we must understand the meanings individuals attribute to their behavior (*verstehen*). While Marx argued for
social activism, Weber argues that scientific research must be
value-free and researchers must not allow their personal biases to affect their work. In addition to his basic argument
that class conflict defines social structure, Marx argued that
the ruling class sets the norms and values that determine the
way members of society think. In what has been termed a
"debate with the ghost of Marx," Weber argues that ideas determine social structure, rather than structure determining
ideas as Marx claimed.

To illustrate his argument, Weber describes one case in
which ideas preceded and promoted the development of social structure. He argues that Protestantism existed before the
capitalist economic institution became dominant. Capitalism
was a natural outcome of Protestant beliefs, including predes-

tination, Martin Luther's concept of a "calling," rationalism, and asceticism. Early Protestants believed that their salvation was predestined—determined from the beginning of life. This belief led them to believe that no one (such as a priest) could effectively intercede for them and this promoted an individualist perspective. A second result of the predestination belief was that people searched for a "sign of divine grace" to indicate what their fate would be. They believed that material success was one such sign. A "calling" is the belief that each person has a divine mandate to perform some earthly duty, and God is best served by working hard at the assigned task.

Early Protestants believed in rational thought instead of emotion and unthinking acceptance of religious doctrine. Adult rather than infant baptism and Bibles printed in the common language rather than Latin demonstrate this belief. Elimination of music and elaborate ritual from their religious services illustrate asceticism, which was most fully developed in the Puritan belief that God should be worshiped with work, not song.

Weber argues that these Protestant ideas combine to produce the Protestant ethic: a belief that work, logical thought, and plain living are moral virtues and that idleness and indulgence are sinful. People would continuously work hard because work is moral, use cost/benefit analyses as a basis for economic decisions, and reinvest rather than spending on luxuries. The probable outcome of such a lifestyle would be accumulation of wealth. Weber concludes that wealth soon became an end in itself and the basis for early capitalism.

QUESTIONS

1. What is the meaning of the term "asceticism" as Weber uses it?
2. According to the way Weber describes the Protestant ethic, is accumulation of wealth good or bad?
3. If capitalism arose from Christian ideas, how does Weber explain the lack of religious domination in modern culture?

■ ■ ■

The Spirit of Capitalism

"He that spends a groat a day idly, spends idly above six pounds a year, which is the price for the use of one hundred pounds.

"He that wastes idly a groat's worth of his time per day, one day with another, wastes the privilege of using one hundred pounds each day.

"He that idly loses five shillings' worth of time, loses five shillings, and might as prudently throw five shillings into the sea.

"He that loses five shillings, not only loses that sum, but all the advantage that might be made by turning it in dealing which by the time that a young man becomes old, will amount to a considerable sum of money."

—Benjamin Franklin

In order to understand the connection between the fundamental religious ideas of ascetic Protestantism and its maxims for everyday economic conduct, it is necessary to examine with especial care such writings as have evidently been derived from ministerial practice. For in a time in which the beyond meant everything, when the social position of the Christian depended upon his admission to the communion, the clergyman, through his ministry, Church discipline, and preaching, exercised an influence which we modern men are entirely unable to picture. In such a time the religious forces which express themselves through such channels are the decisive influences in the formation of national character. . . .

[Within Puritan ethics] wealth as such is a great danger; its temptations never end, and its pursuit is not only senseless as compared with the dominating importance of the Kingdom of God, but it is morally suspect. Here asceticism seems to have turned much more sharply against the acquisition of earthly goods than it did in Calvin, who saw no hindrance to the effectiveness of the clergy in their wealth, but rather a thoroughly desirable enhancement of their prestige. Hence he permitted them to employ their means profitably. Examples of the condemnation of the pursuit of money and goods may be gathered without end from Puritan writings, and may be contrasted with the late mediæval ethical literature, which was much more open-minded on this point.

Moreover, these doubts were meant with perfect seriousness; only it is necessary to examine them somewhat more closely in order to understand their true ethical significance and implications. The real moral objection is to relaxation in the security of possession, the enjoyment of wealth with the consequence of idleness and the temptations of the flesh, above all of distraction from the pursuit of a righteous life. In fact, it is only because possession involves this danger of relaxation that it is objectionable at all. For the saints' everlasting rest is in the next world; on earth man must, to be certain of his state of grace, "do the works of him who sent him, as long as it is yet day." Not leisure and enjoyment, but only activity serves to increase the glory of God, according to the definite manifestations of His will.

Waste of time is thus the first and in principle the deadliest of sins. The span of human life is infinitely short and precious to make sure of one's own election. Loss of time through sociability, idle talk, luxury, even more sleep than is necessary for health, six to at most eight hours, is worthy of absolute moral condemnation. It does not yet hold, with Franklin, that time is money, but the proposition is true in a certain spiritual sense. It is infinitely valuable because every hour lost is lost to labour for the glory of God. Thus inactive contemplation is also valueless, or even directly reprehensible if it is at the expense of one's daily work. For it is less pleasing to God than the active performance of His will in a calling. Besides, Sunday is provided for that, and it is always those who are not diligent in their callings who have no time for God when the occasion demands it.

Accordingly, [the Puritan ethic] is dominated by the continually repeated, often almost passionate preaching of hard, continuous bodily or mental labour. It is due to a combination of two different motives. Labour is, on the one hand, an approved ascetic technique, as it always has been in the Western Church, in sharp contrast not only to the Orient but to almost all monastic rules the world over. It is in particular the specific defence against all those temptations which Puritanism united under the name of the unclean life, whose role for it was by no means small. The sexual asceticism of Puritanism differs only in degree, not in fundamental principle, from that of monasticism; and on account of the Puritan conception of marriage, its practical influence is more far-reaching than that of the latter.

For sexual intercourse is permitted, even within marriage, only as the means willed by God for the increase of His glory according to the commandment, "Be fruitful and multiply." Along with a moderate vegetable diet and cold baths, the same prescription is given for all sexual temptations as is used against religious doubts and a sense of moral unworthiness: "Work hard in your calling." But the most important thing was that even beyond that labour came to be considered in itself the end of life, ordained as such by God. St. Paul's "He who will not work shall not eat" holds unconditionally for everyone. . . .

The Quaker ethic also holds that a man's life in his calling is an exercise in ascetic virtue, a proof of his state of grace through his conscientiousness, which is expressed in the care and method with which he pursues his calling. What God demands is not labour in itself, but rational labour in a calling. In the Puritan concept of the calling the emphasis is always placed on this methodical character of worldly asceticism, not, as with Luther, on the acceptance of the lot which God has irretrievably assigned to man.

Hence the question whether anyone may combine several callings is answered in the affirmative, if it is useful for the common good or one's own, and not injurious to anyone, and if it does not lead to unfaithfulness in one of the callings. Even a change of calling is by no means regarded as objectionable, if it is not thoughtless and is made for the purpose of pursuing a calling more pleasing to God, which means, on general principles, one more useful.

Wealth as a Sign

It is true that the usefulness of a calling, and thus its favour in the sight of God, is measured primarily in moral terms, and thus in terms of the importance of the goods produced in it for the community. But a further, and, above all, in practice the most important, criterion is found in private profitableness. For if that God, whose hand the Puritan sees in all the occurrences of life, shows one of His elect a chance of profit, he must do it with a purpose. Hence the faithful Christian must follow the call by taking advantage of the opportunity. "If God show you a way in which you may lawfully get more than in another way (without wrong to your soul or to any other), if you refuse this, and choose the less gainful way, you cross one of the ends of your calling, and you refuse to be God's steward, and to accept His gifts and use them for Him when He requireth it: you may labour to be rich for God, though not for the flesh and sin."

Wealth is thus bad ethically only in so far as it is a temptation to idleness and sinful enjoyment of life, and its acquisition is bad only when it is with the purpose of later living merrily and without care. But as a performance of duty in a calling it is not only morally permissible, but actually enjoined. The parable of the servant who was rejected because he did not increase the talent which was entrusted to him seemed to say so directly. To wish to be poor was, it was often argued, the same as wishing to be unhealthy; it is objectionable as a glorification of works and derogatory to the glory of God. . . .

When the limitation of consumption is combined with this release of acquisitive activity, the inevitable practical result is obvious: accumulation of capital through ascetic compulsion to save. The restraints which were imposed upon the consumption of wealth naturally served to increase it by making possible the productive investment of capital. . . .

Now naturally the whole ascetic literature of almost all denominations is saturated with the idea that faithful labour, even at low wages, on the part of those whom life offers no other opportunities, is highly pleasing to God. In this respect Protestant Asceticism added in itself nothing new. But it not only deepened this idea most powerfully, it also created the force which was alone decisive for its effectiveness: the psychological sanction of it through the conception of this labour as a calling, as the best, often in the last analysis the only means of attaining certainty of grace. And on the other hand it legalized the exploitation of this specific willingness to work, in that it also interpreted the employer's business activity as a calling. It is obvious how powerfully the exclusive search for the Kingdom of God only through the fulfilment of duty in the calling, and the strict asceticism which Church discipline naturally imposed, especially on the propertyless classes, was bound to affect the productivity of labour in the capitalistic sense of the word. The treatment of labour as a calling became as characteristic of the modern worker as the corresponding attitude toward acquisition of the business man. . . .

41

One of the fundamental elements of the spirit of modern capitalism, and not only of that but of all modern culture: rational conduct on the basis of the idea of the calling, was born—that is what this discussion has sought to demonstrate—from the spirit of Christian asceticism. One has only to re-read the passage from Franklin, quoted at the beginning of this essay, in order to see that the essential elements of the attitude which was there called the spirit of capitalism are the same as what we have just shown to be the content of the Puritan worldly asceticism, only without the religious basis, which by Franklin's time had died away. . . .

The Iron Cage

The Puritan wanted to work in a calling; we are forced to do so. For when asceticism was carried out of monastic cells into everyday life, and began to dominate worldly morality, it did its part in building the tremendous cosmos of the modern economic order. This order is now bound to the technical and economic conditions of machine production which to-day determine the lives of all the individuals who are born into this mechanism, not only those directly concerned with economic acquisition, with irresistible force. Perhaps it will so determine them until the last ton of fossilized coal is burnt. In Richard Baxter's view the care for external goods should only lie on the shoulders of the "saint like a light cloak, which can be thrown aside at any moment." But fate decreed that the cloak should become an iron cage.

Since asceticism undertook to remodel the world and to work out its ideals in the world, material goods have gained an increasing and finally an inexorable power over the lives of men as at no previous period in history. To-day the spirit of religious asceticism—whether finally, who knows?—has escaped from the cage. But victorious capitalism, since it rests on mechanical foundations, needs its support no longer. The rosy blush of its laughing heir, the Enlightenment, seems also to be irretrievably fading, and the idea of duty in one's calling prowls about in our lives like the ghost of dead religious beliefs. Where the fulfilment of the calling cannot directly be related to the highest spiritual and cultural values, or when, on the other hand, it need not be felt simply as economic compulsion, the individual generally abandons the attempt to justify it at all. In the field of its highest development, in the United States, the pursuit of wealth, stripped of its religious and ethical meaning, tends to become associated with purely mundane passions, which often actually give it the character of sport.

No one knows who will live in this cage in the future, or whether at the end of this tremendous development entirely new prophets will arise, or there will be a great rebirth of old ideas and ideals, or, if neither, mechanized petrification, embellished with a sort of convulsive self-importance. For of the last stage of this cultural development, it might well be truly said: "Specialists without spirit, sensualists without heart; this nullity imagines that it has attained a level of civilization never before achieved."

Social Affiliations Define Society

GEORG SIMMEL

Although Marx, Durkheim, and Weber have more influence
on current sociology, Georg Simmel (1858-1918) was much
better known to early U.S. sociologists for his significant
study of interaction within small groups. Simmel was the first
sociologist to focus on interpersonal relations, interconnec-
tions, and interaction. He studied "pure structure," stable
interaction patterns which do not depend on the particular
individuals involved and can be abstracted to "social forms"
independent of content. In this viewpoint, Simmel explains
society as intersecting group memberships that force individuals to interact with others unlike themselves.

One well-known sociological concept is that people tend
to associate with people much like themselves. If you are a
young college student attending a medium-sized public university and working part-time to help pay your own way,
these social positions influence the people with whom you associate. Most of your friends will have similar lifestyles and
similar circumstances. Few of your regular interactions will be

Reprinted with the permission of The Free Press, a division of Simon & Schus-
ter, from *Conflict and the Web of Group Affiliations* by Georg Simmel, translated
by Kurt H. Wolff and Reinhard Bendix. Copyright ©1955 by The Free Press;
copyright renewed 1983 by Kurt H. Wolff.

with Harvard students, or the homeless, or stock-car drivers. However, other of your affiliations—such as attendance at religious events, organizational memberships, and volunteer work—may lead you to associate with some of these people. This is the social "web of affiliations" Simmel believes we should study. These social patterns, apart from concern with specific details, describe and define society.

QUESTIONS

1. In what ways did preindustrial affiliations treat people "as a member of a group rather than as an individual"?
2. Simmel describes personality as "subjectivity par excellence" and claims personality arises from society. How does he say this happens?
3. Two pure forms Simmel mentions in this viewpoint are "concentric" and "intersecting" groups. What examples does he give of each? Define each form.

The number of different social groups in which the individual participates, is one of the earmarks of culture. The modern person belongs first of all to his parental family, then to his family of procreation and thereby also to the family of his wife. Beyond this he belongs to his occupational group, which often involves him in several interest-groups. For example, in an occupation that embraces both supervisory and subordinate personnel, each person participates in the affairs of his particular business, department office, etc., each of which comprises higher and lower employees. Moreover, a person also participates in a group made up of similarly situated employees from several, different firms. Then, a person is likely to be aware of his citizenship, of the fact that he belongs to a particular social class. He is, moreover, a reserve-officer, he belongs to a few clubs and engages in a social life which puts him in touch with different social groups. This is a great variety of groups. Some of these groups are integrated. Others are, however, so arranged that one group appears as the original focus of an individual's affiliation, from which he then turns toward affiliation with other, quite different groups on the basis of his special qualities, which distinguish him from other members of his primary group. His bond with the primary group may well continue to exist, like one aspect of a complex image, which retains its original time-space coordinates though the image itself has long since become established psychologically as an objective configuration in its own right.

During the Middle Ages the individual had certain typical opportunities of group-affiliation, over and above his citizenship in his community. The Hansa League was an association of cities, which permitted the individual to participate in a wide range of activities that not only extended beyond each individual city but far beyond the boundaries of the German Reich. Likewise, the medieval guilds were not organized in accordance with the jurisdiction of towns; instead, affiliation of the individual with the guild had no reference to his status as a citizen within a town but involved him in an organization extending throughout all of Germany. And journeymen-associations extended beyond the boundaries of the guilds, just as the guilds extended their jurisdiction beyond the boundaries of the towns.

These patterns [of group-affiliation] had the peculiarity of treating the individual as a member of a group rather than as an individual, and of incorporating him thereby in other groups as well. An association which is derived from the membership of other associations places the individual in a number of groups. But these groups do not overlap and the problems which they entail for the individual, differ from the problems posed by the sociological constellations which will be discussed subsequently. Group-formation during the Middle Ages was inspired by the idea that only equals could be associated, however often the practice deviated from the theory. This idea obviously was connected with the completeness with which medieval man surrendered himself to his group-affiliation. Hence, cities allied themselves first of all with cities, monasteries with monasteries, guilds with related guilds. This was an extension of the equalitarian principle, even though in fact members of one corporate body may not have been the equals of members from an allied group. But as *members of a corporate body* they were equals. The alliance was valid only in so far as this was the case, and the fact that the members were individually differentiated in other respects was irrelevant. This way of doing things was extended to alliances between *different* groups, but these groups were regarded even then as equal powers within the new alliance. The individual as such was not a fact in such an alliance; hence his indirect participation in it did not add an individuating element to his personality. Nevertheless, as will be discussed later, this was the transitional step from the medieval type to the modern type of group-formation. The medieval group in the strict sense was one which did not permit the individual to become a member in other groups, a rule which the old guilds and the early medieval corporations probably illustrate most clearly. The modern type of group-formation makes it possible for the isolated individual to become a member in whatever number of groups he chooses. Many consequences resulted from this.

Group-Affiliations and the Individual Personality

The groups with which the individual is affiliated constitute a system of coordinates, as it were, such that each new group with which he becomes affiliated circumscribes him more exactly and more unambiguously. To belong to any one of these groups leaves the individual considerable leeway. But the larger the number of groups to which an individual belongs, the more improbable is it that other persons will exhibit the same combination of group-affiliations, that these particular groups will "intersect" once again [in a second individual]. Concrete objects lose their individual characteristics as we subsume them under a general concept in accordance with one of their attributes. And concrete objects regain their individual characteristics as other concepts are emphasized under which their several attributes may be subsumed. To speak Platonically, each thing has a part in as many ideas as it has manifold attributes, and it achieves thereby its individual determination. There is an analogous relationship between the individual and the groups with which he is affiliated.

A concrete object with which we are confronted has been called the synthesis of perceptions. And each object has a more enduring configuration, so to speak, the more various the perceptions are, which have entered into it. Similarly as individuals, we form the personality out of particular elements of life, each of which has arisen from, or is interwoven with, society. This personality is subjectivity par excellence in the sense that it combines the elements of culture in an individual manner. There is here a reciprocal relation between the subjective and the objective. As the person becomes affiliated with a social group, he surrenders himself to it. A synthesis of such subjective affiliations creates a group in an objective sense. But the person also regains his individuality, because his pattern of participation is unique; hence the fact of multiple group-participation creates in turn a new subjective element. Causal determination of, and purposive actions by, the individual appear as two sides of the same coin. The genesis of the personality has been interpreted as the point of intersection for innumerable social influences, as the end-product of heritages derived from the most diverse groups and periods of adjustment. Hence, individuality was interpreted as that particular set of constituent elements which in their quality and combination make up the individual. But as the individual becomes affiliated with social groups in accordance with the diversity of his drives and interests, he thereby expresses and returns what he has "received," though he does so consciously and on a higher level. . . .

Cross-Pressures Arising from Multiple Group-Affiliations

The sociological determination of the individual will be greater when the groups which influence him are juxtaposed than if they are concentric. That is to say, human aggregates such as the nation, a common social position, an occupation, and specific niches within the latter, do not allot any special position to the person who participates in them, because participation in the smallest of these groups already implies participation in the larger groups. But groups which are interrelated in this way do not always control individuals in a unified way. The fact that these associations are related to each other in a concentric way may mean not that they are related organically but that they are in mechanical juxtaposition. Hence, these associations will affect the individual, as if each of them was independent of the other.

This is manifest in earlier systems of law, when a person guilty of a crime is punished twice: by the immediate group to which he belongs and by the wider one which includes the first. If in late medieval Frankfurt a member of a guild had not fulfilled his obligation to render military service, he was punished by the head of his guild, but also by the city council. In a similar way, if in a libel suit the injured party had obtained satisfaction from the guild, it would still seek justice in the regular courts. And conversely, in the older guild systems the guild reserved the right to punish an offender, even though the court had already done so. This two-in-one type of procedure made it clear to the person affected by it that the two groups which enveloped him concentrically in a certain sense were also "intersecting" one another in his person. For his affiliation with the immediate group did not by any means comprise all the obligations which his affiliation with the larger group entailed. This is seen in the example cited above, in which the fact that a person belongs to a special category within a general occupational classification means that all those rules apply to him which apply to this general classification. . . .

Such awkwardness and difficulties arise for the person as a result of his affiliation with groups which surround him concentrically. Yet, this is one of the first and most direct ways in which the individual, who has begun his social existence by being affiliated with one group only, comes to participate in a number of groups. The peculiar character of group-formation in the Middle Ages in contrast with the modern way has been stressed frequently. In the Middle Ages affiliation with a group absorbed the whole man. It served not only a momentary purpose, which was defined objectively. It was rather an association of all who had combined for the sake of that purpose while the association absorbed the whole life of each of them. If the urge to form associations persisted, then it was accompanied by having whole associations combined in confederations of a higher order. This form, which enables the single individual to participate in a number of groups without alienating him from his affiliation with his original locality, may appear simple today, but it was in fact a great social invention. This form could be serviceable as long as men had not invented purposive associations, which made it possible for persons to work together by impersonal means for impersonal ends, and thereby to leave the personality of the individual inviolate. The enrichment of the individual as a social being which was attainable under the Medieval type of group-formation, was to be sure, a limited one, while the enrichment made possible by purposive associations is not limited in this sense.

Still, the enrichment under the Medieval type was considerable, for what the individual obtained from his affiliation with the larger group was in no way contained in the affiliation with his immediate group. By way of contrast, the concept "tree" of which the oak is a part, does contain all the elements of the concept "plant," which comprises the concept "tree" though much else besides. To subsume the oak under the concept "plant" entails a meaning for the oak, which is not revealed by subsuming "oak" under the concept "tree," however much the "tree" includes the conceptual elements of "plant" logically. This meaning is given by relating the oak to everything that is "plant" without being "tree." Much would have been gained in the medieval pattern of group-affiliation, even if nothing else had occurred than what is suggested by this analogy. The concentric pattern of group-affiliations is a systematic and often also an historical stage, which is prior to that situation in which the groups with which persons affiliate are juxtaposed and "intersect" in one and the same person.

The modern pattern differs sharply from the concentric pattern of group-affiliations as far as a person's achievements are concerned. Today someone may belong, aside from his occupational position, to a scientific association, he may sit on a board of directors of a corporation and occupy an honorific position in the city government. Such a person will be more clearly determined sociologically, the less his participation in one group by itself enjoins upon him participation in another. He is determined sociologically in the sense that the groups "intersect" in his person by virtue of his affiliation with them. Whether or not the fact that a person who performs several functions reveals a characteristic combination of his talents, a special breadth of activity depends not only on his participation in several offices and institutions but naturally on the extent of their division of labor. In this way, the objective structure of a society provides a framework within which an individual's non-interchangeable and singular characteristics may develop and find expression, depending on the greater or lesser possibilities which that structure allows. . . .

Individualism and Collectivism in Modern Society

The development of the public mind shows itself by the fact that a sufficient number of groups is present which have form and organization. Their number is sufficient in the sense that they give an individual of many gifts the opportunity to pursue each of his interests in association with others. Such multiplicity of groups implies that the ideals of collectivism and of individualism are approximated to the same extent. On the one hand the individual finds a community for each of his inclinations and strivings which makes it easier to satisfy them. This community provides an organizational form for his activities, and it offers in this way all the advantages of group-membership as well as of organizational experience. On the other hand, the specific qualities of the individual are preserved through the combination of groups which can be a different combination in each case.

Thus one can say that society arises from the individual and that the individual arises out of association. An advanced culture broadens more and more the social groups to which we belong with our whole personality; but at the same time the individual is made to rely on his own resources to a greater extent and he is deprived of many supports and advantages associated with the tightly-knit, primary group. Thus, the creation of groups and associations in which any number of people can come together on the basis of their interest in a common purpose, compensates for that isolation of the personality which develops out of breaking away from the narrow confines of earlier circumstances.

Shared Values Define Society

GEORGE H. MEAD

The social philosopher George Herbert Mead (1863-1931)
taught courses in social psychology at the University of
Chicago and profoundly influenced his students, who published Mead's ideas from their course notes in *Mind, Self and
Society*. Mead combined his interest in self and consciousness
with Simmel's focus on interaction to develop symbolic interactionism as a sociological perspective. Mead argued that the
"conversation of gestures" (communication using mutually
understood symbols) allows the emergence of "mind" (thinking). In this viewpoint, Mead contends that the development
of the "self" results from social interaction, and communities
of mutual understanding define society.

One way to understand Mead's viewpoint is to think
about subcultures in modern society. If your interest lies in
computers, for example, you probably had early exposure to
video games or computer games. Your first exposure to simple games (play stage) advanced to more complex games
(game stage) and perhaps bulletin boards (generalized other).
You learned the language of computers by communicating
with other people who had similar interests or by studying

computers with teachers or books written by someone who "speaks computer." Computer "wizard" or "hacker" has become part of your identity, the way you think about yourself, and the community of hackers is part of our modern culture. Mead's argument is that this same process applies to any group or subculture and explains both the development of self and the reciprocal influence between self and society.

QUESTIONS

1. Define and describe Mead's stages in the development of the self: the play stage, the game stage, and the "generalized other."
2. In other work, Mead defines the self as composed of two parts: "I" and "me." The "I" is the spontaneous creative aspect of the self within the social process, and the "me" is the organized and internalized expectations of others. At which stage would Mead say the "me" develops?
3. If the self is, as Mead argues, a "reflection of the general systematic pattern of social or group behavior," what makes each individual unique?

■ ■ ■

The Play Stage

A child plays at being a mother, at being a teacher, at being a policeman; that is, it is taking different roles, as we say. We have something that suggests this in what we call the play of animals: a cat will play with her kittens, and dogs play with each other. Two dogs playing with each other will attack and defend, in a process which if carried through would amount to an actual fight. There is a combination of responses which checks the depth of the bite. But we do not have in such a situation the dogs taking a definite role in the sense that a child deliberately takes the role of another. This tendency on the part of the children is what we are working with in the kindergarten where the roles which the children assume are made the basis for training. When a child does assume a role he has in himself the stimuli which call out that particular response or group of responses.

He may, of course, run away when he is chased, as the dog does, or he may turn around and strike back just as the dog does in his play. But that is not the same as playing at something. Children get together to "play Indian." This means that the child has a certain set of stimuli which call out in itself the responses that they would call out in others, and which answer to an Indian. In the play period the child utilizes his own responses to these stimuli which he makes use of in building a self. The response which he has a tendency to make to these stimuli organizes them. He plays that he is, for instance, offering himself something, and he buys it; he gives a letter to himself and takes it away; he addresses himself as a parent, as a teacher; he arrests himself as a policeman. He has a set of stimuli which call out in himself the sort of responses they call out in others. He takes this group of responses and organizes them into a certain whole. Such is the simplest form of being another to one's self. It involves a temporal situation. The child says something in one character and responds in another character, and then his responding in another character is a stimulus to himself in the first character, and so the conversation goes on. A certain organized structure arises in him and in his other which replies to it, and these carry on the conversation of gestures between themselves.

The Game Stage

If we contrast play with the situation in an organized game, we note the essential difference that the child who plays in a game must be ready to take the attitude of everyone else involved in that game, and that these different roles must have a definite relationship to each other. Taking a very simple game such as hide-and-seek, everyone with the exception of the one who is hiding is a person who is hunting. A child does not require more than the person who is hunted and the one who is hunting. If a child is playing in the first sense he just goes on playing, but there is no basic organization gained. In that early stage he passes from one role to another just as a whim takes him. But in a game where a number of individuals are involved, then the child taking one role must be ready to take the role of everyone else. If he gets in a ball nine he must have the responses of each position involved in his own position. He must know what everyone else is going to do in order to carry out his own play. He has to take all of these roles. They do not all have to be present in consciousness at the same time, but at some moments he has to have three or four individuals present in his own attitude, such as the one who is going to throw the ball, the one who is going to catch it, and so on. These responses must be, in some degree, present in his own make-up. In the game, then, there is a set of responses of such others so organized that the attitude of one calls out the appropriate attitudes of the other.

This organization is put in the form of the rules of the game. Children take a great interest in rules. They make rules on the spot in order to help themselves out of difficulties. Part of the enjoyment of the game is to get these rules. Now, the rules are the set of responses which a particular attitude calls out. You can demand a certain response in others if you take a certain attitude. These responses are all in yourself as well. There you get an organized set of such responses as that to which I have referred, which is something more elaborate than the roles found in play. Here there is just a set of responses that follow on each other indefinitely. At such a stage we speak of a child as not yet having a fully developed self. The child responds in a fairly intelligent fashion to the immediate stimuli that come to him, but they are not organized. He does not organize his life as we would like to have him do, namely, as a whole. There is just a set of responses of the type of play. The child reacts to a certain stimulus, and the reaction is in himself that is called out in others, but he is not a whole self. In his game he has to have an organization of these roles; otherwise he cannot play the game. The game represents the passage in the life of the child from taking the role of others in play to the organized part that is essential to self-consciousness in the full sense of the term. . . .

The Generalized Other

The fundamental difference between the game and play is that in the latter the child must have the attitude of all the others involved in that game. The attitudes of the other players which the participant assumes organize into a sort of unit, and it is that organization which controls the response of the individual. The illustration used was of a person playing baseball. Each one of his own acts is determined by his assumption of the action of the others who are playing the game. What he does is controlled by his being everyone else on that team, at least in so far as those attitudes affect his own particular response. We get then an "other" which is an organization of the attitudes of those involved in the same process.

The organized community or social group which gives to the individual his unity of self may be called "the generalized other." The attitude of the generalized other is the attitude of the whole community. Thus, for example, in the case of such a social group as a ball team, the team is the generalized other in so far as it enters—as an organized process or social activity—into the experience of any one of the individual members of it.

If the given human individual is to develop a self in the fullest sense, it is not sufficient for him merely to take the attitudes of other human individuals toward himself and toward one another within the human social process, and to bring that social process as a whole into his individual experience merely in these terms: he must also, in the same way that he takes the attitudes of other individuals toward himself and toward one another, take their attitudes toward the various phases or aspects of the common social activity or set of social undertakings in which, as members of an organized society or social group, they are all engaged; and he must then, by generalizing these individual attitudes of that organized society or social group itself, as a whole, act toward different social projects which at any given time it is carrying out, or toward the various larger phases of the general social process which constitutes its life and of which these projects are specific manifestations. This getting of the broad activities of any given social whole or organized society as such within the experiential field of any one of the individuals involved or included in that whole is, in other words, the essential basis and prerequisite of the fullest development of that individual's self: only in so far as he takes the attitudes of the organized social group to which he belongs toward the organized, co-operative social activity or set of such activities in which that group as such is engaged, does he develop a complete self or possess the sort of complete self he has developed. And on the other hand, the complex co-operative processes and activities and institutional function-ings of organized human society are also possible only in so far as every individual involved in them or belonging to that soci-ety can take the general attitudes of all other such individuals with reference to these processes and activities and institu-tional functionings, and to the organized social whole of expe-riential relations and interactions thereby constituted—and can direct his own behavior accordingly.

It is in the form of the generalized other that the social process influences the behavior of the individuals involved in it and carrying it on, i.e., that the community exercises control over the conduct of its individual members; for it is in this form that the social process or community enters as a determining factor into the individual's thinking. In abstract thought the in-dividual takes the attitude of the generalized other toward him-self, without reference to its expression in any particular other individuals; and in concrete thought he takes that attitude in so far as it is expressed in the attitudes toward his behavior of those other individuals with whom he is involved in the given social situation or act. But only by taking the attitude of the general-ized other toward himself, in one or another of these ways, can he think at all; for only thus can thinking—or the internalized conversation of gestures which constitutes thinking—occur. . . .

The Self as Internalized Community

What goes to make up the organized self is the organization of the attitudes which are common to the group. A person is a personality because he belongs to a community, because he takes over the institutions of that community into his own con-duct. He takes its language as a medium by which he gets his personality, and then through a process of taking the different roles that all the others furnish he comes to get the attitude of the members of the community. Such, in a certain sense, is the structure of a man's personality. There are certain common re-sponses which each individual has toward certain common things, and in so far as those common responses are awakened in the individual when he is affecting other persons he arouses his own self. The structure, then, on which the self is built is this response which is common to all, for one has to be a member of a community to be a self. Such responses are abstract attitudes, but they constitute just what we term a man's character. They give him what we term his principles, the acknowledged attitudes of all members of the community toward what are the values of that community. He is putting himself in the place of the generalized other, which represents the organized responses of all the members of the group. It is that which guides conduct controlled by principles, and a person who has such an organized group of responses is a man whom we say has character, in the moral sense.

Several Interdependent Functions Define Society

TALCOTT PARSONS

Talcott Parsons (1902-1979) and his students Robert Merton and Kingsley Davis at Columbia University interpreted the work of Durkheim and Weber to produce the functionalist perspective that dominated sociology in this country through the 1950s. The functionalist perspective defines society as a set of interdependent positions (statuses) each of which has specific expected behavior patterns (roles). Socialized members of society have internalized society's expectation for behavior (norms) and they want to do what society expects. In this viewpoint, Parsons describes society as composed of interdependent parts that meet the needs of the system as a whole, and integrate biology, personality, and culture. Balance among the interdependent parts assures maintenance of society.

Underlying the functionalist argument is the basic idea that all social elements must work together to the benefit of society; the society will not survive otherwise. Therefore, any social element present for a long period of time must be functional (beneficial) for society or it would not be present. From this view, social change occurs gradually, with each of the parts adjusting in a slow and ordered manner to change in any other part. Any disruption not functional for society must subside and disappear, or the society will cease to exist.

Parsons thought that human nature is basically conflictual and society is needed as a civilizing influence. He agreed with Weber that social processes become more rational over time, but Weber emphasized the costs of rationalization (the "iron cage"), and Parsons focused on the benefits that accompany the civilizing process. Of the four functional sectors Parsons describes, he designates culture (the basic value patterns) as the most important and as the sector that regulates the other sectors and generates change in them. Social values are most important and general, and direct formation of norms. Roles consist of the collection of norms that link individuals to the social system. Individuals and groups playing the more highly rewarded roles are those most committed to the benefit of society as a whole, and this force holds the system together.

Functionalism dominated U.S. sociology for more than half a century because it is well-reasoned, broadly applicable, and internally consistent. Parsons and his students applied the same general theory to the "human action system" and the social system, and (in other work) applied the same four functional areas to each sector of the social system. Thus, the theory is applicable at any level or unit of analysis.

QUESTIONS

1. Describe the four parts of the "action system." How are the parts related, according to the author?
2. According to Parsons, how is the social system "the primary link between the culture and the individual"?
3. Identify and explain the functions of each social system component, as Parsons describes them.

"System" is the concept that refers both to a complex of interdependencies between parts, components, and processes that involve discernible regularities of relationship, and to a similar type of interdependency between such a complex and its surrounding environment. System, in this sense, is therefore the concept around which all sophisticated theory in the conceptually generalizing disciplines is and must be organized. This is because any regularity of relationship can be more adequately understood if the whole complex of multiple interdependencies of which it forms part is taken into account.

Social Systems and the Action System

Methodologically, one must distinguish a theoretical system, which is a complex of assumptions, concepts, and propositions having both logical integration and empirical reference, from an empirical system, which is a set of phenomena in the observable world that can be described and analyzed by means of a theoretical system. An empirical system (e.g., the solar system as relevant to analytical mechanics) is never a totally concrete entity but, rather, a selective organization of those properties of the concrete entity defined as relevant to the theoretical system in question. Thus, for Newtonian solar system mechanics, the earth is "only" a particle with a given mass, location in space, velocity, and direction of motion; the Newtonian scheme is not concerned with the earth's geological or human social and cultural characteristics. In this sense, any theoretical system is abstract.

As a theoretical system, the social system is specifically adapted to describing and analyzing social interaction considered as a class of empirical systems. These systems are concerned with the behavior, as distinguished from the metabolic physiology, of living organisms. Among the categories of organisms, our interest in this article centers on human social interaction, which is organized on the symbolic levels we call "cultural." However, one should remember that such interaction is a late evolutionary product and is continuous with a very broad range of interaction phenomena among other organisms. All bisexual reproduction, for example, requires highly structured interactive relations between the organisms of the two sexes. Various kinds of interspecies ecological relations constitute another example, one to which human relations with domesticated animals are relevant.

The aspects of behavior which directly concern "cultural-level" systems I call *action*. Action in this technical sense includes four generic types of subsystems, the differentiation among which has gained fairly clear definition during modern intellectual history.

The first is simply the organism, which though quite properly treated as a concrete entity in one set of terms, becomes, on a more generalized level, a set of abstract components (i.e., a subsystem) in the culturally organized system of action.

A second subsystem is the social system, which is generated by the process of interaction among individual units. Its distinctive properties are consequences and conditions of the specific modes of interrelationship obtaining among the living organisms which constitute its units.

Third is the cultural system, which is the aspect of action organized about the specific characteristics of symbols and the exigencies of forming stable systems of them. It is structured in terms of patternings of meaning which, when stable, imply in turn generalized complexes of constitutive symbolisms that give the action system its primary "sense of direction," and which must be treated as independent of any particular system of social interaction. Thus, although there are many ramifications into such areas as language and communication, the prototypical cultural systems are those of beliefs and ideas. The possibilities of their preservation over time, and of their diffusion from one personality and/or social system into another, are perhaps the most important hallmarks of the independent structure of cultural systems.

Fourth, the analytical distinction between social and cultural systems has a correlative relation to the distinction between the organism and those other aspects of the individual actor which we generally call the personality. With the achievement of cultural levels of the control of behavior, the primary subsystems of action can no longer be organized—or structured primarily—about the organic base, which, in the first instance, is anatomical or "physical." Personality, then, is the aspect of the living individual, as "actor," which *must* be understood in terms of the cultural and social content of the learned patternings that make up his behavioral system. Here, "learned" refers not only to the problem of the origin of the patterns in the heredity-environment sense, but also to the problem of the kind and level of their content. The connection between these two problems partly reflects the fact that we have no evidence that cultural content is, at what we call here the level of pattern, determined through the genes. Thus, there is no evidence of a hereditary "propensity" to speak one language rather than another, although the genetically determined capacities to learn and use language are generally fundamental.

Thus, we treat the social system, when evolved to the action level, as one of four primary subsystems of action, all of which articulate with the organic bases of life and with organic adaptation to the environment in the broadest biological sense.

There is a sense in which the social system is the core of human action systems, being the primary link between the culture and the individual both as personality and as organism—a fact for which "culture and personality" theorists have often not adequately accounted. . . .

Insight into this basic complex of facts constitutes a principal foundation of modern social science theory. It has been attained by convergence from at least four sources: Freud's psychology, starting from a medical-biological base; Weber's sociology, which worked to transcend the problems of the German intellectual tradition concerning idealism-materialism; Durkheim's analysis of the individual actor's relations to the "social facts" of his situation; and the social psychology of the American "symbolic interactionists" Cooley and Mead, who built upon the philosophy of pragmatism.

In dealing with social systems, one must distinguish terminologically between an actor as a unit in a social system and the system as such. The actor may be either an individual or some kind of collective unit. In both cases, the actor *within* a system of reference will be spoken of as acting in a *situation* consisting of other actor-units within the same system of reference who are considered as objects. The system as a whole, however, functions (but does not "act" in a technical sense) in relation to its environment. Of course, the system references are inherently relative to particular scientific problems. When a collective (i.e., social) system is said to act, as in the case of a government conducting foreign relations, this will mean that it and the objects of its action constitute the social system of reference and that these objects are situations, not environment, to the acting collectivity.

The Social System and Its Environments

A social system, like all living systems, is inherently an open system engaged in processes of interchange (or "input-output relations") with its environment, as well as consisting of interchanges among its internal units. Regarding it as an open system is, from some viewpoints, regarding it as a part of—i.e., a subsystem of—one or more superordinate systems. In this sense, it is interdependent with the other parts of the more comprehensive system or systems and, hence, partly dependent on them for essential inputs. Here the dependence of the organism on its physical environment for nutrition and respiration is prototypical. This is the essential basis of the famous concept of *function* as it applies to social systems, as to all other living systems.

For any system of reference, functional problems are those concerning the conditions of the maintenance and/or development of the interchanges with environing systems, both inputs from them and outputs to them. Functional significance may be determined by the simple criterion of the dysfunctional consequences of failure, deficit, or excess of an input to a receiving system, as asphyxiation is the consequence of failure in oxygen input, and so oxygen input is judged to be functionally significant for the organism. Function is the only basis on which a theoretically systematic ordering of the structure of living systems is possible. In this context functional references certainly need beg no question about how structural arrangements have come about, since the biological concepts of variation, selection, and adaptation have long since provided a framework for analyzing the widest variety of change processes.

Goal-attaining processes explicitly intended to fulfill functional requirements constitute a limiting, but very important, case. Outputs in this sense have primary functional significance only for the system which receives them and which is situational or environmental to the system of reference, although they have secondary functional significance to the latter. For example, although economic output ("produced" goods) goes to "consumers," the maintenance of certain levels of salable output clearly has great significance to producing organizations. It is its inputs that have primary functional significance for any given system of reference. The "factors of production" of economic theory are classic examples, being the critical inputs of the economy.

In a crucial sense, the relation between any action system—including the social—and any of its environments is dual. On the one hand, the particular environment constitutes a set of objects which are "exterior" to the system in the Cartesian-Durkheimian sense. On the other hand, through interpenetration, the environmental system is partially and selectively included in the action system of reference. Internalization of cultural and social objects in the personality of the individual is certainly the prototypical case of interpenetration, but the principle it involves should be generalized to all the relations between action systems and their environments.

Thus, neither the individual personality nor the social system has any *direct* relation to the physical environment; their relations with the latter are mediated entirely through the organism, which is action's primary link with the physical world. This, after all, is now a commonplace of modern perceptual and epistemological theory. In essentially the same sense, neither personalities nor social systems have direct contact with the ultimate objects of reference, with the "ultimate reality" which poses "problems of meaning" in the sense sociologists associate above all with the work of Max Weber. The objects that personalities and social systems know and otherwise directly experience are in our terminology cultural objects, which are human artifacts in much the same sense as are the objects of empirical cognition. Hence, the relations of personalities and social systems with ultimate "nonempirical reality" are in a basic sense *mediated* through the cultural system. . . .

Society and Societal Community

On the understanding that all social systems are systems of interaction, the best reference point among their many types, for general theoretical purposes, is the society. The definition of this concept presents considerable difficulties, the history of which cannot occupy us here. For present purposes, I shall define a society as the category of social system embodying, at the requisite levels of evolutionary development and of control over the conditions of environmental relations, the greatest self-sufficiency of any type of social system.

By self-sufficiency (a criterion which has figured prominently in Western thought on the subject since Aristotle at least), I mean the capacity of the system, gained through both its internal organization and resources and its access to inputs from its *environments*, to function autonomously in implementing its normative culture, particularly its values but also its norms and collective goals. Self-sufficiency is clearly a degree of generalized adaptive capacity in the sense of biological theory.

The term "environment" is pluralized here to emphasize the fact that the relevant environment is not just physical, as in most formulations of general biological theory, but also includes the three basic subsystems of action other than the social, which have been outlined above.

The core structure of a society I will call the societal community. More specifically, at different levels of evolution, it is called tribe, or "the people," or, for classical Greece, *polis*, or, for the modern world, *nation*. It is the collective structure in which members are united or, in some sense, associated. Its most important property is the kind and level of solidarity—in Durkheim's sense—which characterizes the relations between its members.

The solidarity of a community is essentially the degree to which (and the ways in which) its collective interest can be expected to prevail over the unit interests of its members wherever the two conflict. It may involve mutual respect among the units for the rights of membership status, conformity with the value and norms institutionalized in the collectivity, or positive contribution to the attainment of collective goals. The character of solidarity varies with the level of differentiation in the society, differentiation which is evident in the structures of the roles in which a given individual is involved, of the system's subcollectivities, and of its norms and specified value orientations. The best-known basis for classifying the types of solidarity is Durkheim's two categories, mechanical and organic.

Both types of solidarity are characterized by common values and institutionalized norms. In the case of mechanical solidarity, however, the patterns of action expected from units are also uniform for all units in the system: relative to one another, the units are *segments*, since they are not functionally differentiated. Durkheim analyzed crime as the prototype violation of the obligations of mechanical solidarity. For full members of the community, no matter how highly differentiated the society, the treatment of the criminal should ideally be always the same, regardless of *who* commits the crime, even though this ideal is frequently and seriously deviated from. At the societal community level in differentiated societies, the core of the system of mechanical solidarity lies in the patterns of citizenship. These patterns can be conveniently subdivided into the components of civil-legal citizenship, political citizenship, and social citizenship. In modern American society, the bill of rights and associated constitutional structures, such as the fourteenth amendment, comprise the most directly relevant institutions in this field.

Organic solidarity concerns those aspects of the societal system in which roles, subcollectivities, and norms are differentiated on a functional basis. Here, though common value patterns remain of the first importance to the various subsystems at the relevant levels of specification, expectations of behavior differ according to role and subcollectivity. Solidarity, then, involves the integration of these differing expectations with respect to the various bases of compatible functioning, from mutual noninterference to positive mutual reinforcement.

Organic solidarity seems to be particularly important in three primary structural contexts. Most familiar is the one Durkheim himself particularly stressed, the economic division of labor, where the most important institutional patterns are contract and property. Second is what we ordinarily call the area of political differentiation, that of both the organization of authority and leadership and the various modes of participation in collective decision making, which involve the interplay of information and influence bearing on collective action. The third is the area of the society's relations with its cultural involvements. This particularly concerns the society's articulation with the religious system, but also (and the more so, the more differentiated both the society and the culture) with the arts, the system of intellectual disciplines and the relationship between the patterns of moral obligation and those of law.

Coercion and Constraint Define Society

RALF DAHRENDORF

Writing in the 1950s, European sociologist Ralf Dahrendorf
was one of the first to apply Marx's work to the study of
modern society. Observing that events take place which are
not able to be explained by the solidarity and equilibrium
emphasized in functional theory, Dahrendorf suggests that
another useful way to analyze society is to examine coercive
forces. Following Marx, he assumes that social structure re-
stricts behavior. Authority structures produce conflict because
what benefits those in charge is different from what benefits
subordinates. Those who have authority benefit from maintaining the social system that gives them that authority, and
those without authority would benefit from changing the system that keeps them subordinate. Dahrendorf's point is that
these opposing forces hold society together and lead to perpetual (and not always orderly) social change.

Dahrendorf's "coercion theory," combined with similar
work by other sociologists, has come to be called "conflict
theory." As you think about Dahrendorf's views, compare

them with the viewpoints from Marx and Parsons. Although Dahrendorf was a Marx scholar and applied Marx's ideas more fully to social analysis than his predecessors in the United States, he is sometimes criticized for not applying the ideas more completely. Conversely, the dominant functional perspective strongly influenced the formulation of Dahrendorf's theory. After you believe you understand Dahrendorf's viewpoint, see whether you can identify the separate influences of Marx and Parsons on the work.

QUESTIONS

1. Dahrendorf uses the example of the "uprising of the 17th of June" as an event better explained by coercion theory than structural functional theory. How does he support this argument?
2. What does Dahrendorf claim the differential distribution of power and authority inevitably produces? How does this happen?
3. According to Dahrendorf, what are "latent and manifest interests"?

Generally speaking, it seems to me that two (meta-)theories can and must be distinguished in contemporary sociology. One of these, the *integration theory of society*, conceives of social structure in terms of a functionally integrated system held in equilibrium by certain patterned and recurrent processes. The other one, the *coercion theory of society*, views social structure as a form of organization held together by force and constraint and reaching continuously beyond itself in the sense of producing within itself the forces that maintain it in an unending process of change. Like their philosophical counterparts, these theories are mutually exclusive. But—if I may be permitted a paradoxical formulation that will be explained presently—in sociology (as opposed to philosophy) a decision which accepts one of these theories and rejects the other is neither necessary nor desirable. There are sociological problems for the explanation of which the integration theory of society provides adequate assumptions; there are other problems which can be explained only in terms of the coercion theory of society; there are, finally, problems for which both theories appear adequate. For sociological analysis, society is Janus-headed, and its two faces are equivalent aspects of the same reality.

Integration Theory

In recent years, the integration theory of society has clearly dominated sociological thinking. In my opinion, this prevalence of one partial view has had many unfortunate consequences. However, it has also had at least one agreeable consequence, in that the very onesidedness of this theory gave rise to critical objections which enable us today to put this theory in its proper place. Such objections have been stimulated with increasing frequency by the works of the most eminent sociological theorist of integration, Talcott Parsons. It is not necessary here to attempt a comprehensive exposition of Parsons' position; nor do we have to survey the sizable literature concerned with a critical appraisal of this position. . . .

For purposes of exposition it seems useful to reduce each of the two faces of society to a small number of basic tenets, even if this involves some degree of oversimplification as well as overstatement. The integration theory of society, as displayed by the work of Parsons and other structural-functionalists, is founded on a number of assumptions of the following type:

1. Every society is a relatively persistent, stable structure of elements.
2. Every society is a well-integrated structure of elements.
3. Every element in a society has a function, i.e., renders a contribution to its maintenance as a system.
4. Every functioning social structure is based on a consensus of values among its members.

In varying forms, these elements of (1) stability, (2) integration, (3) functional coordination, and (4) consensus recur in all structural-functional approaches to the study of social structure. They are, to be sure, usually accompanied by protestations to the effect that stability, integration, functional coordination, and consensus are only "relatively" generalized. Moreover, these assumptions are not metaphysical propositions about the essence of society; they are merely assumptions for purposes of scientific analysis. As such, however, they constitute a coherent view of the social process which enables us to comprehend many problems of social reality.

Coercion Theory

However, it is abundantly clear that the integration approach to social analysis does not enable us to comprehend all problems of social reality. Let us look at two undeniably sociological problems of the contemporary world which demand explanation. (1) In recent years, an increasing number of industrial and commercial enterprises have introduced the position of personnel manager to cope with matters of hiring and firing, advice to employees, etc. Why? And: what are the consequences of the introduction of this new position? (2) On the 17th of June, 1953, the building workers of East Berlin put down their tools and went on a strike that soon led to a generalized revolt against the Communist regime of East Germany. Why? And: what are the consequences of this uprising? From the point of view of the integration model of society, the first of these problems is susceptible of a satisfactory solution. A special position to cope with personnel questions is functionally required by large enterprises in an age of rationalization and "social ethic"; the introduction of this position adapts the enterprise to the values of the surrounding society; its consequence is therefore of an integrative and stabilizing nature. But what about the second problem? Evidently, the uprising of the 17th of June is neither due to nor productive of integration in East German society. It documents and produces not stability, but instability. It contributes to the disruption, not the maintenance, of the existing system. It testifies to dissensus rather than consensus. The integration model tells us little more than that there are certain "strains" in the "system." In fact, in order to cope with problems of this kind we have to replace the integration theory of society by a different and, in many ways, contradictory model.

What I have called the coercion theory of society can also

be reduced to a small number of basic tenets, although here again these assumptions oversimplify and overstate the case:

1. Every society is at every point subject to processes of change; social change is ubiquitous.
2. Every society displays at every point dissensus and conflict; social conflict is ubiquitous.
3. Every element in a society renders a contribution to its disintegration and change.
4. Every society is based on the coercion of some of its members by others.

If we return to the problem of the German workers' strike, it will become clear that this latter model enables us to deal rather more satisfactorily with its causes and consequences. The revolt of the building workers and their fellows in other industries can be explained in terms of coercion. The revolting groups are engaged in a conflict which "functions" as an agent of change by disintegration. A ubiquitous phenomenon is expressed, in this case, in an exceptionally intense and violent way, and further explanation will have to account for this violence on the basis of the acceptance of conflict and change as universal features of social life. . . .

Power and Authority

From the point of view of the integration theory of social structure, units of social analysis ("social systems") are essentially voluntary associations of people who share certain values and set up institutions in order to ensure the smooth functioning of cooperation. From the point of view of coercion theory, however, the units of social analysis present an altogether different picture. Here, it is not voluntary cooperation or general consensus but enforced constraint that makes social organizations cohere. In institutional terms, this means that in every social organization some positions are entrusted with a right to exercise control over other positions in order to ensure effective coercion; it means, in other words, that there is a differential distribution of power and authority. One of the central theses of this study consists in the assumption that this differential distribution of authority invariably becomes the determining factor of systematic social conflicts of a type that is germane to class conflicts in the traditional (Marxian) sense of this term. The structural origin of such group conflicts must be sought in the arrangement of social roles endowed with expectations of domination or subjection. Wherever there are such roles, group conflicts of the type in question are to be expected. Differentiation of groups engaged in such conflicts follows the lines of differentiation of roles that are relevant from the point of view of the exercise of authority. Identification of variously equipped authority roles is the first task of conflict analysis; conceptually and empirically all further steps of analysis follow from the investigation of distributions of power and authority. . . .

So far as the terms "power" and "authority" and their distinction are concerned, I shall follow in this study the useful and well-considered definitions of Max Weber. For Weber, power is the "probability that one actor within a social relationship will be in a position to carry out his own will despite resistance, regardless of the basis on which this probability rests"; whereas authority (*Herrschaft*) is the "probability that a command with a given specific content will be obeyed by a given group of persons." The important difference between power and authority consists in the fact that whereas power is essentially tied to the personality of individuals, authority is always associated with social positions or roles. The demagogue has power over the masses to whom he speaks or whose actions he controls; but the control of the officer over his men, the manager over his workers, the civil servant over his clientele is authority, because it exists as an expectation independent of the specific person occupying the position of officer, manager, civil servant. It is only another way of putting this difference if we say—as does Max Weber—that while power is merely a factual relation, authority is a legitimate relation of domination and subjection. In this sense, authority can be described as legitimate power.

In the present study we are concerned exclusively with relations of authority, for these alone are part of social structure and therefore permit the systematic derivation of group conflicts from the organization of total societies and associations within them. The significance of such group conflicts rests with the fact that they are not the product of structurally fortuitous relations of power but come forth wherever authority is exercised—and that means in all societies under all historical conditions. (1) Authority relations are always relations of super- and subordination. (2) Where there are authority relations, the superordinate element is socially expected to control, by orders and commands, warnings and prohibitions, the behavior of the subordinate element. (3) Such expectations attach to relatively permanent social positions rather than to the character of individuals; they are in this sense legitimate. (4) By virtue of this fact, they always involve specification of the persons subject to control and of the spheres within which control is permissible. Authority, as distinct from power, is never a relation of generalized control over others. (5) Authority being a legitimate relation, noncompliance with authoritative commands can be sanctioned; it is indeed one of the functions of the legal system (and of course of quasi-legal customs and norms) to support the effective exercise of legitimate authority. . . .

For the individual incumbent of roles, domination in one association does not necessarily involve domination in all others to which he belongs, and subjection, conversely, in one association does not mean subjection in all. The dichotomy of positions of authority holds for specific associations only. In a democratic state, there are both mere voters and incumbents of positions of authority such as cabinet ministers, representatives, and higher civil servants. But this does not mean that the "mere voter" cannot be incumbent of a position of authority in a different context, say, in an industrial enterprise; conversely, a cabinet minister may be, in his church, a mere member, i.e., subject to the authority of others. Although empirically a certain correlation of the authority positions of individuals in different associations seems likely, it is by no means general and is in any case a matter of specific empirical conditions. . . .

Latent and Manifest Interests

The analytical process of conflict group formation can be described in terms of a model. Throughout, the categories employed in this model will be used in terms of the coercion theory of social structure. With this restriction in mind, the thesis that conflict groups are based on the dichotomous distribution of authority in imperatively coordinated associations can be conceived of as the basic assumption of the model. To this assumption we now add the proposition that differentially equipped authority positions in associations involve, for their incumbents, conflicting interests. The occupants of positions of domination and the occupants of positions of subjection hold, by virtue of these positions, certain interests which are contradictory in substance and direction. In the case of incumbents of ruling positions, these interests, being "ruling interests" themselves, might also be described as values; however, in the present context I propose to retain the category of interest as a general term for the orientation of dominating and subjected aggregates.

By postulating interests that are given and conditioned by positions, we encounter once again a problem which we must now face squarely. In everyday language, the word "interest" signifies intentions or directions of behavior associated with individuals rather than with their positions. It is not the position, but the individual who "is interested in something," "has an interest in something," and "finds something interesting." It might indeed appear that the notion of interest is not meaningfully conceivable other than in relation to human individuals. Interests would seem to be psychological in the strictest sense. Yet the proposition of certain antagonistic interests conditioned by, even inherent in, social positions contains precisely this apparently meaningless assertion that there can be interests which are, so to say, impressed on the individual from outside without his participation. . . .

For purposes of the sociological analysis of conflict groups and group conflicts, it is necessary to assume certain structurally generated orientations of the actions of incumbents of defined positions. By analogy to conscious ("subjective") orientations of action, it appears justifiable to describe these as "interests." It has to be emphasized, however, that by so doing no assumption is implied about the substance of these interests or the consciousness and articulate orientation of the occupants of the positions in question. The assumption of "objective" interests associated with social positions has no psychological implications or ramifications; it belongs to the level of sociological analysis proper. . . .

In terms of the integration theory of society, social positions, with which we are here concerned, are significant, above all, as social roles. By roles are understood sets of role expectations, "patterned expectations defining the *proper* behavior of persons playing certain roles." "Proper" means, of course, within the frame of reference of integration theory, appropriate for the functioning of the social system and contributing to its integration. The notion of role expectations ascribes an orientation of behavior to social positions or roles. The individual "player" of roles may or may not internalize these role expectations and make them conscious orientations of action. If he does so, he is in terms of integration theory "adapted" or "adjusted"; if he does not do so, he is a "deviant." In any case, the assumption of certain "objective" expectations of behavior proves analytically useful. I suggest that the category of interest in the coercion theory of society must be understood in strict analogy to that of role expectation. The "objective" interests under discussion are in fact role interests, i.e., expected orientations of behavior associated with authority roles in imperatively coordinated associations. Again, the individual incumbent of roles may or may not internalize these expectations. But in our context he behaves in an "adapted" or "adjusted" manner if he contributes to the conflict of contradictory interests rather than to the integration of a social system. The individual who assumes a position in an association finds these role interests with his position, just as he finds certain role expectations from the point of view of the social system. For different purposes of sociological analysis, different aspects of its basic unit—the position-role—are relevant; roles, too, have two faces. In our context they figure primarily as sets of expected interests within imperatively coordinated associations.

For certain purposes of the theory of conflict group formation, it will prove useful to replace the concept of role interests by another one which makes its relation to the incumbents of authority positions even more apparent. Role interests are, from the point of view of the "player" of roles, *latent interests*, i.e., undercurrents of his behavior which are predetermined for him for the duration of his incumbency of a role, and which are independent of his conscious orientations. As such they can, under conditions to be specified presently, become conscious goals which we shall correspondingly call *manifest interests*. By contrast to latent interests, manifest interests are psychological realities. They describe "the fact that emotion, will, and desire of a person are directed toward some goal" (although we presuppose that this goal is "some goal" only in a substantial, not in a formal, sense). The specific substance of manifest interests can be determined only in the context of given social conditions; but they always constitute a formulation of the issues of structurally generated group conflicts of the type in question. In this sense, manifest interests are the program of organized groups.

CHAPTER

2

What Explains
Social Behavior?

Chapter Preface

Sociology is the study of human interaction. Every explanation of society in the first chapter rests upon the fact that humans interact. Although the authors did not agree about the nature of the interaction that makes society possible, they do agree that interpersonal behavior forms the basis for society. If sociologists argue that society is made possible by human interaction, then the next question to ask is, What explains social behavior? Unlike psychologists, who look for causes of behavior within the individual, sociologists study ways two or more social units (individuals, categories, groups, organizations, or societies—or combinations of these) behave toward one another. Sociologists take an interest in explanations of interpersonal behavior from other disciplines, so long as the behavior is *social* and not individual. Viewpoints in this chapter illustrate three forms of the debate over causes of social behavior: nature versus nurture, social structure, and social psychology.

"Nature versus nurture" is a very old debate over the relative importance of heredity and environment (socialization). Does biology influence interpersonal behavior more greatly than social learning? Do hereditary factors such as sex and skin color explain social behavior better than such learned factors as language and religion? Ideally, important questions in a discipline can be answered through scientific analysis, just as a mathematician constructs proofs of theorems and corollaries. Even given great recent progress in biology, however, conclusive evidence of biological determinism, that nature most strongly determines social behavior, does not seem forthcoming.

In the early 1900s, psychologist John B. Watson made a strong claim for social determinism, that nurture most strongly determines social behavior:

> Give me a dozen healthy infants . . . and my own specified world to bring them up in . . . and I will guarantee to take any one at random and train them to become any kind of specialist that I might select—doctor, lawyer, artist, merchant-chief, and, yes, even beggar and thief—regardless of their talent, penchants, tendencies, abilities, vocations, and race of their ancestors.

Since no decisive evidence in support of Watson's argument

has become available either, the debate continues. Recent arguments over the genetic or learned nature of homosexuality provide evidence of ongoing controversy.

Aside from biology and socialization, social structure also influences social behavior. Social structure is the framework or skeleton that gives shape and form to society. People behave differently if they occupy the position of employer or employee, parent or child (young or old), teacher or student. Corporations take different actions when they buy or sell, when they compete or hold a monopoly. It is because these positions exist that people know how to behave; they know what society at large and specific others expect of people in their position. Although there is some latitude for interpretation, expected behavior is generally independent of individual characteristics. For example, students are expected to study, attend class, take notes, and appear interested. This expectation holds regardless of individual physical or personality differences.

Social structure is so important as an indicator of behavior that people are uncomfortable in any situation until they identify their own position relative to the others involved. One sociology professor creatively illustrates this point for students. Everyone knows that professors should dress differently from students and should stand at the front of the room in a dignified manner, especially on the first day of class before students know the professor. This particular professor sometimes wears old clothes and a three-day beard and brings a bucket and rags to clean the board as students enter the room. Students then identify him as the janitor and wonder where their professor is. Since students initially define the situation in this way, they are often reluctant to believe that the "janitor" is actually the professor. In any new situation, people want to clearly identify the other person's sex, race, age, and occupational position so that they know how to behave toward that person and know what behavior to expect of the person.

Nature versus nurture and social structure both take little note of individual variation, but social psychological explanations for social behavior center on individual action in small groups. Exchange theory, conformity, and dramaturgy offer three competing explanations for small group behavior. According to exchange theory, social behavior is best explained by a cost/benefit analysis. Everyone performs actions they found rewarding in the past and avoids actions that were not rewarded or were punished. People make bargains with others all the time, agreeing, for example, to perform a household task in exchange for running an errand or to take in a vacationing neighbor's mail in exchange for the expectation that the neighbor will reciprocate in the future. If such arrangements work well, they will likely be continued, but any problem may block future cooperation.

Conformity processes explain how small groups reach agreement and why individuals comply with expectations for behavior. Many sociologists emphasize shared norms and values without investigating the interpersonal processes in groups of two or more people on which consensus is built. People in pairs or small groups expect to agree or to amicably disagree, and this expectation holds for couples in long-term relationships and for committees of strangers brought together to accomplish a task. Despite the high value placed on individualism in U.S. culture, most people do conform to general expectations and this conformity brings order and regularity to social relationships. People conform in ordinary daily situations, but conform even more strongly when the situation is unfamiliar and ambiguous.

Dramaturgy theorists agree with Shakespeare that "all the world's a stage, and all the men and women merely players," and argue that interpersonal behavior can best be explained as expressions of social actors to an audience. "Impression management" is the idea that people determine how they want others to see them and perform the behavior necessary to produce the desired image. Others involved in the interaction form the audience which receives an impression and provides feedback to the actor. If the actor is not satisfied with the feedback, the interaction modifies the actor's behavior. Dramaturgy includes the idea that people behave differently when they are "onstage" or "backstage." Comparing a job interview with a casual discussion about work with friends readily illustrates this point.

Viewpoints in this chapter again demonstrate sociological diversity. Each explanation for social behavior is logical and internally consistent, and each applies to a wide range of behavior. Reserve judgment about whether you agree with each viewpoint until you read and understand each author's more complete explanation. Some of the explanations are compatible, that is, one does not exclude the other. After you read the viewpoints, imagine that each is the absolute truth. Given that, which other explanations are complementary? Which are impossible? Another issue to consider is the extent to which the competing explanations allow for individual free choice. Everyone has considerable experience interacting with others—consider your own experience as you read these viewpoints.

Early Socialization Explains Social Behavior

KINGSLEY DAVIS

One problem with trying to study society is that we are all immersed in it. It is very difficult to gain a detached perspective on something into which we are born and live our everyday lives. The very concept of socialization is the idea that society—represented first by parents and then by such others as teachers, friends, the media, neighbors, employers, and coworkers—teaches each new member how to think, feel, and live. Take, for example, the concept of "individualism" that we value so highly in our culture. There could be no "individualism" without thorough knowledge of what "everyone else does," the behavioral norms that exist. "Individualism" is meaningless for an individual in total isolation. Learning cultural norms is an ordinary part of growing up.

Ethics also seriously limits the study of society. Social scientists do not perform the kinds of experiments needed to provide an answer, for example, to the "nature versus nur-

Excerpted from Kingsley Davis, "Final Note on a Case of Extreme Isolation," *American Journal of Sociology* 50: 432-37 (1947).

ture" debate. To resolve this issue would require a series of carefully controlled experiments where some persons experience socialization and some do not. This last is the limiting factor, since social scientists are not willing to deprive anyone of socialization even to resolve so fundamental an issue. This viewpoint, however, reports the results of two "natural" experiments where scientists gained knowledge of two cases where parents denied their children opportunities for socialization.

Kingsley Davis, a student of Talcott Parsons's at Columbia University, first reported on "Anna" in 1940, two years after she had been found "tied to an old chair in a storage room on the second floor of a farm home seventeen miles from a small Pennsylvania city" (Davis 1940:554). When found, Anna was taken to a "county home" where she was "completely apathetic" and "had lain in a limp, supine position, immobile, expressionless, indifferent to everything" (Davis 1940:555). Information in this viewpoint comes from Davis's second article after Anna's death in 1942 from "hemorrhagic jaundice." Scientists estimated that Anna was about ten years old when she died. Davis compares Anna's progress with that of another child, "Isabelle," who experienced isolation for a similar period of time but who received different treatment when found. Before you read this viewpoint, try to imagine not learning language and never playing with other children, let alone learning to interact socially. As Davis notes, "it is small wonder" that specialists considered both children "feeble-minded" (1947:436). These natural experiments do not resolve the nature versus nurture debate, but do offer evidence that almost complete lack of socialization ("extreme isolation") has dire consequences.

QUESTIONS

1. Can you draw conclusions from this viewpoint about standardized psychological and IQ testing?
2. Other than natural experiments such as the ones described, is there another way to test the "nature versus nurture" debate?
3. Do these natural experiments support "nature" or "nurture" as more important influences?

Anna's Early History

The first few days and weeks of Anna's life were complicated by frequent changes of domicile. It will be recalled
that she was an illegitimate child, the second such child born
to her mother, and that her grandfather, a widowed farmer in
whose house her mother lived, strongly disapproved of this
new evidence of the mother's indiscretion. This fact led to the
baby's being shifted about.

Two weeks after being born in a nurse's private home,
Anna was brought to the family farm, but the grandfather's
antagonism was so great that she was shortly taken to the
house of one of her mother's friends. At this time a local minister became interested in her and took her to his house with an
idea of possible adoption. He decided against adoption, however, when he discovered that she had vaginitis. The infant
was then taken to a children's home in the nearest large city.
This agency found that at the age of only three weeks she was
already in a miserable condition, being "terribly galled and
otherwise in very bad shape." It did not regard her as a likely
subject for adoption but took her in for a while anyway, hop-
ing to benefit her. After Anna had spent nearly eight weeks in
this place, the agency notified her mother to come to get her.
The mother responded by sending a man and his wife to the
children's home with a view to their adopting Anna, but they
made such a poor impression on the agency that permission
was refused. Later the mother came herself and took the child
out of the home and then gave her to the couple. It was in the
home of this pair that a social worker found the girl a short
time thereafter. The social worker went to the mother's home
and pleaded with Anna's grandfather to allow the mother to
bring the child home. In spite of threats, he refused. The child,
by then more than four months old, was next taken to another
children's home in a near-by town. A medical examination at
this time revealed that she had impetigo, vaginitis, umbilical
hernia, and a skin rash.

Anna remained in this second children's home for nearly
three weeks, at the end of which time she was transferred to a
private foster-home. Since, however, the grandfather would not,
and the mother could not, pay for the child's care, she was finally taken back as a last resort to the grandfather's house (at the

age of five and a half months). There she remained, kept on the second floor in an attic-like room because her mother hesitated to incur the grandfather's wrath by bringing her downstairs.

The mother, a sturdy woman weighing about 180 pounds, did a man's work on the farm. She engaged in heavy work such as milking cows and tending hogs and had little time for her children. Sometimes she went out at night, in which case Anna was left entirely without attention. Ordinarily, it seems, Anna received only enough care to keep her barely alive. She appears to have been seldom moved from one position to another. Her clothing and bedding were filthy. She apparently had no instruction, no friendly attention.

It is little wonder that, when finally found and removed from the room in the grandfather's house at the age of nearly six years, the child could not talk, walk, or do anything that showed intelligence. She was in an extremely emaciated and undernourished condition, with skeleton-like legs and a bloated abdomen. She had been fed on virtually nothing except cow's milk during the years under her mother's care. . . .

Anna's Later History

In 1939, nearly two years after being discovered, Anna had progressed, as previously reported, to the point where she could walk, understand simple commands, feed herself, achieve some neatness, remember people, etc. But she still did not speak, and, though she was much more like a normal infant of something over one year of age in mentality, she was far from normal for her age.

On August 30, 1939, she was taken to a private home for retarded children, leaving the county home where she had been for more than a year and a half. In her new setting she made some further progress, but not a great deal. . . .

More than five months later, on April 25, 1940, a clinical psychologist, the late Professor Francis N. Maxfield, examined Anna and reported the following: large for her age; hearing "entirely normal"; vision apparently normal; able to climb stairs; speech in the "babbling stage" and "promise for developing intelligible speech later seems to be good." He said further that "on the Merrill-Palmer scale she made a mental score of 19 months. On the Vineland social maturity scale she made a score of 23 months."

Professor Maxfield very sensibly pointed out that prognosis is difficult in such cases of isolation. "It is very difficult to take scores on tests standardized under average conditions of environment and experience," he wrote, "and interpret them in a case where environment and experience have been so unusual." With this warning he gave it as his opinion at that time that Anna would eventually "attain an adult mental level of six or seven years."

The school for retarded children, on July 1, 1941, reported that Anna had reached 46 inches in height and weighed 60 pounds. She could bounce and catch a ball and was said to conform to group socialization, though as a follower rather than a leader. Toilet habits were firmly established. Food habits were normal, except that she still used a spoon as her sole implement. She could dress herself except for fastening her clothes. Most remarkable of all, she had finally begun to develop speech. She was characterized as being at about the two-year level in this regard. She could call attendants by name and bring in one when she was asked to. She had a few complete sentences to express her wants. The report concluded that there was nothing peculiar about her, except that she was feeble-minded—"probably congenital in type."

A final report from the school, made on June 22, 1942, and evidently the last report before the girl's death, pictured only a slight advance over that given above. It said that Anna could follow directions, string beads, identify a few colors, build with blocks, and differentiate between attractive and unattractive pictures. She had a good sense of rhythm and loved a doll. She talked mainly in phrases but would repeat words and try to carry on a conversation. She was clean about clothing. She habitually washed her hands and brushed her teeth. She would try to help other children. She walked well and could run fairly well, though clumsily. Although easily excited, she had a pleasant disposition.

Such was Anna's condition just before her death. It may seem as if she had not made much progress, but one must remember the condition in which she had been found. One must recall that she had no glimmering of speech, absolutely no ability to walk, no sense of gesture, not the least capacity to feed herself even when the food was put in front of her, and no comprehension of cleanliness. She was so apathetic that it was hard to tell whether or not she could hear. And all this at the age of nearly six years. Compared with this condition, her capacities at the time of her death seem striking indeed, though they do not amount to much more than a two-and-a-half-year mental level. One conclusion therefore seems safe, namely, that her isolation prevented a considerable amount of mental development that was undoubtedly part of her capacity. Just what her original capacity was, of course, is hard to say; but her development after her period of confinement (including the ability to walk and run, to play, dress, fit into a social situation, and, above all, to speak) shows that she had at least this much capacity—capacity that never could have been realized in her original condition of isolation. . . .

Comparison with Another Case: Isabelle

Perhaps more to the point than speculations about Anna's ancestry would be a case for comparison. If a child could be discovered who had been isolated about the same length of time as Anna but had achieved a much quicker recovery and a greater mental development, it would be a stronger indication that Anna was deficient to start with.

Such a case does exist. It is the case of a girl found at about the same time as Anna and under strikingly similar circumstances. A full description of the details of this case has not been published, but, in addition to newspaper reports, an excellent preliminary account by a speech specialist, Dr. Marie K. Mason, who played an important role in the handling of the child, has appeared. Also the late Dr. Francis N. Maxfield, clinical psychologist at Ohio State University, as was Dr. Mason, has written an as yet unpublished but penetrating analysis of the case. Some of his observations have been included in Professor Zingg's book on feral man. The following discussion is drawn mainly from these enlightening materials. The writer, through the kindness of Professors Mason and Maxfield, did have a chance to observe the girl in April, 1940, and to discuss the features of her case with them.

Born apparently one month later than Anna, the girl in

question, who has been given the pseudonym Isabelle, was discovered in November, 1938, nine months after the discovery of Anna. At the time she was found she was approximately six and a half years of age. Like Anna, she was an illegitimate child and had been kept in seclusion for that reason. Her mother was a deaf-mute, having become so at the age of two, and it appears that she and Isabelle had spent most of their time together in a dark room shut off from the rest of the mother's family. As a result Isabelle had no chance to develop speech; when she communicated with her mother, it was by means of gestures. Lack of sunshine and inadequacy of diet had caused Isabelle to become rachitic. Her legs in particular were affected; they "were so bowed that as she stood erect the soles of her shoes came nearly flat together, and she got about with a skittering gait." Her behavior toward strangers, especially men, was almost that of a wild animal, manifesting much fear and hostility. In lieu of speech she made only a strange croaking sound. In many ways she acted like an infant. "She was apparently utterly unaware of relationships of any kind. When presented with a ball for the first time, she held it in the palm of her hand, then reached out and stroked my face with it. Such behavior is comparable to that of a child of six months." At first it was even hard to tell whether or not she could hear, so unused were her senses. Many of her actions resembled those of deaf children.

It is small wonder that, once it was established that she could hear, specialists working with her believed her to be feeble-minded. Even on nonverbal tests her performance was so low as to promise little for the future. Her first score on the Stanford-Binet was 19 months, practically at the zero point of the scale. On the Vineland social maturity scale her first score was 39, representing an age level of two and a half years. "The general impression was that she was wholly uneducable and that any attempt to teach her to speak, after so long a period of silence, would meet with failure."

In spite of this interpretation, the individuals in charge of Isabelle launched a systematic and skilful program of training. It seemed hopeless at first. The approach had to be through pantomime and dramatization, suitable to an infant. It required one week of intensive effort before she even made her first attempt at vocalization. Gradually she began to respond, however, and, after the first hurdles had at last been overcome, a curious thing happened. She went through the usual stages of learning characteristic of the years from one to six not only in proper succession but far more rapidly than normal. In a little over two months after her first vocalization she was putting sentences together. Nine months after that she could identify words and sentences on the printed page, could write well, could add to ten, and could retell a story after hearing it. Seven months beyond this point she had a vocabulary of 1,500–2,000 words and was asking complicated questions. Starting from an educational level of between one and three years (depending on what aspect one considers), she had reached a normal level by the time she was eight and a half years old. In short, she covered in two years the stages of learning that ordinarily require six. Or, to put it another way, her I.Q. trebled in a year and a half. The speed with which she reached the normal level of mental development seems analogous to the recovery of body weight in a growing child after an illness, the recovery being achieved by an extra fast rate of growth for a period after the illness until normal weight for the given age is again attained.

When the writer saw Isabelle a year and a half after her discovery, she gave him the impression of being a very bright, cheerful, energetic little girl. She spoke well, walked and ran without trouble, and sang with gusto and accuracy. Today she is over fourteen years old and has passed the sixth grade in a public school. Her teachers say that she participates in all school activities as normally as other children. Though older than her classmates, she has fortunately not physically matured too far beyond their level.

Differences Between Isabelle and Anna

Clearly the history of Isabelle's development is different from that of Anna's. In both cases there was an exceedingly low, or rather blank, intellectual level to begin with. In both cases it seemed that the girl might be congenitally feeble-minded. In both a considerably higher level was reached later on. But the Ohio girl achieved a normal mentality within two years, whereas Anna was still marked inadequate at the end of four and a half years. This difference in achievement may suggest that Anna had less initial capacity. But an alternative hypothesis is possible.

One should remember that Anna never received the prolonged and expert attention that Isabelle received. The result of such attention, in the case of the Ohio girl, was to give her speech at an early stage, and her subsequent rapid development seems to have been a consequence of that. "Until Isabelle's speech and language development she had all the characteristics of a feeble-minded child." Had Anna, who, from the standpoint of psychometric tests and early history, closely resembled this girl at the start, been given a mastery of speech at an earlier point by intensive training, her subsequent development might have been much more rapid. . . .

Consideration of Isabelle's case serves to show, as Anna's case does not clearly show, that isolation up to the age of six, with failure to acquire any form of speech and hence failure to grasp nearly the whole world of cultural meaning, does not preclude the subsequent acquisition of these. Indeed, there seems to be a process of accelerated recovery in which the child goes through the mental stages at a more rapid rate than would be the case in normal development. Just what would be the maximum age at which a person could remain isolated and still retain the capacity for full cultural acquisition is hard to say. Almost certainly it would not be as high as age fifteen; it might possibly be as low as age ten. Undoubtedly various individuals would differ considerably as to the exact age.

Anna's is not an ideal case for showing the effects of extreme isolation, partly because she was possibly deficient to begin with, partly because she did not receive the best training available, and partly because she did not live long enough. Nevertheless, her case is instructive when placed in the record with numerous other cases of extreme isolation. This and the previous article about her are meant to place her in the record. It is to be hoped that other cases will be described in the scientific literature as they are discovered (as unfortunately they will be), for only in these rare cases of extreme isolation is it possible "to observe *concretely separated* two factors in the development of human personality which are always otherwise only analytically separated, the biogenic and the sociogenic factors."

Ongoing Socialization Explains Social Behavior

PETER L. BERGER AND THOMAS LUCKMANN

Sociologists Peter L. Berger and Thomas Luckmann, writing in one of the most influential and widely read theory books of the 1960s, define and describe two forms of socialization in this viewpoint: primary and secondary. Most children receive primary socialization from their immediate families through the daily interaction that begins at birth. Children learn language through primary socialization and also to care for their own physical needs. They learn how their parents expect them to behave, and thereby also begin to learn what society expects. Through this process, children establish an identity, what Mead called a "self," a sense of "who am I?" and "how do I fit into society?" In describing primary socialization, Berger and Luckmann rely on Mead's viewpoint, an excerpt from which you read in Chapter 1.

Functionalists often portray socialization as something society applies to children to teach them to function effectively, but symbolic interactionists argue that socialization is an interactive process that continues throughout life. Neither children nor adults passively accept what is taught but actively interpret the information offered. Berger and Luckmann explain that people understand secondary socialization, learning a new occupation for example, based on their primary socialization. While children have no choice about initially accepting their families' definition of reality, people can and do choose whether to accept a new set of values and beliefs.

Think about the social change you have experienced during your lifetime. Do you passively adopt or critically evaluate change in clothing styles, popular music, media offerings, and political platforms? All of these are examples of the secondary socialization this viewpoint describes. Secondary socialization is not limited to learning a new occupation, but would also include, for example, examining your family's religious beliefs and accepting or rejecting them for yourself.

QUESTIONS

1. Berger and Luckmann refer often to "definition of the situation." Explain this term.
2. What is the major means by which primary socialization takes place? When does primary socialization end?
3. How do primary socialization, biology, and identification relate to secondary socialization? When does secondary socialization end?

■ ■ ■

Primary Socialization

Every individual is born into an objective social structure within which he encounters the significant others who are in charge of his socialization. These significant others are imposed upon him. Their definitions of his situation are posited for him as objective reality. He is thus born into not only an objective social structure but also an objective social world. The significant others who mediate this world to him modify it in the course of mediating it. They select aspects of it in accordance with their own location in the social structure, and also by virtue of their individual, biographically rooted idiosyncrasies. The social world is "filtered" to the individual through this double selectivity. Thus the lower-class child not only absorbs a lower-class perspective on the social world, he absorbs it in the idiosyncratic coloration given it by his parents (or whatever other individuals are in charge of his primary socialization). The same lower-class perspective may induce a mood of contentment, resignation, bitter resentment, or seething rebelliousness. Consequently, the lower-class child will not only come to inhabit a world greatly different from that of an upper-class child, but may do so in a manner quite different from the lower-class child next door. . . .

Primary socialization creates in the child's consciousness a progressive abstraction from the roles and attitudes of specific others to roles and attitudes *in general*. For example, in the internalization of norms there is a progression from "Mummy is angry with me *now*" to "Mummy is angry with me *whenever* I spill the soup." As additional significant others (father, grandmother, older sister, and so on) support the mother's negative attitude toward soup-spilling, the generality of the norm is subjectively extended. The decisive step comes when the child recognizes that *everybody* is against soup-spilling, and the norm is generalized to "*One* does not spill soup"—"one" being himself as part of a generality that includes, in principle, *all* of society insofar as it is significant to the child. This abstraction from the roles and attitudes of concrete significant others is called the generalized other. Its formation within consciousness means that the individual now identifies not only with concrete others but with a generality of others, that is, with a society. Only by virtue of this generalized identification does his own self-identification attain stability and continuity. He now has not only an identity *vis-à-vis* this or that significant other, but an identity *in general*, which is subjectively apprehended as remaining the same no matter what others, significant or not, are encountered. This newly coherent identity incorporates within itself all the various internalized roles and attitudes—including, among many other things, the self-identification as a non-spiller of soups.

Primary socialization ends when the concept of the generalized other (and all that goes with it) has been established in the consciousness of the individual. At this point he is an effective member of society and in subjective possession of a self and a world. But this internalization of society, identity and reality is not a matter of once and for all. Socialization is never total and never finished. . . .

Secondary Socialization

The formal processes of secondary socialization are determined by its fundamental problem: it always presupposes a preceding process of primary socialization; that is, that it must deal with an already formed self and an already internalized world. It cannot construct subjective reality *ex nihilo*. This presents a problem because the already internalized reality has a tendency to persist. Whatever new contents are now to be internalized must somehow be superimposed upon this already present reality. There is, therefore, a problem of consistency between the original and the new internalizations. The problem may be more or less difficult of solution in different cases. Having learned that cleanliness is a virtue in one's own person it is not difficult to transfer the same virtue to one's horse. But having learned that certain obscenities are reprehensible as a pedestrian child, it may need some explanation that they are now *de rigueur* as a member of the cavalry. To establish and maintain consistency secondary socialization presupposes conceptual procedures to integrate different bodies of knowledge.

In secondary socialization, biological limitations become decreasingly important to the learning sequences, which now come to be established in terms of intrinsic properties of the knowledge to be acquired; that is, in terms of the foundational structure of that knowledge. For example, in order to learn certain hunting techniques one must first learn mountain climbing; or in order to learn calculus one must first learn algebra. The learning sequences can also be manipulated in terms of the vested interests of the personnel administering the body of knowledge. For example, it can be established that one must learn divination from animal entrails before one can learn divination from the flight of birds, or that one must have a high-school diploma before one can enroll in an embalming school, or that one must pass an examination in Gaelic before being eligible for a position in the Irish civil service. Such stipulations are extrinsic to the knowledge pragmatically required for the performance of the roles of diviner, embalmer, or Irish civil servant. They are established institutionally to enhance the prestige of the roles in question or to meet other ideological interests. A grade-school education may be perfectly sufficient to grasp the curriculum of an embalming school, and Irish civil servants carry on their normal business in the English language. It may even happen that the learning sequences thus manipulated are pragmatically dysfunctional. For instance, it may be stipulated that a college background in "general culture" should precede the professional training of research sociologists, while their actual activities might in fact be more efficiently carried on if they were unburdened with "culture" of this sort.

Identification with Significant Others

While primary socialization cannot take place without an emotionally charged identification of the child with his significant others, most secondary socialization can dispense with this kind of identification and proceed effectively with only the amount of mutual identification that enters into any communication between human beings. Put crudely, it is necessary to love one's mother, but not one's teacher. Socialization in later life typically begins to take on an affectivity reminiscent of childhood when it seeks radically to transform the subjective reality of the individual. This posits special problems that we shall analyze a little further on.

In primary socialization the child does not apprehend his significant others as institutional functionaries, but as mediators of reality *tout court*; the child internalizes the world of his parents as *the* world, and not as the world appertaining to a specific institutional context. Some of the crises that occur after primary socialization are indeed caused by the recognition that the world of one's parents is *not* the only world there is, but has a very specific social location, perhaps even one with a pejorative connotation. For example, the older child comes to recognize that the world represented by his parents, the same world that he had previously taken for granted as inevitable reality, is actually the world of uneducated, lower-class, rural Southerners. In secondary socialization, the institutional context is usually apprehended. Needless to say, this need not involve a sophisticated understanding of all the implications of the institutional context. Yet the Southern child, to stay within the same example, does apprehend his school teacher as an institutional functionary in a way he never did his parents, and he understands the teacher's role as representing institutionally specific meanings—such as those of the nation as against the region, of the national middle-class world as against the lower-class ambience of his home, of the city as against the countryside. Hence the social interaction between teachers and learners can be formalized. The teachers need not be significant others in any sense of the word. They are institutional functionaries with the formal assignment of transmitting specific knowledge. The roles of secondary socialization carry a high degree of anonymity; that is, they are readily detached from their individual performers. The same knowledge taught by one teacher could also be taught by another. Any functionary of this type could teach this type of knowledge. The individual functionaries may, of course, be subjectively differentiated in various ways (as more or less congenial, better or worse teachers of arithmetic, and so on), but they are in principle interchangeable.

This formality and anonymity are, of course, linked with the affective character of social relations in secondary socialization. Their most important consequence, however, is to bestow on the contents of what is learned in secondary socialization much less subjective inevitability than the contents of primary socialization possess. Therefore, the reality accent of knowledge internalized in secondary socialization is more easily bracketed (that is, the subjective sense that these internalizations are real is more fugitive). It takes severe biographical shocks to disintegrate the massive reality internalized in early childhood; much less to destroy the realities internalized later. Beyond this, it is relatively easy to set aside the reality of the secondary internalizations. The child lives willy-nilly in the world as defined by his parents, but he can cheerfully leave the world of arithmetic behind him as soon as he leaves the classroom.

This makes it possible to detach a part of the self and its concomitant reality as relevant only to the role-specific situation in question. The individual then establishes distance between his total self and its reality on the one hand, and the role-specific partial self and its reality on the other. This important feat is possible only after primary socialization has taken place.

Put crudely once more, it is easier for the child "to hide" from his teacher than from his mother. Conversely, it is possible to say that the development of this capacity "to hide" is an important aspect of the process of growing into adulthood. . . .

The Nature of Learning Sequences

The facts that the processes of secondary socialization do not presuppose a high degree of identification and its contents do not possess the quality of inevitability can be pragmatically useful because they permit learning sequences that are rational and emotionally controlled. But because the contents of this type of internalization have a brittle and unreliable subjective reality compared to the internalizations of primary socialization, in some cases special techniques must be developed to produce whatever identification and inevitability are deemed necessary. The need for such techniques may be intrinsic in terms of learning and applying the contents of internalization, or it may be posited for the sake of the vested interests of the personnel administering the socialization process in question. For example, an individual who wants to become an accomplished musician must immerse himself in his subject to a degree quite unnecessary for an individual learning to be an engineer. Engineering education can take place effectively through formal, highly rational, emotionally neutral processes. Musical education, on the other hand, typically involves much higher identification with a maestro and a much more profound immersion in musical reality. This difference comes from the intrinsic differences between engineering and musical knowledge, and between the ways of life in which these two bodies of knowledge are practically applied. A professional revolutionary, too, needs an immeasurably higher degree of identification and inevitability than an engineer. But here the necessity comes not from intrinsic properties of the knowledge itself, which may be quite simple and sparse in content, but from the personal commitment required of a revolutionary in terms of the vested interests of the revolutionary movement. Sometimes the necessity for the intensifying techniques may come from both intrinsic and extrinsic factors. The socialization of religious personnel is one example.

The techniques applied in such cases are designed to intensify the affective charge of the socialization process. Typically, they involve the institutionalization of an elaborate initiation process, a novitiate, in the course of which the individual comes to commit himself fully to the reality that is being internalized. When the process requires an actual transformation of the individual's "home" reality it comes to replicate as closely as possible the character of primary socialization, as we shall see a little later. But even short of such transformation, secondary socialization becomes affectively charged to the degree to which immersion in and commitment to the new reality are institutionally defined as necessary. The relationship of the individual to the socializing personnel becomes correspondingly charged with "significance," that is, the socializing personnel take on the character of significant others *vis-à-vis* the individual being socialized. The individual then commits himself in a comprehensive way to the new reality. He "gives himself" to music, to the revolution, to the faith, not just partially but with what is subjectively the whole of his life. The readiness to sacrifice oneself is, of course, the final consequence of this type of socialization. . . .

The institutionalized distribution of tasks between primary and secondary socialization varies with the complexity of the social distribution of knowledge. As long as it is relatively uncomplicated, the same institutional agency can proceed from primary to secondary socialization and carry on the latter to a considerable extent. In cases of very high complexity, specialized agencies for secondary socialization may have to be developed, with full-time personnel specially trained for the educational tasks in question. Short of this degree of specialization, there may be a sequence of socializing agencies combining this task with others. In the latter case, for example, it may be established that at a certain age a boy is transferred from his mother's hut to the warriors' barracks, where he will be trained to become a horseman. This need not entail full-time educational personnel. The older horsemen may teach the younger ones. The development of modern education is, of course, the best illustration of secondary socialization taking place under the auspices of specialized agencies. The resultant decline in the position of the family with regard to secondary socialization is too well known to require further elaboration here.

VIEWPOINT

3

Statuses and Roles Explain Social Behavior

RALPH LINTON

Anthropologist Ralph Linton (1893-1953) was the first to distinguish the important sociological concepts of status and role. Here, he contends that functioning societies require reciprocal behavior patterns for interpersonal interaction. A status is a set of rights and duties that defines the positions people in society occupy. Statuses include work occupations, but also such social positions as mother, voter, and driver. When people carry out the rights and duties associated with a status, they perform a role. As in the example of mother, one status can have many associated roles (housekeeper, cook, teacher, physician, disciplinarian, etc.). A status can be ascribed—assigned without regard for choice—or achieved— acquired by choice. Most societies ascribe status on the basis of sex, age, family, and social class. Linton argues that societies experiencing change offer more achieved status opportunities than less dynamic societies. Most important is the viewpoint that the concepts of status and role link individuals with their societies.

Excerpted from Ralph Linton, *The Study of Man*, ©1936, renewed 1964, pp. 113-18, 128-30. Reprinted by permission of Prentice Hall, Englewood Cliffs, New Jersey.

100

QUESTIONS

1. According to Linton's definitions, is "student" a status or a role?
2. Again by Linton's definitions, is an "overweight" status ascribed or achieved?
3. Can a role exist without a corresponding status, according to Linton?

■ ■ ■

The functioning of societies depends upon the presence of patterns for reciprocal behavior between individuals or groups of individuals. The polar positions in such patterns of reciprocal behavior are technically known as *statuses*. The term *status*, like the term *culture*, has come to be used with a double significance. A *status*, in the abstract, is a position in a particular pattern. It is thus quite correct to speak of each individual as having many statuses, since each individual participates in the expression of a number of patterns. However, unless the term is qualified in some way, *the status* of any individual means the sum total of all the statuses which he occupies. It represents his position with relation to the total society. Thus the status of Mr. Jones as a member of his community derives from a combination of all the statuses which he holds as a citizen, as an attorney, as a Mason, as a Methodist, as Mrs. Jones's husband, and so on.

A status, as distinct from the individual who may occupy it, is simply a collection of rights and duties. Since these rights and duties can find expression only through the medium of individuals, it is extremely hard for us to maintain a distinction in our thinking between statuses and the people who hold them and exercise the rights and duties which constitute them. The relation between any individual and any status he holds is somewhat like that between the driver of an automobile and the driver's place in the machine. The driver's seat with its steering wheel, accelerator, and other controls is a constant with ever-present potentialities for action and control, while the driver may be any member of the family and may exercise these potentialities very well or very badly.

A *role* represents the dynamic aspect of a status. The individual is socially assigned to a status and occupies it with relation to other statuses. When he puts the rights and duties which constitute the status into effect, he is performing a role. Role and status are quite inseparable, and the distinction between them is of only academic interest. There are no roles without statuses or statuses without roles. Just as in the case of *status*, the term *role* is used with a double significance. Every individual has a series of roles deriving from the various patterns in which he participates and at the same time *a role*, general, which represents the sum total of these roles and determines what he does for his society and what he can expect from it.

Although all statuses and roles derive from social patterns and are integral parts of patterns, they have an independent function with relation to the individuals who occupy particular statuses and exercise their roles. To such individuals the combined status and role represent the minimum of attitudes and behavior which he must assume if he is to participate in the overt expression of the pattern. Status and role serve to reduce the ideal patterns for social life to individual terms. They become models for organizing the attitudes and behavior of the individuals so that these will be congruous with those of the other individuals participating in the expression of the pattern. Thus if we are studying football teams in the abstract, the position of quarter-back is meaningless except in relation to the other positions. From the point of view of the quarter-back himself it is a distinct and important entity. It determines where he shall take his place in the line-up and what he shall do in various plays. His assignment to this position at once limits and defines his activities and establishes a minimum of things which he must learn. Similarly, in a social pattern such as that for the employer-employee relationship the statuses of employer and employee define what each has to know and do to put the pattern into operation. The employer does not need to know the techniques involved in the employee's labor, and the employee does not need to know the techniques for marketing or accounting.

It is obvious that, as long as there is no interference from external sources, the more perfectly the members of any society are adjusted to their statuses and roles the more smoothly the society will function. In its attempts to bring about such adjustments every society finds itself caught on the horns of a dilemma. The individual's formation of habits and attitudes begins at birth, and, other things being equal, the earlier his training for a status can begin the more successful it is likely to be. At the same time, no two individuals are alike, and a status which will be congenial to one may be quite uncongenial to another. Also, there are in all social systems certain roles which require more than training for their successful performance. Perfect technique does not make a great violinist, nor a thorough book knowledge of tactics an efficient general. The utilization of the special gifts of individuals may be highly important to society, as in the case of the general, yet these gifts usually show themselves rather late, and to wait upon their manifestation for the assignment of statuses would be to forfeit the advantages to be derived from commencing training early.

Ascribed and Achieved Statuses

Fortunately, human beings are so mutable that almost any normal individual can be trained to the adequate performance of almost any role. Most of the business of living can be conducted on a basis of habit, with little need for intelligence and none for special gifts. Societies have met the dilemma by developing two types of statuses, the *ascribed* and the *achieved*. *Ascribed* statuses are those which are assigned to individuals without reference to their innate differences or abilities. They can be predicted and trained for from the moment of birth. The *achieved* statuses are, as a minimum, those requiring special qualities, although they are not necessarily limited to these. They are not assigned to individuals from birth but are left open to be filled through competition and individual effort. The majority of the statuses in all social systems are of the ascribed type and those which take care of the ordinary day-to-day business of living are practically always of this type.

In all societies certain things are selected as reference points for the ascription of status. The things chosen for this purpose are always of such a nature that they are ascertainable at birth, making it possible to begin the training of the individual for his potential statuses and roles at once. The simplest and most universally used of these reference points is sex. Age is used with nearly equal frequency, since all individuals pass through the same cycle of growth, maturity, and decline, and the statuses whose occupation will be determined by age can be forecast and trained for with accuracy. Family relationships, the simplest and most obvious being that of the child to its mother, are also used in all societies as reference points for the establishment of a whole series of statuses. Lastly, there is the matter of birth into a particular socially established group, such as a class or caste. The use of this type of reference is common but not universal. In all societies the actual ascription of statuses to the individual is controlled by a series of these reference points which together serve to delimit the field of his future participation in the life of the group.

Sex as an Ascribed Status

The division and ascription of statuses with relation to sex seems to be basic in all social systems. All societies prescribe different attitudes and activities to men and to women. Most of them try to rationalize these prescriptions in terms of the physiological differences between the sexes or their different roles in reproduction. However, a comparative study of the statuses ascribed to women and men in different cultures seems to show that while such factors may have served as a starting point for the development of a division the actual ascriptions are almost entirely determined by culture. Even the psychological characteristics ascribed to men and women in different societies vary so much that they can have little physiological basis. Our own idea of women as ministering angels contrasts sharply with the ingenuity of women as torturers among the Iroquois and the sadistic delight they took in the process. Even the last two generations have seen a sharp change in the psychological patterns for women in our own society. The delicate, fainting lady of the middle eighteen-hundreds is as extinct as the dodo.

When it comes to the ascription of occupations, which is after all an integral part of status, we find the differences in various societies even more marked. Arapesh women regularly carry heavier loads than men "because their heads are so much harder and stronger." In some societies women do most of the manual labor; in others, as in the Marquesas, even cooking, housekeeping, and baby-tending are proper male occupations, and women spend most of their time primping. Even the general rule that women's handicap through pregnancy and nursing indicates the more active occupations as male and the less active ones as female has many exceptions. Thus among the Tasmanians seal-hunting was women's work. They swam out to the seal rocks, stalked the animals, and clubbed them. Tasmanian women also hunted opossums, which required the climbing of large trees.

Although the actual ascription of occupations along sex lines is highly variable, the pattern of sex division is constant. There are very few societies in which every important activity has not been definitely assigned to men or to women. Even when the two sexes coöperate in a particular occupation, the field of each is usually clearly delimited. Thus in Madagascar rice culture the men make the seed beds and terraces and prepare the fields for transplanting. The women do the work of transplanting, which is hard and back-breaking. The women weed the crop, but the men harvest it. The women then carry it to the threshing floors, where the men thresh it while the women winnow it. Lastly, the women pound the grain in mortars and cook it.

When a society takes over a new industry, there is often a period of uncertainty during which the work may be done by either sex, but it soon falls into the province of one or the other. In Madagascar, pottery is made by men in some tribes and by women in others. The only tribe in which it is made by both men and women is one into which the art has been introduced within the last sixty years. I was told that during the fifteen years preceding my visit there had been a marked decrease in the number of male potters, many men who had once practised the art having given it up. The factor of lowered wages, usually advanced as the reason for men leaving one of our own occupations when women enter it in force, certainly was not operative here. The field was not overcrowded, and the prices for men's and women's products were the same. Most of the men who had given up the trade were vague as to their reasons, but a few said frankly that they did not like to compete with women. Apparently the entry of women into the occupation had robbed it of a certain amount of prestige. It was no longer quite the thing for a man to be a potter, even though he was a very good one. . . .

Achieved Statuses Compared
with Ascribed Statuses

Ascribed statuses, whether assigned according to biological or to social factors, compose the bulk of all social systems. However, all these systems also include a varying number of statuses which are open to individual achievement. It seems as though many statuses of this type were primarily designed to serve as baits for socially acceptable behavior or as escapes for the individual. All societies rely mainly on their ascribed statuses to take care of the ordinary business of living. Most of the statuses which are thrown open to achievement do not touch this business very deeply. The honored ones are extremely satisfying to the individuals who achieve them, but many of them are no more vital to the ordinary functioning of the society than are honorary degrees or inclusions in "Who's Who" among ourselves.

Most societies make only a grudging admission of the fact that a limited number of statuses do require special gifts for their successful performance. Since such gifts rarely manifest themselves in early childhood, these statuses are, of necessity, thrown open to competition. At the same time, the pattern of ascribing all vital statuses is so strong that all societies limit this competition with reference to sex, age, and social affiliations. Even in our own society, where the field open to individual achievement is theoretically unlimited, it is strictly limited in fact. No woman can become President of the United States. Neither could a Negro nor an Indian, although there is no formal rule on this point, while a Jew or even a Catholic entering the presidential race would be very seriously handicapped from the outset. Even with regard to achievable statuses which are of much less social importance and which, perhaps, require more specific gifts, the same sort of limited competition is evident. It would be nearly if not quite impossible for either a woman or a Negro to become conductor of our best symphony orchestra, even if better able to perform the duties involved than any one else in America. At the same time, no man could become president of the D. A. R. [Daughters of the American Revolution], and it is doubtful whether any man, unless he adopted a feminine *nom de plume* [pen name], could even conduct a syndicated column on advice to the lovelorn, a field in which our society assumes, *a priori*, that women have greater skill.

These limitations upon the competition for achieved statuses no doubt entail a certain loss to society. Persons with special talents appear to be mutants and as such are likely to appear in either sex and in any social class. At the same time, the actual loss to societies through this failure to use their members' gifts to the full is probably a good deal less than persons reared in the American tradition would like to believe. Individual talent is too sporadic and too unpredictable to be allowed any important part in the organization of society. Social systems have to be built upon the potentialities of the average individual, the person who has no special gifts or disabilities. Such individuals can be trained to occupy almost any status and to perform the associated role adequately if not brilliantly. The social ascription of a particular status, with the intensive training that such ascription makes possible, is a guarantee that the role will be performed even if the performance is mediocre. If a society waited to have its statuses filled by individuals with special gifts, certain statuses might not be filled at all. The ascription of status sacrifices the possibility of having certain roles performed superlatively well to the certainty of having them performed passably well.

When a social system has achieved a good adjustment to the other sectors of the group's culture and, through these, to the group's environment, it can get along very well without utilizing special gifts. However, as soon as changes within the culture or in the external environment produce maladjustments, it has to recognize and utilize these gifts. The development of new social patterns calls for the individual qualities of thought and initiative, and the freer the rein given to these the more quickly new adjustments can be arrived at. For this reason, societies living under new or changing conditions are usually characterized by a wealth of achievable statuses and by very broad delimitations of the competition for them. Our own now extinct frontier offered an excellent example of this. Here the class lines of the European societies from which the frontier population had been drawn were completely discarded and individuals were given an unprecedented opportunity to find their place in the new society by their own abilities.

As social systems achieve adjustment to their settings, the

social value of individual thought and initiative decreases. Thorough training of the component individuals becomes more necessary to the survival and successful functioning of society than the free expression of their individual abilities. Even leadership, which calls for marked ability under conditions of change, becomes largely a matter of routine activities. To ensure successful training, more and more statuses are transferred from the achieved to the ascribed group, and the competition for those which remain is more and more rigidly delimited. To put the same thing in different terms, individual opportunities decrease. There is not an absolute correlation between the degree of adjustment of a social system to its setting and the limitation of individual opportunity. Thus if the group attaches a high value to individual initiative and individual rights, certain statuses may be left open to competition when their ascription would result in greater social efficiency. However, well-adjusted societies are, in general, characterized by a high preponderance of ascribed over achieved statuses, and increasing perfection of adjustment usually goes hand in hand with increasing rigidity of the social system.

VIEWPOINT

4

Social Structure Explains Social Behavior

Bruce H. Mayhew

Bruce Mayhew, a widely published sociologist who followed the structuralist tradition of Georg Simmel, performed dozens of research projects that demonstrated the influence of social structure on social behavior. For example, Mayhew demonstrates mathematically in one article (1976) that power concentrates in a group of people as the group size increases. This finding supports Michels's concept of oligarchy, which you will read about in Chapter 4. Mayhew maintains that interaction patterns can and *should* be studied apart from their content. Patterned relationships, whether of individuals, groups, organizations, or institutions, can be mapped and the interaction networks studied.

In this viewpoint, Mayhew argues that patterned social relationships explain interpersonal interaction. For example, society specifies that professors and students communicate in expected ways regardless of which individuals the interaction involves: Professor Smith or Professor Gomez or student Jai Ling or student Chris Jones. Psychologists (or, in Mayhew's

Reprinted, with permission, from *Social Forces* 59:627-48 (March 1981). "Structuralism vs. Individualism: Part 2, Ideological and Other Obfuscations" by Bruce H. Mayhew. Copyright © The University of North Carolina Press.

terms, "individualists") study individual behavior. Structuralists acknowledge that individuals behave, but study the ways social structure regulates interaction between individuals in various social positions. The same social principles that regulate interaction between individuals also apply to interaction between corporations or nations, depending on the positions they occupy in the social structure. Therefore, structuralists conclude that social structure determines social behavior.

QUESTIONS

1. How does Mayhew support his claim that studying organizational forms is more productive than studying individual actions?
2. What does Mayhew say about network size?
3. According to Mayhew, what is the primary task of sociology?

■ ■ ■

Writing in 1847, Karl Marx formulated the view of society which I take to be fundamental: "Society does not consist of individuals, but expresses the sum of interrelations in which individuals stand with respect to one another". In this view, the individual is never the unit of analysis in either research or theory construction. Rather, in this *structuralist* conception of social life, sociologists are studying a communication network mapped on some human population. That network, the interaction which proceeds through it, and the social structures which emerge in it are the subject matter of sociology. Sociology is therefore the study of this network's *organization*. It is an attempt to construct and test explanations of variation in social organization.

Of course, structuralists conceive of their task in somewhat broader terms than "social organization" alone would suggest. They are also concerned with determining how social organization is related to other forms of organization. At a minimum, the latter include (1) the *organization of information* (symbols)—commonly called the cultural or ideological system—and (2) the *organization of materials* (tools)—commonly called the technological system. Most structuralists would also insist that explaining social organization presupposes a knowledge of the social network's underlying demographic structure as well as its ecological context (bio-physical and social environment).

In studying organization, structuralists are concerned with at least two kinds of phenomena: (1) aggregate properties of populations and (2) *emergent* (purely structural) properties of organization itself. An aggregate property is one which can be used to construct a variable by simple addition of bio-physical characteristics of individual population elements, e.g., population size. However, an emergent property can only be constructed from relations between population elements. In the case of social organization, an emergent property is one defined on the overall connectivity of the network, and is not, therefore, derived from characteristics of individual population elements. The division of labor and the degree of stratification are emergent properties of social organization.

The Primary Task of Sociology

Structuralists do not study human behavior. The behavior they do study is that of the variables which define various aspects of social organization, its population, environment, ideological and technological subsystems. For structuralists, a general sociological theory is a set of theorems stated in terms of these variables, theorems which will predict and explain the structure and dynamics of societal phenomena. This is a rather large task—coextensive with sociology itself—and it has few workers in the United States.

Most American sociologists do not study sociology in the structuralist sense of the term indicated above. Rather, they merely assume the existence of social structures in order to study their impact on *individuals*, that is, in order to study *social psychology* (the study of the behavior and experience of individuals in social stimulus situations). In this subfield of psychology the objectives are expected to be aligned with those of general psychology, not necessarily with the objectives of sociology. In other words, most American sociologists adopt the *individualist* perspective in that the individual is their unit of analysis and so-called "human behavior" (in both its subjective and objective aspects) is the individual level phenomena they seek to explain or interpret.

To a very large degree, this means that structuralists and individualists are asking different questions. They are attempting to explain different things. I would not say (as individualists often do) that structuralists and individualists are merely studying different aspects of the same phenomena. This may happen in a few instances, but generally their paths of inquiry diverge to such a marked degree that no shared language and no line of communication unites them in any common discourse. From my structuralist point of view, the psychological concerns of American sociologists do not bear on questions of social structure and organization, and at best would have only a secondary relevance to them. The reason for this is quite simple (say the structuralists). If one assumes the structure of society in order to examine its impact on the immediate acts, thoughts, and feelings of individuals, one has assumed most of what has to be explained (indeed, about 95 percent of the variation in human society) in order to study a small part of human activity and experience (about 5 percent—and as such, difficult to distinguish from random noise). Whereas, in the structuralist view, the primary task of sociology is not to assume the empirical conditions of social structure, but to explain its existence in the first place (the opposite of social psychology's concerns). The reason for this, of course, is that structural sociologists are interested in explaining most of what happens in human society, not some minute fraction of it.

Structuralists Study Relationships

Individualists and structuralists, each within their respective domains of inquiry, can examine various relationships. However, I will select for illustration here only one for each. Out of all the types of relations between phenomena they may examine, the two shown in Figure 1 are exclusive to each approach. That is, as shown in Figure 1-A, structuralists may examine relations between one form of organization and another (at the same or different points in time), but individualists would never do this. Similarly, as shown in Figure 1-B, individualists may examine relations between one individual action and another (at the same or different points in time), but structuralists would never do this. The two extreme cases shown in Figure 1 are intended to indicate just how far apart the two approaches can be (although Figure 1 does not exhaust the possibilities for either). To mention concrete cases, Figure 1-A is exemplified in Offe's treatment of the *relation* between the organization of occupational positions in a bureaucratic hierarchy (social organization) and the organization of ideas (information) about the way these positions are reputedly filled through rules of performance (ideological system). Figure 1-B is exemplified in Collins' discussion of the *relation* between what an individual talks about at one point in time (individual action) and what the same individual talks about at a later point in time (individual action).

Many individualists do not believe there is any difference between the phenomena distinguished in Figure 1. They would probably say that the organization in Figure 1-A is nothing more than the actions (behaviors) of individuals in Figure 1-B. Structuralists would reply that the individualists are wrong, or that any existing correspondence between the two is irrelevant. I will try to illustrate (very briefly) why structuralists see a difference between the two.

Figure 2 illustrates two forms of organization in social networks. Each is comprised of points and directed lines. Points may be interpreted as positions (not individuals) and directed lines as asymmetric social relations defining each network. The positions may be occupied by individuals, households, communities, associations, and the like. But—for the benefit of example—I will assume they are occupied by individual humans. The social relations may refer to any kind of communi-

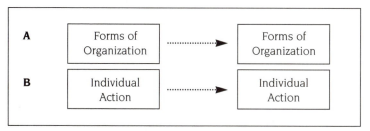

FIGURE 1. Structuralists relate forms of organization to one another (*A*), while individualists relate individual actions to one another (*B*).

cation link (direct or indirect) between positions (as long as their asymmetric quality is preserved). They could, for example, be interpreted to mean "has authority over." In this case, we would call the two forms of organization *dominance structures*, because they are defined by dominance relations, but also because they carry no identification of the concrete population elements occupying each of their positions.

The particular way concrete (identifiable) individuals are placed in the Figure 2 structures generates six *patterns* for the transitive form and two *patterns* for the cyclical form, as shown in Figure 3. The fact that these different patterns of individual arrangement can be identified means that individuals can change positions with respect to one another in a wide variety of ways *without altering the structure* at all. Not only can such form-preserving shifts in individual position occur, they have in fact been observed. And, since the shifts in position between concrete individuals can come about as a result of a wide variety of different actions (behaviors) of individuals, this indicates that *there can be a wide divergence between the actions of persons and the forms of organization they participate in.* In Figures 2 and 3, there is a much wider divergence between action and form in the transitive than in the cyclical configuration. Not only, therefore, may there be a disjunction between concrete behavior and organizational form, the degree of divergence is determined by the structure itself. And, the larger the set of population elements drawn together in such networks, the wider this divergence becomes.

Consider one more illustration of this difference. Figure 4

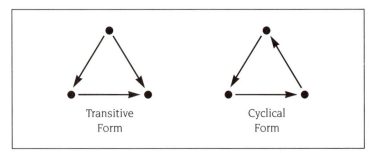

Transitive
Form

Cyclical
Form

FIGURE 2. Two different forms of network organization.

shows six interaction networks drawn as points and lines. Points represent positions (or locations) and lines represent communication (and/or transportation) links between positions. For the moment, I will assume that the positions are occupied by individuals who communicate with one another along the indicated lines. The three networks on the left-hand side of Figure 4 all have the property that they can be disrupted by the removal of at least one point (position). That is, all three have at least one point which, if removed, will break off communication between other positions in the network. Points which can produce such disruption are called cut-points and networks containing cut-points are said to be point-vulnerable. Thre three networks on the right-hand side of Figure 4 have no cut-points and are, therefore, point-invulnerable. Regardless of which point we remove from them, the remaining positions are still in communication with one another.

Point-vulnerability and point-invulnerability are purely structural properties of social networks. They are derived from the organization of the network itself, not from the characteristics of individuals occupying various positions in them, nor from the characteristics of the positions themselves. A cut-point is a cut-point not by virtue of its own characteristics, but because of the way in which the network is organized. Whether a cut-point exists at all depends entirely on the struc-

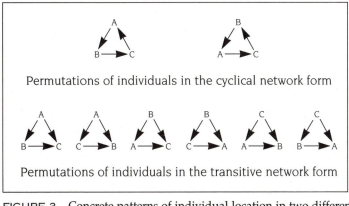

FIGURE 3. Concrete patterns of individual location in two different network forms.

ture of the network itself.

Social networks may vary a great deal in the number of cut-points they contain. The proportion of cut-points in a network is a measure of the a priori likelihood that it will be disrupted by a break in communication. It is also possible to assign a cutting-number to each cut-point. This cutting-number refers to the number of network pairs (of positions) which cease to communicate after the cut-point is removed (excluding pairs involving the cut-off point itself). The average cutting-number is a measure of the *magnitude* of a network's disruption potential, that is, of the degree of communicative disruption which is potentially contained in the *organization of the network*.

The amount of variability in all the above network properties depends primarily on the size of the network (the number of positions it defines). The larger the number of positions, the

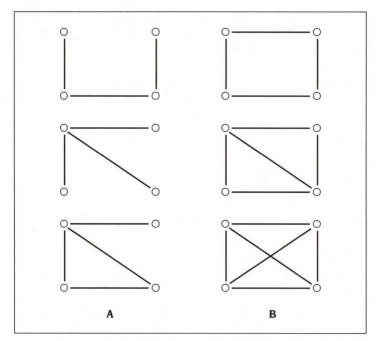

FIGURE 4. Point-vulnerable (*A*) and point-invulnerable (*B*) forms of organization in social networks.

greater the variability. In any case, all of these network properties depend directly on how the network is organized *and on nothing else*. The structuralist's concern with these properties involves relating them to other forms of organization, such as the division of labor and the degree of social stratification. That such concerns do not require paying attention to the concrete behaviors (actions) of individuals is easily discerned from Figure 4. Each of the networks in Figure 4 can channel wide varieties of individual action. These networks can map the flow of rumors, or business transactions, or moves in chess games, or any number of other concrete activities *without in any way altering the structural properties of each communication system.* In other words, there can be a wide divergence between activities of individuals and the structural relations through which these activities are expressed. It is for this reason (as well as for those mentioned in discussion of Figures 2 and 3) that structuralists consider the individualist equation of behavior = structure to be either false or irrelevant.

A Projected Individualist Rebuttal

Dyed-in-the-wool individualists will have no trouble doubting everything I have just said about the illustrations in Figure 2 and 4. Perhaps they will want to reflect on the consequences of filling the network positions in Figures 2 and 4 with groups instead of individuals. In that case, the positions might be occupied by villages, factories, or battleships. Each position would then contain its own internal network of social relations. Under these circumstances, the connection between structure in the larger network and items of individual behavior within each position's micro-network admits an even wider divergence between network properties and individual action than anything I have mentioned before. The huge gap between the two indicates just how far individualists are from sociology.

The usual response of individualists to the kinds of differences I have been discussing here is to ignore them. Homans tells us that "the arbitrary lines we draw between the psychological and the social will disappear" if we are willing to adopt the psychological priority of studying individuals, while ignoring other considerations. If he had said "sociology will disappear," I would agree with him. But, since these other considerations are what structuralists study, I am more inclined to agree with Znanlecki's contention: "We deny that the theories of psychology or of biology or of any other science can form the premises of sociological propositions." As I have attempted to illustrate, structuralists do not endorse this statement on the basis of some hypothetical possibility that there *might be* some difference between action at the level of the individual organism and structure at the level of the social network. Those who continue to believe that social structure can be reduced to the characteristics of individuals may wish to examine Krippendorff's mathematical proof of their error.

Structuralists conceive of sociology much in the fashion of [Georg] Simmel (a) as being concerned with forms of human association abstracted from their *specific* content. But they would not agree with his assumption that social phenomena require an "explication psychologique." Instead, they would concur with Marx (a) that relations among people have a material character which is largely independent of individual control or conscious action. Accordingly, there is a vast distance between the structuralist and the Weberian definitions of sociology.

Rewards and Punishments Explain Social Behavior

GEORGE C. HOMANS

Sociologist George C. Homans, president of the American Sociological Association in 1963-64 and a prolific theorist, contributed importantly to the development of exchange theory as applied in sociology. Exchange theory had its roots in the psychological reinforcement theory tradition that began with Pavlov's research using dogs and more recently was extended by B. F. Skinner. The basic idea from psychology was that external events determine behavior rather than internal psychological states. Any phenomenon that produces behavioral change is called a stimulus, and the behavioral change is called a response. Homans uses these terms to describe social interaction, arguing that individuals repeat actions they find rewarding and avoid actions with undesirable results. Theory from Homans and other early exchange theorists—Harold Kelley and John Thibaut (1959), Peter Blau (1964), and Richard Emerson (1981)—founded a sociological exchange theory tradition that remains influential in sociology today.

1. List Homans's success, perception, value, deprivation-satiation, and frustration-aggression propositions.
2. How does Homans's behavioral psychology differ from learning theory and the rational choice model?
3. According to Homans, why do people conform?

■ ■ ■

The characteristic problems of social science are problems of explanation, and the first of them is, What are its general propositions? Before the rise of academic anthropology and sociology at the end of the nineteenth century, the nature of the answer would have seemed obvious to most scholars. They would have answered: propositions about "human nature," about the psychic characteristics men share as members of a single species. It was anthropology and sociology, as we shall see, that first raised the possibility of there being an alternative answer. But at the very time the alternative was being put forward, the work that would furnish a reply to it was in progress—work in modern psychology. My contention will be that the original answer was correct, provided we accept the view modern psychology takes as to the essentials of human nature. It is not really a new view, except that it eliminates from the list of essentials some things that might have been considered such in the past. . . .

Behavioral Psychology

One proposition from B. Berelson and G. Steiner, *Human Behavior: An Inventory of Scientific Findings* is: "When a response is followed by a reward (or 'reinforcement'), the frequency or probability of its recurrence increases." This I call a proposition about the effect of the *success* of a person's action on its recurrence. Several other propositions in the same field ought to have been included. Thus, if a response (action) was followed by a reward under particular conditions (stimuli) in the past, the reappearance of similar conditions makes more frequent or probable the recurrence of the action. This I call a proposition about the effect on a person's action of his *perception* of the situation attending his action. Again, the higher the *value* a person sets on the reward, the more likely he is to take the action or repeat it; and the value of the reward increases the more the person has been *deprived* of it, as in hunger, and decreases the more nearly he has been *satiated* with it. If the reward has a negative value, that is, if the action has been punished, the probability of the action's recurring decreases. Several propositions about emotional behavior ought also to be included, such as the familiar one that, if a person is *frustrated*, he is apt to take action that may be described as aggressive.

Scholars in the field of "learning and thinking" would not agree as to just what propositions should be included on a list of fundamental ones. Nor, since like all scholars they set a high value on their own special terminologies, would they agree on the wording of the propositions. But most of them would agree that some of the propositions on the above list should be included, and most of them would agree on their substance.

"Learning Theory" or "Rational Choice"?

Propositions like these constitute what is often called "learning theory," but the name is misleading, for they continue to hold good of human responses long after the responses have, in every usual sense of the word, been learned. Though a man may learn quickly that he can buy food cheaply at a supermarket, his behavior does not for that reason cease to be governed by the value-proposition, and he will go back to the supermarket whenever he needs to buy food. Accordingly I prefer to speak of behavioral psychology rather than learning theory.

These propositions refer to voluntary behavior. A more complete set should include propositions about involuntary actions, the reflexes, such as the familiar knee-jerk. If I say no more about the reflexes, the reason is that they do not include the features of behavior of most interest to social scientists.

What has been called the "rational-choice model" of human behavior coincides in part with the body of propositions of behavioral psychology. The coincidence has not always been recognized, because the rational theory has usually been put forward not by psychologists but by other scholars, such as economists and mathematicians interested in explaining the process of decision-making. The main proposition of the rational theory in one of its forms may be stated as follows: In choosing between alternative courses of action, a person will choose the one for which, as perceived by him, the mathematical value of $p \times v$ is the greater, where p is the probability that the action will be successful in getting a given reward and v is the value to the person of that reward. The effect of value on action in the rational theory is embodied in the value-proposition of behavioral psychology; the effect of the probability of success, in the success-proposition. But the rational theory is obviously more limited than behavioral psychology. Though it recognizes the importance of perception, and assumes that a man is rational in acting in accordance with his perceptions even though in the eyes of persons better informed his perceptions may be incorrect, it simply takes the perceptions as given and does not tie them back, as behavioral psychology does, to past experience. In the same way, it takes a person's values as given and does not tie them back to deprivation and to the process by which new values are learned. Nor is it at all clear how the rational theory would deal with emotional behavior. But we need not worry about the limitations of the rational theory, so long as we recognize that it is not an alternative to behavioral psychology; the two are in fact largely the same. This, I argue, is a first point in favor of the view that the social sciences share the same body of general propositions.

This Is Behavioral Psychology

I cannot embark here on a treatise on behavioral psychology and spell out all the implications of the propositions. All I want to do is emphasize their main characteristics, and, above all, that they are psychological. They are psychological in two senses. First, they are usually stated and empirically tested by persons who call themselves psychologists. Though they are, as we shall see, used in explanation by all the social sciences, the field of research in which they lie is the special concern of only one of these sciences, psychology. Second, they are propositions about the behavior of individual human beings, rather than propositions about groups or societies as such; and the behavior of men, as men, is generally considered the province of psychology.

The propositions are not new, in the sense that they were once unknown and have had to be discovered. Though the language in which psychologists state them is unfamiliar because it aims at precision, their content is not. When we know what they mean, they do not surprise us, though some of their further implications may do so. Nor, we may guess, would they have surprised Cro-Magnon men. Indeed they are part of the traditional psychology of common sense.

Improvements on Traditional Psychology

Another part of that psychology this body of propositions leaves out or, better, de-emphasizes. The traditional psychology tended to argue that "human nature was the same the world over" in the sense that all human beings, or all of certain main kinds, shared certain very specific values. Thus all women were supposed to feel for their children something called "mother love"; they were supposed to find the care of their children naturally rewarding, and this was supposed to account, for instance, for universal features of the family as an institution. Human nature is certainly not concretely the same the world over, and modern anthropology and psychiatry have forced us to recognize many surprising ways in which it differs from society to society, from group to group, and from individual to individual. Faced with facts like these, the new psychology has not abandoned the idea of the universality of human nature, but has given up specific similarities for more general ones. It tends to emphasize, not that men hold similar values, but that, whatever their values may be, these values have similar effects on their behavior. A particular kind of reward may be valuable to one man or to the members of one group, a different kind valuable to another; and since the pursuit of different rewards often requires different actions, what the two men or groups do may differ concretely. Yet the proposition: the more valuable the reward, the more frequent or probable the action that gets the reward, holds good for both. Even if many men and women do share in some degree values built into them genetically and biologically—even if in this sense there is indeed something to be called "mother love"—still the actions they can learn to adopt in attaining these values are very varied: the actions are specified by instinct to a far lower degree than was assumed by the traditional psychology. There are also values, like that of money, that are not genetically determined but are themselves acquired by learning; different persons in different circumstances may acquire different ones, and yet the process is the same for all: like money, they become values in themselves by proving to be the means to other, more primordial values. It is often said that the new psychology emphasizes the plasticity of human behavior. It has kept—and extended and tested—just that part of the old psychology which, stressing how similar men are in *how* they learn, accounts paradoxically for how different they can be in *what* they learn. . . .

Psychological Explanation of Conformity

Institutions are among the main concerns of anthropology, sociology, political science, and history. Their defining characteristic is a set of rules or, as sociologists call them, norms: statements specifying how persons ought, or ought not, to behave in particular circumstances. Thus money as an institution is accompanied by rules against counterfeiting coins and bills, and the market, by rules against one form or another of rigging the market, of conspiracies in restraint of trade. One can make much progress in anthropology and sociology by working directly with the institutions, showing how they are related to one another within a particular society or across many societies, without ever worrying about whether the institutional rules are obeyed. But sooner or later one must ask why the rules are obeyed at all; one must raise the question of conformity to norms. For if its rules are not obeyed by some persons and to some extent, the institution in question does not effectively exist and is not worth studying. Accordingly the question of conformity is fundamental to much of social science.

How to explain why people—all people at some time or other—obey rules? If one thing is clear it is that rules are not obeyed automatically: they are not obeyed just because they are rules. We know this from experience in our own societies, and

Malinowski taught us long ago in one of the great books of social science that it is just as true of the so-called primitive societies. Speaking of the "compulsory obligations of one individual or group towards another individual or group" he wrote: "The fulfilment of such obligations is usually rewarded according to the measure of its perfection, while non-compliance is visited upon the remiss agent." Should the rewards or punishments fail, the primitive man does not continue to comply: "Whenever the native can evade his obligations without the loss of prestige, or without the prospective loss of gain, he does so, exactly as a civilized business man would do."

As two more recent writers on the subject of conformity put it: "The greater and more valued the reward, the oftener it is achieved through conformity behavior, the more conformist the behavior is likely to become, and the more likely it is to become a generalized way of behaving in new situations." In other words, if conforming to a norm brings a man success in attaining a reward, he is likely to conform. He is the more likely to do so, the more valuable he finds the reward. His success and the value of his success on one occasion makes his conformity more probable on other, similar occasions. But all these statements about the particular action of conforming follow directly from the propositions about actions in general that we have called the propositions of behavioral psychology. That is, the behavior that makes possible the very existence of institutions, which are in turn the things of most interest to the more "social" of social scientists, can only be explained through psychological propositions. . . .

The General Explanation for Human Behavior

Since the appearance of some of the same propositions in a variety of different deductive systems is evidence of the generality of these propositions for the explanation of findings within a particular field, I infer that propositions of behavioral psychology are the general explanatory propositions in the field of human behavior, that is, the field of social science. This does not mean of course that they are the only propositions that will appear in the explanations. Particular deductive systems will require particular propositions about the effects of given conditions. Nor does it mean that they allow us to explain every-thing. We shall never be able to explain many things because we have, and can get, no adequate information about the given conditions within which the general propositions are to be applied. I argue only that when we think we can explain, our general principles turn out to be psychological.

Conformity Explains Social Behavior

ROGER BROWN

An important sociological concept states that people conform to social expectations (norms) for their behavior, and that conformity to normative prescriptions provides order in society. If you are an employee and you know that another person is a vice president of your company, you communicate with that person differently from the way you communicate with your younger sibling. In these examples, you (wisely) conform to the vice president's expectations but most likely expect your younger sister or brother to conform to your expectations. But how does conformity operate within small groups of people who are alike? Researchers performed many small group experiments with, for example, groups of students at the same university, to try to find out.

In this viewpoint taken from his widely used textbook on social psychology, Roger Brown describes two of the most influential conformity experiments: Sherif's autokinetic effects and Asch's line length comparisons. In the 1930s and 1940s, Muzafer Sherif and his colleagues performed a series of ex-

Excerpted from *Social Psychology* by Roger Brown. New York: Free Press, 1965. Copyright Roger Brown. Reprinted by permission of the author.

periments in involving a most unfamiliar situation: participants watched a small spot of light in a dark room. The purpose of these experiments was to determine whether the participants would agree on whether and how much the light moved. Since none of the participants had prior experience in similar situations and only an optical illusion makes the light appear to move at all, these experiments provided an excellent test of conformity processes. Solomon Asch performed his conformity experiments in the 1950s using a more familiar scenario. At some time or other, most people have the experience of being asked to answer a question and then having their answer contradicted. When the person doing the contradicting is in a position of authority (for example, a parent or teacher), it is likely that the person agrees with the new answer. Asch's experiments showed what happens when those disagreeing are previously unacquainted peers and again demonstrated how conformity influences social interaction. Later experiments based on those from Sherif and Asch support the argument that people conform in small groups because they want to be liked and they want to be right. To this extent, conformity explains social behavior.

QUESTIONS

1. Brown offers one alternative to positive bonds as an explanation for conformity: that "consensus is the only reality." What does he mean?
2. Do the Sherif and Asch experiments both illustrate the emergence of norms?
3. From this research, would you qualify the argument that conformity explains social behavior? Why or why not?

The classical [conformity] study is that of Sherif. Sherif set his subjects the task of estimating the extent of movement of a single point of light in a completely dark room. A light of this kind cannot be definitely localized because there is nothing in reference to which one can locate it. Such a light, though it is in fact perfectly stationary, will seem to move and these movements are likely to appear erratic in direction and extent. This effect, called the autokinetic effect, was discovered by astronomers staring at a single star in the night sky, before psychology began. Sherif used it to explore the emergence of group standards.

The subject was told: "When the room is completely dark, I shall give you the signal *Ready* and then show you a point of light. After a short time the light will start to move. A few seconds later the light will disappear. Then tell me the distance it moved." The light was exposed to the subject by a small shutter controlled by the experimenter. Any subject's first judgments were likely to range rather widely but in the course of one hundred trials Sherif found that each subject settled down to a rather narrow range with a consistent central value. These ranges and standard values were quite different from one subject to another but very consistent for a given subject, even across several series of judgments made on different days. . . .

What happened when individuals who had established individual ranges in private sessions were combined into groups of two or three and asked to report their judgments aloud? Their judgments converged. In one group of three, individual A started by guessing that the light moved about seven inches; B guessed that it moved two inches and C that it moved less than one inch. After several sessions together all three subjects were consistently guessing in the range between two and four inches. Sometimes judgments converged on a value nearer the larger extreme and sometimes on a value nearer the smaller extreme but the general outcome was convergence toward the central tendency of the group. In these groups there was no request for unanimity, no argument, no effort to persuade, no clear sanctions for disagreement and often no awareness of any social influence. Nevertheless the individuals were much closer together in their judgments after they had been convened as groups than before.

In the groups created by Sherif there is only the expression of individual judgment to produce convergence and this would seem to be a minimal condition. How can individuals converge unless they know one another's position?

Sherif's situation, however, is not the simplest social condition imaginable. The simplest condition would seem to be one in which individuals work in one another's presence but without any explicit communication, the coworking group. The empirical study of group processes began with the coworking group, with comparisons between the performance of individuals working alone and working side by side. In one of these F.H. Allport (1924) had subjects judge the degree of pleasantness of odors in a series and the heaviness of a series of weights. He obtained a result which suggests that the wish to agree, to establish a norm, exists even in the coworking group. Subjects made fewer extreme judgments, that is judgments toward the ends of the scale, in the "together" condition than they did when working alone. It is as if they were trying to avoid deviation from a presumed central tendency of the group. . . .

There seems to be an almost ineradicable tendency for members of a group to move toward agreement. It occurs when there is no instruction to reach a consensus. It occurs when there is no opportunity to argue. It even occurs, incipiently, when the members do not know one another's opinions but can only guess at them. It occurs when the positive relations among the members are very weak. Leon Festinger and John Thibaut varied "pressure toward uniformity" in groups but found some change toward uniformity following a discussion in all groups under all conditions. Sherif's subjects . . . introduced to one another on the occasion of the experiment, must have had minimally strong positive bonds.

The autokinetic effect and Allport's aesthetic judgments do not have objectively correct answers and that may be the reason why opinions converged. I say that the problems do not have objectively correct answers because individuals, who understand them and who possess the relevant allowable information, if they work in isolation will not necessarily arrive at the same answer. On matters of this kind a consensus may be essential because the consensus is the only reality. Asch, in a vastly influential series of experiments (1956), has studied conformity effects with problems that do have objective answers.

The Asch Experiment

If you were a subject for Asch you would have been recruited for an experiment in visual perception. On arriving at the designated room you find Dr. Asch already there and also some other subjects like yourself. Subjects are to be seated in a row and you take the position next to the far left (actually you have been jockeyed into that position). Dr. Asch says that the experiment will involve the discrimination of length of lines. Before you, in the front of the room, is a single vertical line and just to the right of it, on cards, are three lines differing in length and numbered 1, 2, and 3. The cards will change but one of the three lines at the right will always be equal to a standard line on the left and it will be your job to select the correct line and report it by number. Judgments are to be spoken aloud, which seems to you a rather poor experimental procedure, but then that is the way with these pseudo-sciences. The order of reporting is from right to left down the row of subjects so you will be next to the last.

The first lines appear and the match is an obvious one. In fact the standard is 10 inches tall and the comparison lines are: Number 1 = 8¾ inches; Number 2 = 10 inches; Number 3 = 8 inches. It is quite easy to see that Number 2 is the correct answer, and apparently it is easy for everyone since the judges all report that number and so, when your turn comes, do you. The second trial is equally easy and the judgments are equally consistent and you begin to wonder whether the experimenter has not made some mistake and selected stimuli that are too obvious. The third set of lines appears and the match is as easily made as on the first two trials; it is Number 3 this time. The first subject in order calls out his answer. He says, "Number one." Number 1 is *obviously* longer than the standard; in fact it is three-quarters of an inch longer. But the second subject says "Number one" and so does the third and so do they all and now it is your turn. On subsequent trials a unanimous majority very frequently reports an answer you know to be incorrect. This happened, you will later learn, because all the "subjects" other than yourself were confederates of the experimenter reporting falsely on a prearranged schedule.

The situation is an epistemological nightmare. The judgments involved concern the nature of physical reality and they are not the sort of near-threshold difficult judgment on which some variation is to be expected. The equivalence between the standard line and the line you perceive to be of the same length is an objective fact. The proof of its objectivity is a set of comparison data Asch collected for the case in which subjects judged the same lines but each subject worked all alone. They almost invariably reported correctly; of thirty-seven subjects one made one error and one made two errors. These are judgments on which one expects a unanimous opinion. Sherif's subjects, working alone, did not all make the same judgments of the extent of movement in a pinpoint of light and had F.H. Allport's subjects made their aesthetic judgments in isolation we can be sure that they would not have perfectly agreed with one another. To separate unanimity and the clear evidence of one's senses is to set in opposition the two means by which we recognize reality. It is a powerful situation.

One can see the power of the Asch situation in the distress of subjects who are in the presence of a false majority. Morton D. Bogdonoff and his associates (1961) working at the Duke University Medical Center, have obtained evidence that there are physiological effects consequent upon deviance. While the subjects were working at the perceptual-judgment task sequential physiological measures were taken of the increase in plasma-free fatty acid level which is an index of central nervous system arousal. When a naïve subject was confronted with the majority opposition the level of the fatty acids went up. For those who yielded to the majority the level was reduced, but for those who resisted the group the level remained high.

About one-third of the reports made by subjects in the Asch situation are not correct but are in accordance with the group judgment. Subjects can be characterized as largely independent or as largely conforming though the greater number by far conform on some trials and are independent on others. . . .

The Sherif and Asch Research Compared

The differences of length presented by Asch are real and sizeable. A subject working all alone at these judgments can feel greater confidence in his decisions than can a subject who is all alone with the autokinetic phenomenon. Because Sherif's subjects could not be quite sure what they saw one would expect the opinions of others to be more influential with them than with Asch's subjects. However, the Asch case balances the objectivity of the judgment by increasing the power of the majority. In Sherif's groups of three there was no majority opinion but simply three opinions. Subjects were not confronted with a norm; they were given the occasion to forge a norm, and this could be done by converging on a central tendency since judgments were free to assume any value on the continuum of distance. Asch's subjects had only three discontinuous alternatives and usually there was no compromise position available. Sherif's is a study of the emergence of norms and Asch's is a study of the impact of norms with absolute conformity the only alternative to deviance on a particular trial.

The Sherif subject in the group situation found himself with only one or two others whereas Asch has sometimes arrayed majorities as large as fifteen against one subject. However, Asch has tried the effects of majorities of different sizes. The case most comparable to that of Sherif's subject is that in which a single confederate disagrees with a single naïve subject. Here there is no norm or majority opinion but simply, as in Sherif's studies, a single other opinion. It is very interesting to find that the one opposing opinion produces a few more false responses in the subject than occur when he is all alone. The result suggests again, as do F.H. Allport's findings with coworking individuals, that the impulse to agree is coincident with the creation of interpersonal bonds. Even when the task in no sense requires agreement this is so and even when agreement means the assertion of manifest falsehoods.

Asch's inquiries into the importance of the size of the majority resulted in an interesting discovery. The strength of the conformity effect increases as the number of confederates increases only up to a majority of three. Beyond that value, increasing the size of the majority results in no further significant increments in conformity. . . .

What can conformity account for in the behavior of the groups? . . . It can account for the convergence of individual judgments toward a central value. That is in fact exactly what happened to the judgments of Sherif's subjects. Probably the impulse to agree is coincidental with the creation of a group. However new the acquaintance, however temporary the aggregation, however restricted their common concerns, there seems always to be enough of a positive bond among the members to motivate a balancing convergence of opinions.

Audience Reaction Explains Social Behavior

ERVING GOFFMAN

The ideas of Durkheim and Simmel influenced sociologist Erving Goffman (1922-1982), a main developer of symbolic interactionist thought. Based on extensive observational research, for example in a mental institution, Goffman developed his own variation of symbolic interactionism that he called dramaturgical theory. Goffman argued that we present ourselves to others who serve as an audience, just as we serve as an audience for their presentations. People behave differently in the presence of others (an audience) from ways they behave when alone. Actors (individuals) perform expressions of the way they want to be seen by others, audiences form impressions, and together actors and audiences define ordinary social situations. In this viewpoint, Goffman outlines these and other ideas from his dramaturgical perspective, which compares social interaction to a staged drama.

1. According to Goffman, what kinds of situations need to be defined?
2. What is "impression management"? What examples of impression management does Goffman provide?
3. What does Goffman claim happens when interaction is disrupted and how do people prevent disruption?

I mean this viewpoint to serve as a sort of handbook detailing one sociological perspective from which social life can be studied, especially the kind of social life that is organized within the physical confines of a building or plant. . . .

The perspective employed in this viewpoint is that of the theatrical performance; the principles derived are dramaturgical ones. I shall consider the way in which the individual in ordinary work situations presents himself and his activity to others, the ways in which he guides and controls the impression they form of him, and the kinds of things he may and may not do while sustaining his performance before them. In using this model I will attempt not to make light of its obvious inadequacies. The stage presents things that are make-believe; presumably life presents things that are real and sometimes not well rehearsed. More important, perhaps, on the stage one player presents himself in the guise of a character to characters projected by other players; the audience constitutes a third party to the interaction—one that is essential and yet, if the stage performance were real, one that would not be there. In real life, the three parties are compressed into two; the part one individual plays is tailored to the parts played by the others present, and yet these others also constitute the audience. . . .

Dramaturgy

When an individual enters the presence of others, they commonly seek to acquire information about him or to bring into play information about him already possessed. They will be interested in his general socio-economic status, his conception of self, his attitude toward them, his competence, his trustworthiness, etc. Although some of this information seems to be sought almost as an end in itself, there are usually quite practical reasons for acquiring it. Information about the individual helps to define the situation, enabling others to know in advance what he will expect of them and what they may expect of him. Informed in these ways, the others will know how best to act in order to call forth a desired response from him.

For those present, many sources of information become accessible and many carriers (or "sign-vehicles") become available for conveying this information. If unacquainted with the individual, observers can glean clues from his conduct and appearance which allow them to apply their previous experience with individuals roughly similar to the one before them or, more important, to apply untested stereotypes to him. They can also assume from past experience that only individuals of a particular kind are likely to be found in a given social setting. They can rely on what the individual says about himself or on documentary evidence he provides as to who and what he is. If they know, or know of, the individual by virtue of experience prior to the interaction, they can rely on assumptions as to the persistence and generality of psychological traits as a means of predicting his present and future behavior.

However, during the period in which the individual is in the immediate presence of the others, few events may occur which directly provide the others with the conclusive information they will need if they are to direct wisely their own activity. Many crucial facts lie beyond the time and place of interaction or lie concealed within it. For example, the "true" or "real" attitudes, beliefs, and emotions of the individual can be ascertained only indirectly, through his avowals or through what appears to be involuntary expressive behavior. Similarly, if the individual offers the others a product or service, they will often find that during the interaction there will be no time and place immediately available for eating the pudding that the proof can be found in. They will be forced to accept some events as conventional or natural signs of something not directly available to the senses. The individual will have to act so that he intentionally or unintentionally *expresses* himself, and the others will in turn have to be *impressed* in some way by him.

Individual Expression

The expressiveness of the individual (and therefore his capacity to give impressions) appears to involve two radically different kinds of sign activity: the expression that he *gives*, and the expression that he *gives off*. The first involves verbal symbols or their substitutes which he uses admittedly and solely to convey the information that he and the others are known to attach to these symbols. This is communication in the traditional and narrow sense. The second involves a wide range of action that others can treat as symptomatic of the actor, the expectation being that the action was performed for reasons other than the information conveyed in this way. As we shall have to see, this distinction has an only initial validity. The individual does of course intentionally convey misinformation by means of both of these types of communication, the first involving deceit, the second feigning.

Taking communication in both its narrow and broad sense, one finds that when the individual is in the immediate presence of others, his activity will have a promissory character. The others are likely to find that they must accept the individual on faith, offering him a just return while he is present before them in exchange for something whose true value will not be established until after he has left their presence. (Of course, the others also live by inference in their dealings with the physical world, but it is only in the world of social interaction that the objects about which they make inferences will purposely facilitate and hinder this inferential process.) The security that they justifiably feel in making inferences about the individual will vary, of course, depending on such factors as the amount of information they already possess about him, but no amount of such past evidence can entirely obviate the necessity of acting on the basis of inferences. As William I. Thomas suggested:

> It is also highly important for us to realize that we do not as a matter of fact lead our lives, make our decisions, and reach our goals in everyday life either statistically or scientifically. We live by inference. I am, let us say, your guest. You do not know, you cannot determine scientifically, that I will not steal your money or your spoons. But inferentially I will not, and inferentially you have me as a guest.

Definition of the Situation

Let us now turn from the others to the point of view of the individual who presents himself before them. He may wish them to think highly of him, or to think that he thinks highly of them, or to perceive how in fact he feels toward them, or to obtain no clear-cut impression; he may wish to ensure sufficient harmony so that the interaction can be sustained, or to defraud, get rid of, confuse, mislead, antagonize, or insult them. Regardless of the particular objective which the individual has in mind and of his motive for having this objective, it will be in his interests to control the conduct of the others, especially their responsive treatment of him. This control is achieved largely by influencing the definition of the situation which the others come to formulate, and he can influence this definition by expressing himself in such a way as to give them the kind of impression that will lead them to act voluntarily in accordance with his own plan. Thus, when an individual appears in the presence of others, there will usually be some reason for him to mobilize his activity so that it will convey an impression to others which it is in his interests to convey. Since a girl's dormitory mates will glean evidence of her popularity from the calls she receives on the phone, we can suspect that some girls will arrange for calls to be made, and Willard Waller's finding can be anticipated:

> It has been reported by many observers that a girl who is called to the telephone in the dormitories will often allow herself to be called several times, in order to give all the other girls ample opportunity to hear her paged. . . .

The Audience Receives Impressions

I have said that when an individual appears before others his actions will influence the definition of the situation which they come to have. Sometimes the individual will act in a thoroughly calculating manner, expressing himself in a given way solely in order to give the kind of impression to others that is likely to evoke from them a specific response he is concerned to obtain. Sometimes the individual will be calculating in his activity but be relatively unaware that this is the case. Sometimes he will intentionally and consciously express himself in a particular way, but chiefly because the tradition of his group or social status requires this kind of expression and not because of any particular response (other than vague acceptance or approval) that is likely to be evoked from those impressed by the expression. Sometimes the traditions of an individual's role will lead him to give a well-designed impression of a particular kind and yet he may be neither consciously nor unconsciously disposed to create such an impression. The others, in their turn, may be suitably impressed by the individual's efforts to convey something, or may misunderstand the situation and come to conclusions that are warranted neither by the individual's intent nor by the facts. In any case, in so far as the others act *as if* the individual had conveyed a particular impression, we may take a functional or pragmatic view and say that the individual has "effectively" projected a given definition of the situation and "effectively" fostered the understanding that a given state of affairs obtains.

There is one aspect of the others' response that bears special comment here. Knowing that the individual is likely to present himself in a light that is favorable to him, the others may divide what they witness into two parts; a part that is relatively easy for the individual to manipulate at will, being chiefly his verbal assertions, and a part in regard to which he seems to have little concern or control, being chiefly derived from the expressions he gives off. The others may then use what are considered to be the ungovernable aspects of his expressive behavior as a check upon the validity of what is conveyed by the governable aspects. In this a fundamental asymmetry is demonstrated in the communication process, the individual presumably being aware of only one stream of his communication, the witnesses of this stream and one other. For example, in Shetland Isle one crofter's wife, in serving native dishes to a visitor from the mainland of Britain, would listen with a polite smile to his polite claims of liking what he was eating; at the same time she would take note of the rapidity with which the visitor lifted his fork or spoon to his mouth, the eagerness with which he passed food into his mouth, and the gusto expressed in chewing the food, using these signs as a check on the stated feelings of the eater. The same woman, in order to discover what one acquaintance (A) "actually" thought of another acquaintance (B), would wait until B was in the presence of A but engaged in conversation with still another person (C). She would then covertly examine the facial expressions of A as he regarded B in conversation with C. Not being in conversation with B, and not being directly observed by him, A would sometimes relax usual constraints and tactful deceptions, and freely express what he was "actually" feeling about B. This Shetlander, in short, would observe the unobserved observer. . . .

Given the fact that the individual effectively projects a definition of the situation when he enters the presence of others, we can assume that events may occur within the interaction which contradict, discredit, or otherwise throw doubt upon this projection. When these disruptive events occur, the interaction itself may come to a confused and embarrassed halt. Some of the assumptions upon which the responses of the participants had been predicated become untenable, and the participants find themselves lodged in an interaction for which the situation has been wrongly defined and is now no longer defined. At such moments the individual whose presentation has been discredited may feel ashamed while the others present may feel hostile, and all the participants may come to feel ill at ease, nonplussed, out of countenance, embarrassed, experiencing the kind of anomy that is generated when the minute social system of face-to-face interaction breaks down. . . .

One cannot judge the importance of definitional disruptions by the frequency with which they occur, for apparently they would occur more frequently were not constant precautions taken. We find that preventive practices are constantly employed to avoid these embarrassments and that corrective practices are constantly employed to compensate for discrediting occurrences that have not been successfully avoided. When the individual employs these strategies and tactics to protect his own projections, we may refer to them as "defensive practices"; when a participant employs them to save the definition of the situation projected by another, we speak of "protective practices" or "tact." Together, defensive and protective practices comprise the techniques employed to safeguard the impression fostered by an individual during his presence before others. It should be added that while we may be ready to see that no fostered impression would survive if defensive practices were not employed, we are less ready perhaps to see that few impressions could survive if those who received the impression did not exert tact in their reception of it.

In addition to the fact that precautions are taken to prevent disruption of projected definitions, we may also note that an intense interest in these disruptions comes to play a significant role in the social life of the group. Practical jokes and social games are played in which embarrassments which are to be taken unseriously are purposely engineered. Fantasies are created in which devastating exposures occur. Anecdotes from the past—real, embroidered, or fictitious—are told and retold, detailing disruptions which occurred, almost occurred, or occurred and were admirably resolved. There seems to be no grouping which does not have a ready supply of these games, reveries, and cautionary tales, to be used as a source of humor, a catharsis for anxieties, and a sanction for inducing individuals to be modest in their claims and reasonable in their projected expectations. The individual may tell himself through dreams of getting into impossible positions. Families tell of the time a guest got his dates mixed and arrived when neither the house nor anyone in it was ready for him. Journalists tell of times when an all-too-meaningful misprint occurred, and the paper's assumption of objectivity or decorum was humorously discredited. Public servants tell of times a client ridiculously misunderstood form instructions, giving answers which implied an unanticipated and bizarre definition of the situation. Seamen, whose home away from home is rigorously he-man, tell stories of coming back home and inadvertently asking mother to "pass the fucking butter.". . .

To summarize, then, I assume that when an individual appears before others he will have many motives for trying to control the impression they receive of the situation.

CHAPTER

3

Does Inequality Exist?

Chapter Preface

Each time a new baby is born, parents have great hopes for the child's success and rewards in life. Will the baby become president of the United States, a corporate executive, a scientist, or a famous entertainer or professional athlete? Will the baby at least gain enough resources for a long and satisfying life free from poverty and hunger? Sociologists formally study these questions and use the term "life chances" to describe the outcome of such studies. Do all new babies have equal life chances? Which of the baby's characteristics make a difference in the probability of any successful outcome? Put another way, who gets what and why? Study results consistently suggest that resources are distributed unequally according to statuses over which people have no control: age, gender, and skin color. Life chances also vary by education and occupation, statuses over which people have *some* control, but people have variable access to resources that expand opportunities.

Most people recognize that various segments of the population have differing amounts of wealth, power, and prestige. Nevertheless, many people in the United States resist the idea that social classes exist within our society. One reason is that our culture strongly values individualism and equality, and many of our most basic ideas revolve around everyone being "created equal" and "liberty and justice for all." Our favorite legends are about the triumph of accomplishment over adversity—the poor person who becomes rich and powerful, "pulling ourselves up by our own bootstraps." We treasure "rags to riches" success stories such as those about Abraham Lincoln, Andrew Carnegie, John D. Rockefeller, and J.P. Morgan. Belief in upward social mobility motivates ambition and hard work as key to the American Dream. Research shows, however, that the dream rarely becomes reality and average upward mobility is limited to small gains between generations.

Another reason people resist the notion of "class" is that people tend to associate with others like themselves and usually have little exposure to lifestyles different from their own. One student described ways her family struggles to send four children to a university with an annual household income of $100,000. This struggle contrasts sharply with those for whom the dream of enough food and medical care remains hopelessly elusive.

Contrary to the ideal, neither equality of resources nor equality of opportunity exists, and segments of the population have varying amounts of wealth, power, and prestige. Wealth includes both income from wages or salaries and from income-producing holdings such as stocks, bonds, and other investments. Power is the ability to accomplish personal goals, even facing opposition, or the ability to allocate scarce resources. While it is more difficult to measure, power combined with wealth can lead to increased prestige. Sociologists measure prestige using a series of surveys that ask people to evaluate occupations from poor to excellent. Respondents in large, randomly selected samples ranked occupations similarly in 1947 and 1963, and again in the 1970s and 1980s. Sociologists often measure "class" as "socioeconomic status" (SES): some combination of income, education, and occupational prestige scores.

Most significantly, distribution of wealth, power, and prestige is not random in stratified societies. As sociologist Leonard Beeghley notes, real life is not a Monopoly game where everyone begins with the same resources and plays by the same rules. Life chances vary systematically by social category rather than strictly by skill and luck. Stratification in the United States is an open system; some do win the lottery or manage to improve their positions at least slightly. Consider, however, ways in which wealth, power, and prestige influence the aspirations people have. Are people plagued by hunger more likely to hope for election to the Senate or merely enough to eat? Clearly, aspirations precede achievement—no one can reach a goal to which they do not aspire. And, in our culture, achievement is the source of wealth, power, and prestige. This circularity should make stratification of interest to everyone.

Many People Deny That Inequality Exists

ROBERT S. LYND AND HELEN MERRELL LYND

A good way to begin the study of social stratification is by examining the ways people discuss inequality in everyday life. Sociologists Robert and Helen Lynd spent eighteen months of 1924 and 1925 in "Middletown" (actually Muncie, Indiana) researching everyday life and documenting its history. They returned to Middletown in June 1935 to identify change after the economic boom times of the late 1920s and six years of economic depression. In this viewpoint from the second study, the Lynds report that most people in Middletown avoid talking about differences among themselves as "class differences" despite the fact that divisions exist.

As you read this viewpoint, think about whether you believe the United States in the 1990s is a "classless society." Do you hear comments today similar to those from the Middletown residents? How would your life be different if you lived in a household with $15,000 annual income or $150,000? Are there parts of your city where you would not go after dark?

Are there stores or restaurants you would not patronize because they are too exclusive or too shabby? Imagine either category as the only stores and restaurants you frequent. As in Middletown, most people in the 1990s still live their lives without consciousness of class distinctions even though inequality—differences in income, wealth, and lifestyles—continues to increase in our society.

QUESTIONS

1. Do some statements by Middletown residents indicate that they identify individuals as the problem rather than the "reigning system" as the Lynds suggest? If so, list at least three such statements.
2. What evidence do the Lynds provide of the emergence of a "small, self-conscious upper class"?
3. What distinguishes Middletown's "middle class" from the "working class"?

■ ■ ■

To quote a full-page advertisement by another automotive plant greeting the return of General Motors: "[Middletown] is a good town to live in! A good town to work in!" This happy, "constructive" note is very characteristic. In 1932, the high-school dean proposed that high-school girls wear a simple uniform "in order to eliminate class distinctions in high school and to place the poor on an equal footing with the rich"—a proposal addressed to a problem that distresses many South Side girls acutely (some of them to the point of withdrawing from high school), many parents of all classes, and high-school teachers sensitive to conditions affecting personality. But the evening paper promptly shuddered editorially at such regimentation and denial of democratic principles, taking the high ground that "The purpose of the educational system is to build personality by stimulating thought rather than to force students to accept ideas unthinkingly"; and it then shunted off the whole problem by announcing cheerfully that "Little distinction is found today between rich and poor dress in so far as high-school girls are concerned. The only difference is in taste." In 1935 the same editor commented with satisfaction in his column, ". . . naturally [factory girls] cannot indulge in the feminine furbelows of some other working girls, which is too bad. But in the evenings, the work day over, they cannot be distinguished in appearance from the clerks, bookkeepers, and other 'white collar' workers. The American melting pot does a better job of melting women than men."

In August 1936, this denial of class differences was made still more explicit in a local editorial:

THE MIDDLE CLASS RULES AMERICA

. . . The United States never was a feudal nation. . . . As a result, while some became very rich and others very poor, the sovereign authority rested with a great middle class, whom we like to term the typical Americans. They were the people whose ideal of life was to own a home, and rear and educate a family in the fear of the Lord and in obedience to law. It is from the children of these middle-class families that our industrial and political leaders have come. They have been neither revolutionists nor class baiters. They have held the government on an even keel. That is why the radicals have hated them so—the Reds well know that this middle class is the great obstacle to revolution.

So long as the United States eschews class division and maintains this great middle-class America, we shall be free of such troubles as now beset unhappy Spain. But once we permit the middle class to be destroyed by taxation or other form of confiscation, giving us only class consciousness instead, then we may expect bitterness and hatred, even revolution, to take the place of the American ideals of free government. . . .

Middletown's working class does not, for the most part, spend its time thinking of itself as different from the people on the North Side. In the main it has followed the same symbols, trying intermittently, as work allows, to affirm them as loudly as does the business class, and to narrow the gap between symbol and reality. It, like the business class, is busy living, manipulating the poker chips at its command, and trying to get more. Its drives are largely those of the business class: both are caught up in the tradition of a rising standard of living and lured by the enticements of salesmanship; and the modern merchandising device of "price-lining," coupled with installment selling, enables the workingman to have many things that "look like" the possessions seen in the "nice" store windows uptown and in the movies. Class ideologies are foreign to Middletown's working class, and, without identifying oneself as a member of one class as over against another, one lives along, in the pursuit of what plums one can contrive to get in one's porridge. . . .

In a word, what Middletown's business class wants is to be let alone to run its own business, and what the working class wants is a job so that it can pay the rent, own a car, and go to the movies. As a small businessman—one of the two private individuals in Middletown in 1934 (including students at the college) who subscribed to the *New Republic*—remarked: "These workers here don't want to 'steal the works,' but just to have a job, security, and the chance to bring up their kids and have some fun. If the employing crowd here could just realize that and act accordingly toward their men, it'd be worth money to them." Like most other people, Middletown folk don't want to have to think too much. They reluctantly ask "Why?" And the occasional persons who do keep their questions to themselves. A leading lawyer remarked, "We can't solve all these problems. They're too big for us. We've our own problems, and we send men to Congress to try to solve the big problems." Occupied with personal immediacies, Middletown generalizes the succession of daily experiences with difficulty. To most of its people, of whatever group, "class differences" and "class consciousness" are vague, unfamiliar, and, if recognized, unpleasant and sinister terms. And above all, Middletown people avoid questioning the assumed adequacy of the reigning system under which they live. It is much less troublesome and more congenial to attribute troubles to personal devils. Thus, in commenting on the unrest in France in 1936, a local editorial noted simply that conditions there are attributable "mainly to machinations of politicians rather than to capitalism." By the same process any talk about "class differences," a "class struggle," and similar unpleasant things is attributed to "reckless outside troublemakers." Officially, Middletown scoffs at the "class struggle." "Remnants of that notion [of the class struggle] are still with us," said a local editorial in 1935. "Indeed, many people do not realize that that theory has been exploded once and for all." And a local pundit, in a "guest editorial" in one of the papers, voiced the conviction commonly held by Middletown businessmen that "As a scheme for society and as a plan for the government of a state, *Das Kapital* is a flop. . . . For a quarter of a century [Marx and his followers] wisecracked against the existing order, and then disappeared as a social force."

And yet—despite the fact that tradition, inertia, and intent combine to blur any potential class differences, indications of a sharpening of awareness of some class lines continually break through tendencies to bury them.

Businessmen frequently forget in conversation their formal denials of the separate existence of a working class; they tend to speak of it as a group apart, people who are "different from us." From a number of business-class persons one picked up impatient characterizations of the working class as having a high percentage of "intellectually inferior" members. Characteristic, too, is the impatient remark of a local real-estate man on "the impossibility of inculcating any aesthetic values in people like that. Why, give 'em a brand-new house, and in a few months it'll look like a pigstye." One intelligent man said, "It seems to me that the working class are different here from any other place. They are more incapable, stupid—just a crummy lot, biologically inferior, with a lot of these dopes from Kentucky and Tennessee. They never do anything." Another man, protesting to the investigator against the treatment of the monotony of certain types of jobs in the 1925 study, exclaimed, "Those people aren't like us! They *love* that kind of job. Why, there isn't anything there in those fellows to begin with.". . .

From conversations with the South Siders themselves one got still more keenly an occasional awareness not of definitely antagonistic interests but of growing social distance, and in some cases the definite voicing of the question, "Where is this going to lead us?"

This apparently arises not from any formulated theory of divergent class interests or of an "exploited" working class, but from the fact that workers feel that in one situation after another they find themselves on the opposite side of the fence from the business class and pulling in an opposite direction. The contrasts have been rubbed in in the homes whose juniors must run the gantlet of high-school life. The alert principal of the large junior high school on the South Side replied to the question as to whether class consciousness between North and South Sides is growing with the following concrete instances:

I have noticed two things recently: Our parents have been coming to me urging that we have our own senior high school down on the South Side, "so that our children won't have to go up to Central High School where they don't like it—the dressing, clubs, and social contrasts."

And the second thing I've run against in urging our boys to keep their records clear so that they'll be eligible for the Central High School Bearcat basketball team. They say to me: "Mr. ——, you *know* we don't have a chance to make teams up there against the North Side boys." And that's true—they *are* handicapped. . . .

In connection with this incipient drawing apart of business class and working class, two other significant tendencies should be noted here. One is the emergence of a small, self-conscious upper class from the earlier more democratic situation, in which the few wealthy families tended to avoid ostentation and to merge themselves in the general business class. The presence of this group is tending to focus some of the conflicts in values. Middletown's new upper class tends to cultivate the unusual rather than always the homely middle-of-the-road things; it plays more than its parents did, and its play is more sporty and expensive; it reads the *New Yorker*, *Esquire*, and *Fortune*; it enjoys swank with just a touch of laughing at itself for doing so; its children go to Eastern schools; it can talk about New York's "Rainbow Room" and the "Sert Room" from first-hand knowledge; it opens its garage doors by an electric button; and it laughs at Eddie Guest and takes Rotary casually. Middletown's top sliver of families who constitute this emerging upper class are neither lazy, undemocratic, immoral, nor blatantly "different"; but their ways of living may as time goes on bring out into the open some of the alternatives to Middletown's traditional values which have hitherto existed locally only in occasional exceptional individuals. Furthermore, the very existence in the community of their riding clubs, airplanes, and expansive new homes in the correct Westwood section heightens the contrasts with the working class and makes it more difficult to maintain the symbols of the unified city, in which each is simply on a different rung of the same ladder with the top accessible to all.

The other tendency, accompanying the drawing away of the top group of the business class into a nascent "upper class," is the apparently clearer demarcation of another and larger group of families at the lower end of the business class as a Middletown "middle class." These are the "small" white-collar folk—struggling manufacturers with no particular future, the smaller retailers and tradespeople, salesmen, officeholders, schoolteachers, and many of the growing group of hired professional assistants. These minor white-collar people are beginning to realize as the city grows larger that they definitely do not belong with the small new upper class and that even in relation to the central bloc of substantial business people they are hangers-on rather than of their number. They are courted by this more successful group when a membership drive for the Chamber of Commerce is on or when a Community Fund has to be raised. But their contacts are intermittent and on terms which the more important businessfolk elect. The depression has brought home to all Middletown businessmen the extreme degree to which extension of credit depends upon the "Yes" or "No" of a few individuals; but whereas the more "well-fixed" business and professional folk can rub elbows socially with such central sources of power, the white-collar small fry are, more today than in 1925, out of easy reach of these power controls. And these dependent persons seemed to the investigator to be more sharply aware of their dependent position, below both the upper class and the bloc of influential business people who jointly prescribe the city's central values.

Few people in Middletown are articulate about this. From a few persons in this group one gleaned statements like the following:

> . . . Classes certainly are drawing apart here. Many of the lower business class are beginning to realize that they are permanently blocked and won't go any further. Some men who were making good modest livings before the depression, belonging to the less prominent civic clubs, and generally feeling themselves as "one of the boys," now feel uneasy and self-conscious and not so sure that they "belong." (*A man from this group with a degree from the local college.*)

Undoubtedly this crystallizing of a "middle class" somewhat apart from Middletown's dominant business class is not an entirely new tendency. There were in 1925, as today, plenty of sober business-class folk who were "outsiders" and cheerfully accepted themselves as such. It is the impression of the investigator, however, based upon frankly tenuous data and brief observation, that this trend toward the separating out of a middle class is definitely increasing in Middletown. . . .

If the nascent "class" system of "Magic [Middletown]" appears to follow somewhat the above lines, Middletown itself will turn away from any such picture of the fissures and gullies across the surface of its social life. It is far more congenial to the mood of the city, proud of its traditions of democratic equality, to think of the lines of cleavage within its social system as based not upon class differences but rather upon the entirely spontaneous and completely individual and personal predilections of the 12,500 families who compose its population. [Groups of business leaders] even express impatience over the fact that various groups of inconspicuous folk keep breaking off from the central big-business drive of the Chamber of Commerce and setting up bitter little pressure groups to try to protect their interests. These things are regarded as "disloyal," as "stirring up dissensions," and as the work of "troublemakers." Thus the dominant business group is annoyed by the organization among the schoolteachers of a Teachers' Federation to fight, in Middletown and at the state capital, against business pressure groups bent on hammering down teachers' salaries along with the tax rate; it also objects to the teachers' "mixing in politics" by endorsing a Democratic candidate for governor. Much more congenial to Middletown than such emphases on differences within itself is the harmonizing, friendly proposal made in jest in a local editorial to start a "Patched Pants Club, to be composed only of men who in their youth were forced because of poverty to wear patched trousers to school." Such a proposal brings a warm sense of neighborliness back to the hearts of parents who are worried because their daughter is excluded from the recently organized Junior Cotillion, and to those who must look from a wistful distance at the new homes of the wealthy springing up in the exclusive Westwood subdivision.

Inequality Exists and Benefits Society

Kingsley Davis
and Wilbert E. Moore

Sociologists Kingsley Davis and Wilbert E. Moore, structural functional theorists and students of Talcott Parsons, present the functional perspective on stratification in this viewpoint. The core concepts are that unequal rewards motivate people to prepare for and work at tasks needed by society. Less difficult work that requires little preparation offers fewer rewards. Tasks more vital to society must be more greatly rewarded. Davis and Moore explain that society's needs continue as individuals perform their tasks and "die off." Stratification assures that positions most functionally important to the society continue to be filled by the most capable and qualified individuals.

Many people accept this view of inequality in the 1990s even as they deny class distinctions in our society. People usually believe it is appropriate that school principals receive more pay than teachers and that state governors are more highly paid than mayors. Greater rewards for innovation seem proper, even when corporate executives' incomes reach

From Kingsley Davis and Wilbert E. Moore, "Some Principles of Stratification," *American Sociological Review* 10:242-49 (1945).

seven figures and workers accept pay cuts to avoid joining the unemployed. Few people protest any means today's giant corporations use to increase their income. The functional perspective on stratification fits very well with strongly held values in a capitalist economy.

QUESTIONS

1. What are the major points in the argument that stratification is necessary?
2. Davis and Moore identify three kinds of rewards "built into" positions. What are they?
3. In what two ways can the relative importance of positions be determined?

■　■　■

Starting from the proposition that no society is "classless," or unstratified, an effort is made to explain, in functional terms, the universal necessity which calls forth stratification in any social system. Next, an attempt is made to explain the roughly uniform distribution of prestige as between the major types of positions in every society. . . .

Throughout, it will be necessary to keep in mind one thing—namely, that the discussion relates to the system of positions, not to the individuals occupying those positions. It is one thing to ask why different positions carry different degrees of prestige, and quite another to ask how certain individuals get into those positions. Although, as the argument will try to show, both questions are related, it is essential to keep them separate in our thinking. Most of the literature on stratification has tried to answer the second question (particularly with regard to the ease or difficulty of mobility between strata) without tackling the first. The first question, however, is logically prior and, in the case of any particular individual or group, factually prior.

The Functional Necessity of Stratification

Curiously, however, the main functional necessity explaining the universal presence of stratification is precisely the requirement faced by any society of placing and motivating individuals in the social structure. As a functioning mechanism a society must somehow distribute its members in social positions and induce them to perform the duties of these positions. It must thus concern itself with motivation at two different levels: to instill in the proper individuals the desire to fill certain positions, and, once in these positions, the desire to perform the duties attached to them. Even though the social order may be relatively static in form, there is a continuous process of metabolism as new individuals are born into it, shift with age, and die off. Their absorption into the positional system must somehow be arranged and motivated. This is true whether the system is competitive or non-competitive. A competitive system gives greater importance to the motivation to achieve positions, whereas a non-competitive system gives perhaps greater importance to the motivation to perform the duties of the positions; but in any system both types of motivation are required.

If the duties associated with the various positions were all equally pleasant to the human organism, all equally important to societal survival, and all equally in need of the same ability or talent, it would make no difference who got into which positions, and the problem of social placement would be greatly reduced. But actually it does make a great deal of difference who gets into which positions, not only because some positions are inherently more agreeable than others, but also because some require special talents or training and some are functionally more important than others. Also, it is essential that the duties of the positions be performed with the diligence that their importance requires. Inevitably, then, a society must have, first, some kind of rewards that it can use as inducements, and, second, some way of distributing these rewards differentially according to positions. The rewards and their distribution become a part of the social order, and thus give rise to stratification.

One may ask what kind of rewards a society has at its disposal in distributing its personnel and securing essential services. It has, first of all, the things that contribute to sustenance and comfort. It has, second, the things that contribute to humor and diversion. And it has, finally, the things that contribute to self-respect and ego expansion. The last, because of the peculiarly social character of the self, is largely a function of the opinion of others, but it nonetheless ranks in importance with the first two. In any social system all three kinds of rewards must be dispensed differentially according to positions.

In a sense the rewards are "built into" the position. They consist in the "rights" associated with the position, plus what may be called its accompaniments or perquisites. Often the rights, and sometimes the accompaniments, are functionally related to the duties of the position. (Rights as viewed by the incumbent are usually duties as viewed by other members of the community.) However, there may be a host of subsidiary rights and perquisites that are not essential to the function of the position and have only an indirect and symbolic connection with its duties, but which still may be of considerable importance in inducing people to seek the positions and fulfil the essential duties.

If the rights and perquisites of different positions in a society must be unequal, then the society must be stratified, because that is precisely what stratification means. Social inequality is thus an unconsciously evolved device by which societies insure that the most important positions are conscientiously filled by the most qualified persons. Hence every society, no matter how simple or complex, must differentiate persons in terms of both prestige and esteem, and must therefore possess a certain amount of institutionalized inequality.

It does not follow that the amount or type of inequality need be the same in all societies. This is largely a function of factors that will be discussed presently.

The Two Determinants of Positional Rank

Granting the general function that inequality subserves, one can specify the two factors that determine the relative rank of different positions. In general those positions convey the best reward, and hence have the highest rank, which (a) have the greatest importance for the society and (b) require the greatest training or talent. The first factor concerns function and is a matter of relative significance; the second concerns means and is a matter of scarcity.

Differential Functional Importance

Actually a society does not need to reward positions in proportion to their functional importance. It merely needs to give sufficient reward to them to insure that they will be filled competently. In other words, it must see that less essential positions do not compete successfully with more essential ones. If a position is easily filled, it need not be heavily rewarded, even though important. On the other hand, if it is important but hard to fill, the reward must be high enough to get it filled anyway. Functional importance is therefore a necessary but not a sufficient cause of high rank being assigned to a position.

Differential Scarcity of Personnel

Practically all positions, no matter how acquired, require some form of skill or capacity for performance. This is implicit in the very notion of position, which implies that the incumbent must, by virtue of his incumbency, accomplish certain things.

There are, ultimately, only two ways in which a person's qualifications come about: through inherent capacity or through training. Obviously, in concrete activities both are always necessary, but from a practical standpoint the scarcity may lie primarily in one or the other, as well as in both. Some positions require innate talents of such high degree that the persons who fill them are bound to be rare. In many cases, however, talent is fairly abundant in the population but the training process is so long, costly, and elaborate that relatively few can qualify. Modern medicine, for example, is within the mental capacity of most individuals, but a medical education is so burdensome and expensive that virtually none would undertake it if the position of the M.D. did not carry a reward commensurate with the sacrifice.

If the talents required for a position are abundant and the training easy, the method of acquiring the position may have little to do with its duties. There may be, in fact, a virtually accidental relationship. But if the skills required are scarce by reason of the rarity of talent or the costliness of training, the position, if functionally important, must have an attractive power that will draw the necessary skills in competition with other positions. This means, in effect, that the position must be high in the social scale—must command great prestige, high salary, ample leisure, and the like.

How Variations Are to Be Understood

In so far as there is a difference between one system of stratification and another, it is attributable to whatever factors affect the two determinants of differential reward—namely, functional importance and scarcity of personnel. Positions important in one society may not be important in another, because the conditions faced by the societies, or their degree of internal development, may be different. The same conditions, in turn, may affect the question of scarcity; for in some societies the stage of development, or the external situation, may wholly obviate the necessity of certain kinds of skill or talent. Any particular system of stratification, then, can be understood as a product of the special conditions affecting the two aforementioned grounds of differential reward.

VIEWPOINT

3

Unequal Power and Prestige Maintain Social Order

W. LLOYD WARNER, MARCHIA MEEKER, AND KENNETH EELLS

In this viewpoint, social anthropologists W. Lloyd Warner and his colleagues describe three extensions to the functionalist theory of stratification. First, they distinguish between power and prestige as two rewards for difficult work. Functionalist theory implicitly assumes that greater rewards for more important work include income, power, and prestige concurrently, but power and prestige do not always coincide. Second, society does not operate exclusively in an economic environment but requires three different functional environments to survive: the physical environment controlled by technology (the economy), the "human species environment" regulating how people behave toward each other, and the "supernatural environment" ordered by religion. Individuals may have power and/or prestige in one of these environments but not the others.

In their third extension to the functionalist view, Warner et al. argue that power and prestige can occur as an integral

Excerpted from pp. 265-73 of *Social Class in America* by W. Lloyd Warner, Marchia Meeker, and Kenneth Eells. New York: Harper & Row, 1960. Reprinted with permission.

part of the statuses people occupy or be accorded to the status by other members of the society. Police, for example, have the *power* to arrest citizens; however, cultural values determine whether police have prestige in the society, and these values may fluctuate over time. Members of the society as a whole may confer prestige and esteem on police officers or they may not. The main point is that all components of stratification maintain order and equilibrium in society.

QUESTIONS

1. How do the authors define power and prestige?
2. According to the authors, what positions have power and/or prestige in each of the three environments?
3. How does stratification maintain order in society?

Power may be simply defined for our immediate purposes as the possession of control over other beings and objects in the social and natural environments, making it possible to act on them to achieve outcomes that would not take place if control were not exerted. Prestige is the kind and amount of value socially attributed to objects, activities, persons, and statuses. The two are usually interrelated; power can derive from prestige and prestige from power. However, a man may have power with little prestige or high prestige with little power. The kinds and amount of power and prestige vary from one territorial group to another. They also differ among the several forms of rank and status. The problem of how forms of rank are related to prestige and power as well as the nature of sources of power and prestige must be considered.

The Marxians and others have founded their system of class analysis on the assumption that power is *only* a product of *one* kind of status control over *one* kind of environment; that the statuses which control the means of production and the distribution of their products hold the power and are thus given the prestige which determine class alignments; it is argued that since the technological adjustments to the natural environment are moving in a given, predetermined direction, the dependent society, its mental and cultural life, the class forms, their composition and relations are perforce moving in a predictable sequence to a classless society.

Clearly such economic determinists are correct in pointing out the importance of the statuses which control the natural environment and the real power inherent in such statuses or those superordinate statuses which control them. They are wrong, however, in assuming that technological control is the *only* source of power. The sources of power are *multiple*, not one. To properly understand the problems of power and prestige we must use the knowledge of sociology, social anthropology, and the psychological sciences that has accumulated since Marx and Engels. We must re-examine the whole question of the relation of power to the human adaptive controls of the several environments, and man's dependence on them.

Control over Three Environments

Human survival universally depends on two and, it is believed, three environments. The first is the so-called natural environment which in varying degrees is controlled by the technology; the second, the human species environment which is controlled by (part of) the moral order, a system of social organization; and the third, real or not, the supernatural environment, ordered and controlled, it is believed, by the "myths" and rituals of religion and magic, a system of sacred symbols. . . .

The second, the control over the species, by imposing the pressures of moral forms on animal behavior, regulates the discharge of species energy; it controls the interactions of individuals and structures their access to each other. Thus it orders the basic life-flow of the species and of each individual, including the procreative processes and the relations of the adult and immature; it orders the expression of hostility, aggression, and violence, the disposition of prized objects, and the imposition of unpleasant tasks among the members of the group. Control over the species environment means an exercise of real power; it also means the presence of power in every socially organized species group and a *sense* of social power (in Durkheim's sense) within the group among those who live in it. The meanings and social representations of what social power is vary from group to group; the forms by which it is utilized and expressed also vary enormously. . . .

The *supernatural* adaptations controlling, it is believed, man's ultimate fate, govern those activities and outcomes over which the other two have insufficient power. Sickness, death, obliteration of the self, social disaster, and the ill- or well-being of man are in its compass. Each society has fashioned its own adaptive controls to meet as best it can the terrible and absolute power of this other world and thereby reduce human anxiety and dread. . . .

Status, Power, and Prestige

The power of an adaptive status, or hierarchy of statuses, may be *intrinsic* and directly applied or *extrinsic* to its activities and functions. In other words, the force it possesses and applies may be an integral and necessary part of its adaptive activity, or it may be ("given") attributed to it by all, or some, members of the society. The power to kill a kangaroo with a spear by a hunter (who does or does not keep its meat for himself, his family, and clan) is at least partly intrinsic, but the man may also be accorded by his group increased power beyond his ability to kill and keep. The first is an intrinsic and integral part of his technical status as a hunter and of his moral status as a member of his family and clan; the latter power, not necessary for the execution of his technical and moral acts, is of course attributed to him.

The prestige of a status, the esteem in which it is held, or the derogation, is attributable and extrinsic. The values of the group, or some part of it, are projected upon the status and determine its social worth. Much of what are popularly and scientifically termed prestige and power are products of the larger group's feelings. The facts of the adaptive actions of a status become evaluated symbols which accumulate and attract other negative or positive social values that may have little to do with the activities of the status.

Since the statuses of adaptation are integral parts of a social system, they are in a position of mutual influence. No one system of adaptation is entirely free from the others. . . . When the technology is complex the kinds and number of statuses (occupations, for example) are necessarily numerous and highly diverse. Such economic status systems may be scientifically classified into types and arranged along a continuum of simple to complex. In many primitive societies, occupations are largely undifferentiated. Each man performs many productive functions which are not classifiable occupationally. Occupational ranking is therefore not possible. In such a society as ours where the division of labor is exceedingly great, ranking of occupations is one of the principal forms of stratification; and the accumulation of wealth and the sources of wealth are also ranked in "separate" systems. . . .

The moral order's family, age, and sex statuses control and regulate some of the most powerful activities and energies of the species environment. The status of the parent, the father particularly, subordinates the statuses of the sons and daughters. The foundations of authority, its use by the one and submission to it by the other, are in this universal relation. The usual superordination of males and subordination of females and the similar relation of the mature to the young are forms of authority where social power is exercised. Rudimentary systems of rank are part of all family, kinship, and age grade systems. . . .

Since the children are identified with the social status of the parents, both the closed and open general systems initially place the child's status in this system of rank. In the closed system like color caste the child remains by moral rule at the parents' and his ancestors' level; in the open he may stay or move out of it.

If the general inclusive type is an open system, the parent-child relation and the sibling relations often assume most diverse forms and are subject to great stress and distortion. The son may move to superior position, or the daughter marry into one, thus subordinating the parent and placing the family's superior adult in an inferior position of rank. Some of the siblings may move up, others down, and still others remain at the parents' level. Open systems with free competition disperse the members of many families over distant parts of the rank order. Ordinarily they must if the systems are to continue. Closed fixed systems tend to hold the members of the family together and add their influence to maintaining family solidarity. In an open system the family of orientation quickly yields its maturing young to the larger world and to their own families of procreation; in a closed system the older generations are more likely to be related to the younger ones. The two families, often forming into a *grosse* family, hold together in primary interaction biologically, territorially, and socially. They provide the hard core of fixed position for their members and closure for movement beyond their limits. . . .

The statuses associated with the control of the unknown which reduce human anxieties about their life chances by the use of myth and ritual are religious and magical. They are ordinarily centered in the church. They include such ritual statuses as priests, magicians, some doctors and psychiatrists, and occasionally other statuses to which such power is attributed.

They, too, may be simple or complex. They, too, may be in societies where the religious life dominates, or is subordinate to, the technological or secular organization. In the simpler societies there may be no more than a temporary ritual leader with little power and prestige, his tenure being only during the ceremony. In many of the complex societies there may be a hierarchy of statuses from local ones up through a hierarchy that integrates and controls the supernatural activities of a whole nation or those of many nations. The vertical height may be exceedingly great or not, the area of social activity limited, or in a theocracy it may include the whole society.

The powers of the supernatural environment which can harm or benefit men are often dualistically conceived. The problem confronting the statuses related to these beings and the forces of sacred good and evil is to control them and to adapt their power to man's ends. The forces of good must be harnessed to assist men; the forces of evil must be diverted, quarantined, or weakened. When it is believed that the statuses manipulating myth and ritual accomplish these ends and they "control" the uncontrollable, the statuses of magicians, priests, and others like them are attributed some of the power of the environment they control. They and their statuses derive power and prestige both from their knowledge and ability to use the symbols effectively and from the power that comes from the sacred world itself. As Durkheim pointed out, supernatural forces are comparable to physical forces; the words and objects of the rites of religion have social force and strength attached to them. They have the power to kill or cure. The priest or magician can benefit man or the sorcerer can cause sickness and death in his victim. They control the forces that can take or give life. The power that the sacred statuses possess tends to be absolute. . . .

Sources of Power and Prestige

The sources of power and prestige accordingly are multiple. They derive from all powerful environments and from their adaptive controls. The statuses which function to organize the activities of these controls possess their power. In all societies social power expressed in secular or sacred terms is present and distributed among statuses, persons, and things. Power, like prestige, may not be intrinsic to the activities of the status but attributed by the group to the status and its activities.

VIEWPOINT

Inequality Disadvantages Minorities

JONATHAN H. TURNER, ROYCE SINGLETON JR., AND DAVID MUSICK

Sociologist Jonathan Turner is the author of dozens of books
and articles on sociological theory and social structure. In this
viewpoint, Turner and his colleagues describe social conditions during the twentieth century that have influenced popular beliefs about race. Early in the century, "scientific" research
generated racial theories that the authors call "a stigma of inferiority more damaging and more humiliating" than slavery.
Scientists rejected these theories beginning in the 1920s, but
the public opinion polling that originated in the 1930s shows
that such beliefs endure in the population. Racism, the authors
argue, continues to perpetuate discrimination today and
blacks receive fewer benefits because of this prejudice.

Excerpted from *Oppression: A Socio-History of Black-White Relations in America* by
Jonathan H. Turner, Royce Singleton Jr., and David Musick. Chicago: Nelson-
Hall, 1984. Copyright 1984 by Jonathan H. Turner. Reprinted with permission.

1. In what ways do the authors say early biologists, psychologists, and sociologists contributed to racism? When did this change?
2. What early twentieth century population factors contributed to racism?
3. What is "symbolic racism"?

■ ■ ■

Entering the twentieth century, Americans were probably less disposed to accept the social equality of blacks than at any other period in their history. Racist thought was respectable among all social classes and in all sections of the country. The South, defending its efforts to disenfranchise and legally segregate blacks, was inundating the nation with a mass of anti-Negro literature. The North, concerned with the nation's imperialistic ventures and channeling its reformist energies into other areas, mounted no serious challenge to southern race policies. Finally, American interest in "scientific" racism blossomed after 1900, receiving wide attention from those who, in the burgeoning age of science, felt compelled to give their ideas an elaborate scientific rationale. As a result, during the first quarter of the century, sociologists, psychologists, and biologists developed a comprehensive science of race that firmly affixed upon blacks a stigma of inferiority more damaging and more humiliating in many respects than that of slavery. To this day, blacks still suffer from that stigma.

Racism in Science

The source of racism in biology was the newly developing fields of genetics and eugenics. Darwin's theories had convinced biologists that evolution accounted for race differences and hence for racial inequality. It remained for the science of heredity to explain the mechanisms underlying the evolution of these differences. Experiments with plant genetics and hybridization were believed to demonstrate the overwhelming importance of heredity in the transmission of human characteristics, supporting the notion of innate black inferiority. Eugenicists warned that racial intermixture led to biological abnormalities, and urged the adoption of public policies that would curtail the birthrate of undesirable races such as Negroes. Even biologists who did not accept the theory of racial "abnormalities" sometimes deplored race intermixture, reasoning that crosses between inferior and superior races must produce offspring intermediate between the two parent groups.

In psychology, a parallel development in the assessment of mental and emotional differences between the races was also thought to support the assumption of the black's innate inferiority. Intelligence testing, which originated in France in 1905 and developed rapidly in the following decade, was applied on a massive scale to men coming into the armed services after American entry into World War I. The tests, particularly the "army beta" test designed for illiterates and immigrants unfamiliar with English, were claimed to be objective measures of innate intellectual ability. Consequently, when blacks' scores turned out to be lower than whites' on the average, a powerful tool was placed in the hands of racists who would argue that the racial inferiority of blacks was an established scientific fact.

Sociologists also contributed, often unwittingly, to the body of scientific knowledge upon which racists drew at this time. For example, the famous University of Chicago sociologist William I. Thomas maintained that race prejudice was "an instinct originating in the tribal stage of society, when solidarity in feeling and action were essential to the preservation of the group," and that it would "probably never disappear completely." Others lent support to the notion of instinctive intergroup antipathy by arguing that the vast physical and psychical differences between the races fostered a "caste feeling" and "consciousness of kind" that was strongest among the "superior" white race. Finally, Robert Park, a sociological authority on race relations in the period between the wars, celebrated black artistic achievements during the "Harlem Renaissance" of the 1920s as an expression of the black's superior emotionalism and sensuality, thus confirming part of the traditional stereotype of blacks as "expressive" and "sensual."

During the first quarter of the twentieth century, then, reputable scientists in several fields furnished an abundance of authoritative "proof" of black inferiority and instinctive racial antipathy. Although many of these scientists maintained a purely academic interest in the subject of race and argued against the use of their ideas to justify discriminatory policies toward blacks, their ideas nonetheless became the foundation of sophisticated defenses of segregation and social inequality. Popular writers such as Lothrop Stoddard, who felt that as a "scientific humanist" he was morally obligated to warn the nation about the perils of race, made the "new 'truths' of science concerning race available to great numbers of people. Against the backdrop of the events of this period, these "truths" gained heightened significance.

The Great Migration

The mass migration of southern blacks to the North during World War I had a great impact on racial attitudes toward blacks. This movement caused deep resentment among working-class people with whom blacks competed for jobs. The result was the outbreak of several race riots in 1919 and the surfacing of racial prejudices. The great wave of foreign immigration in the late nineteenth and early twentieth centuries also raised concern over race, making restrictive immigration legislation the chief political objective of racists in the 1920s and inviting the usual invidious comparisons between white and black races. In the end, such events were to make the problem of black-white relations national in scope and to cause reflective people in the sciences to question the scientific truths to which racists appealed.

A New Attitude

The scientific backing that racists had received was finally revoked in the 1920s and 1930s. Throughout the history of the United States, there had always been a few whites who were able to see through the illogic and irrationality of racism; but not until the anthropologist Franz Boas led the attack in the 1920s did the opponents of racism gain a sizable following. Boas forcefully exposed the mass of contradictory evidence, errors of judgment, and faulty generalizations associated with studies of race. At the same time, he offered a well-reasoned cultural explanation of why races all over the world reveal diversity. Engaged in the study of aboriginal peoples, Boas argued that the intelligence and temperament of individuals are not associated with the racial inheritance of bodily characteristics and could only be meaningfully interpreted in terms of the language, beliefs, and customs of their culture. Boas was also highly critical of the assumption of inferiority and superiority among races or cultures and of the failure of scientists to dissociate their judgments from the standards of their own culture, a criticism that psychologists soon applied to intelligence tests.

By the late 1920s, the tide had turned against racism in all the sciences. Psychologists disclosed the biases inherent in mental tests. Careful analysis of the results of these tests clearly demonstrated the powerful effect of the environment, leading to the conclusion that there is no evidence of inherent racial differences in intelligence. Among biologists, arguments against the harmful effects of miscegenation gained force, as did the idea that both heredity and environment collectively determine the traits of an organism. In a similar vein, sociologists shifted their emphasis from the biological and instinctive basis of human relationships to one based upon social and cultural factors, with the result that racial prejudice was no longer understood as an innate aversion but as a consequence of social forces.

From these scientific developments there emerged a new enlightened perspective in white racial thinking that George M. Fredrickson has labeled "liberal environmentalism." The major tenet of this view is that all apparent social, cultural, and intellectual differences between the races are the product of environment. Hence, blacks are seen as the products of an oppressive environment that creates discontent, frustration, and a sense of powerlessness. By World War II such thinking completely dominated the fields of sociology and anthropology and was becoming increasingly influential among the liberal public.

Adding force to this perspective was the growth of socialist thinking, which recognized the harmful effects of economic and social deprivation. Further, the emergence of black political power as evidenced by the shift of black voters to the Democratic party in the election of 1936 and the threatened march on Washington in 1942 began to awaken the public to the oppression of blacks. During World War II, when the horrors of Nazi racism were revealed and the democratic-egalitarian ideology of the "American creed" was once again called forth, the liberal environmentalist doctrine finally triumphed as the respectable thought in intellectual and academic circles.

The importance of this triumph for race relations in America is inestimable. The new egalitarian doctrine provided the theoretical basis of the civil rights movement of the 1950s and 1960s and was influential in the legislative and court decisions that this movement produced. It offered the first serious challenge to the most fundamental racist belief in America—that blacks are inherently inferior to whites. Although millions of Americans still associate race with character, intelligence, and human worth, blatant racist beliefs are no longer respectable, and today only a small segment of the population will publicly acknowledge a belief in black intellectual inferiority. Perhaps of even greater ultimate significance, the thorough debunking of racial theories of human differences has meant that racists have found it increasingly difficult to invoke the authority of science to support their views. . . .

Contemporary Attitudes Towards Blacks

In 1942 only 42 percent of a nationwide sample of whites said they believed that "Negroes are as intelligent as white people . . . if they are given the same education and training." This is a very important belief, for it is central to the white image of black inferiority. When the National Opinion Research Center (NORC) asked the same question in subsequent national surveys, the percentage increased to 53 percent in 1946 and then to 77 percent in 1956 before dipping slightly to 76 percent in 1963 as reported by Herbert Hyman and Paul Sheatsley. The question has not been included in NORC surveys since 1963. However, Louis Harris and Associates have addressed the same issue throughout the 1960s and 1970s with a differently worded question. In this case, respondents were asked whether they personally tended to agree or disagree that "blacks have less native intelligence than whites," a statement, respondents were told, that "people sometimes make about black people." Apparently because of the different way the question was asked, the responses to the Harris survey were less "liberal" than responses to the NORC polls of 1956 and 1963. Still, the percentage of people who disagreed with the Harris statement rose from 61 percent in 1963 to 75 percent in 1978. Thus, the two sets of polling results together show a substantial decline between 1942 and 1978 in a publicly stated belief that is central to the inherent-inequality doctrine. . . .

Public Versus Private Beliefs

At the same time, there is reason to question the depth of these changes in beliefs and attitudes. For one thing, such surveys may be more a measure of what people are willing to say publicly than of what they really feel. White Americans simply may have "improved their conformity to the increasingly institutionalized normative standards of an officially 'liberal' society" according to John. In fact, there is evidence of indirect resistance and incomplete acceptance of racial integration among those who publicly appear tolerant.

For example, while the polling data show that whites have become much more willing to accept black neighbors, continuing residential segregation seems to be largely a matter of white preference for segregated neighborhoods. When a Detroit area survey by Reynolds Farley and his colleagues presented white respondents with diagrams of a variety of neighborhoods, a majority said they were not willing to move into a nice, affordable house in a neighborhood that is 20 percent black, and three quarters were unwilling to move to a neighborhood that is 33 percent black. On the other hand, there was widespread acceptance of residential integration on the usual indicators such as willingness to sell to a black or to have a "black on your block." Thus, when the question went beyond abstract values and moved toward how respondents personally felt in specific situations, whites were much less tolerant.

A similar pattern exists with respect to racial integration in the schools. In contrast to support for the principle of integrated schools, the number of whites opposed to having their child attend a school where the majority of pupils are blacks actually increased in the 1970s after a period of decline in the 1960s. Closely related, upwards of 80 percent of whites have remained strongly opposed, throughout the 1970s, to the busing of white school children from one district to another, usually the only realistic method for achieving school integration.

In contrast to the sanguine polling results showing a reduction in white opposition to formal racial equality, then, these responses suggest that white racism has far from disappeared. Rather, there appears to have been a shift in the manifest content of white racism coincident with the change in racial policy issues in the late 1960s as demonstrated in a study by Donald Kinder and David Sears. With the passage of civil rights legislation in the 1960s and explicit legal discrimination no longer at issue, the struggle for racial progress became concentrated on "forcing" institutions to be actively egalitarian. The symbols of this shift in policy—affirmative action, busing, and racial quotas—have become the focus of what has been called "symbolic racism." According to Kinder and Sears' formulation, this style of racism combines antiblack anxiety and hostility with traditional American moral values such as individualism and self-reliance. Placing their faith in the Protestant work ethic, whites have become indignant over the sense that blacks are playing by a different and easier set of rules as a result of "unfair" government assistance. Symbolic racism therefore finds its clearest expression on such issues as: welfare ("welfare cheats could find work if they tried"); affirmative action ("blacks should not be given a status they have not earned"); busing ("whites have worked hard for their . . . neighborhood schools"); and "free" abortions for the poor ("if blacks behaved morally, they would not need abortions").

Ample evidence exists that something akin to symbolic racism is the dominant form of racial beliefs in American society today. As we noted earlier, a vast majority of whites continue to express antiblack sentiments on the symbolic issue of busing for racial integration. Kinder and Sears found similar strong opposition to quotas for black college students, as well as widespread beliefs that blacks get more than they deserve and that blacks on welfare could get along without it if they tried. Moreover, national polls throughout the 1970s and early 1980s consistently showed that though most Americans favored equal rights and equal opportunity, they overwhelmingly rejected any form of "forced" integration and preferential treatment. In recent years, over 70 percent of the American public has endorsed the statement, "Blacks shouldn't push themselves where they are not wanted." A majority of whites have been disturbed by the pace of change in race relations. Finally, whites have generally favored "integration in some areas of life" over "full racial integration" and have said that they would feel "uneasy" if a close relative were planning to marry someone of another race. In short, while Americans support racial equality, they have been slow to accept full racial integration; they tend to resent efforts to force it on them: and they are concerned about programs that violate the values of individual freedom and fair individual competition.

Kinder and Sears found that their own measures of symbolic racism were unrelated to whites' current social status or to direct racial threats to whites' private lives such as neighborhood desegregation and the likelihood of having a child bused to achieve school desegregation. This latest version of white racism has less to do with the current realities of whites' lives than with racial attitudes and moral values learned years ago. To the extent that this accurately characterizes contemporary beliefs, it simply reflects the latent racial hostility that over three hundred fifty years of racism has imbued in American culture. And as long as this hostility persists, it will threaten America's commitment to racial equality.

Inequality Disadvantages Women

HELEN MAYER HACKER

Over forty years ago, sociologist Helen Hacker was among the first to suggest that women do not receive benefits in the workplace equal to those of men. Writing during the economic boom following World War II when two (or one and a half) incomes were beginning to be required to support an increasingly affluent lifestyle, Hacker observes that women were treated as a workforce minority. She notes that women themselves perpetuate this discrimination. This viewpoint also contains Hacker's classic comparison of treatment of women with treatment of blacks.

As you read this viewpoint, contemplate the following question: Do women in the 1990s still face the expectation that they appear deferential and content in subordinate roles? On first thought, some people would argue that conditions have changed considerably since 1951. Such recent phenomena as the "glass ceiling" and the "revolving door," however, would cause many to be less optimistic. Although women filled more than twice the number of business management positions in 1990 as they did in 1972 (almost 40 percent as compared with 19 percent, according to *Fortune* magazine), less than one-half of 1 percent of the top four thousand officials of 1990 U.S. corporations were women. On their way up the corporate ladder, women regularly encounter what the *Wall Street Journal* calls the "glass ceiling"—they can see but are unable to reach the top jobs because of traditional corporate cultures and gender stereotypes. Sociologist Jerry Jacobs reported in his 1989 book on the "revolving door," another problem women face in the job market. Current statistics consistently show more women in higher-paid, previously male-dominated professions, but many women leave these fields as they meet with discriminatory treatment. Obviously, sexism is still a problem and women are still a minority treated differently on the basis of their sex.

QUESTIONS

1. How does Hacker define a "minority group"?
2. According to Hacker, what causes women not to identify as a minority group?
3. What are the similarities and differences between the status of women and the status of blacks?

■ ■ ■

In defining the term "minority group," the presence of discrimination is the identifying factor. As Louis Wirth has pointed out, "minority group" is not a statistical concept, nor need it denote an alien group. Indeed for the present discussion I have adopted his definition: "A minority group is any group of people who because of their physical or cultural characteristics, are singled out from the others in the society in which they live for differential and unequal treatment, and who therefore regard themselves as objects of collective discrimination." It is apparent that this definition includes both objective and subjective characteristics of a minority group; the fact of discrimination and the awareness of discrimination, with attendant reactions to that awareness. A person who on the basis of his group affiliation is denied full participation in those opportunities which the value system of his culture extends to all members of the society satisfies the objective criterion, but there are various circumstances which may prevent him from fulfilling the subjective criterion.

In the first place, a person may be unaware of the extent to which his group membership influences the way others treat him. He may have formally dissolved all ties with the group in question and fondly imagine his identity is different from what others hold it to be. Consequently, he interprets their behavior toward him solely in terms of his individual characteristics. Or, less likely, he may be conscious of his membership in a certain group but not be aware of the general disesteem with which the group is regarded. A final possibility is that he may belong in a category which he does not realize has group significance. An example here might be a specific peculiarity which has come to have unpleasant connotations in the minds of others. Or a lower class child with no conception of "class as culture" may not understand how his manners act as cues in eliciting the dislike of his middle class teacher. The foregoing cases all assume that the person believes in equal opportunities for all in the sense that one's group affiliation should not affect his role in the larger society. We turn now to a consideration of situations in which this assumption is not made.

It is frequently the case that a person knows that because of his group affiliation he receives differential treatment, but feels that this treatment is warranted by the distinctive characteristics of his group. A Negro may believe that there are significant differences between whites and Negroes which justify a different role in life for the Negro. A child may accept the fact that physical differences between him and an adult require his going to bed earlier than they do. A Sudra knows that his lot in life has been cast by divine fiat, and he does not expect the perquisites of a Brahmin. A woman does not wish for the rights and duties of men. In all these situations, clearly, the person does not regard himself as an object of collective discrimination.

For the two types presented above: (1) those who do not

know that they are being discriminated against on a group basis; and (2) those who acknowledge the propriety of differential treatment on a group basis, the subjective attributes of a minority group member are lacking. They feel no minority group consciousness, harbor no resentment, and, hence, cannot properly be said to belong in a minority group. Although the term "minority group" is applicable to both types, the term "minority group status" may be substituted. This term is used to categorize persons who are denied rights to which they are entitled according to the value system of the observer. An observer, who is a firm adherent of the democratic ideology, will often consider persons to occupy a minority group status who are well accommodated to their subordinate roles. . . .

Still women often manifest many of the psychological characteristics which have been imputed to self-conscious minority groups. Kurt Lewin has pointed to group self-hatred as a frequent reaction of the minority group member to his group affiliation. This feeling is exhibited in the person's tendency to denigrate other members of the group, to accept the dominant group's stereotyped conception of them, and to indulge in "mea culpa" breast-beating. He may seek to exclude himself from the average of his group, or he may point the finger of scorn at himself. Since a person's conception of himself is based on the defining gestures of others, it is unlikely that members of a minority group can wholly escape personality distortion. Constant reiteration of one's inferiority must often lead to its acceptance as a fact.

Certainly women have not been immune to the formulations of the "female character" throughout the ages. From those, to us, deluded creatures who confessed to witchcraft to modern sophisticates who speak disparagingly of the cattiness and disloyalty of women, women reveal their introjection [acceptance] of prevailing attitudes toward them. Like those minority groups whose self-castigation outdoes dominant group derision of them, women frequently exceed men in the violence of their vituperations of their sex. They are more severe in moral judgments, especially in sexual matters. A line of self-criticism may be traced from Hannah More, a blue-stocking herself, to Dr. Marynia Farnham, who lays most of the world's ills at women's door. Women express themselves as disliking other women, as preferring to work under men, and as finding exclusively female gatherings repugnant. The *Fortune* polls conducted in 1946 show that women, more than men, have misgivings concerning women's participation in industry, the professions, and civic life. And more than one-fourth of women wish they had been born in the opposite sex! . . .

Minority Group Status of Women

Formal discriminations against women are too well-known for any but the most summary description. In general they take the form of being barred from certain activities or, if admitted, being treated unequally. Discriminations against women may be viewed as arising from the generally ascribed status "female" and from the specially ascribed statuses of "wife," "mother," and "sister." (To meet the possible objection that "wife" and "mother" represent assumed, rather than ascribed statuses, may I point out that what is important here is that these statuses carry ascribed expectations which are only ancillary in the minds of those who assume them.)

As female, in the economic sphere, women are largely confined to sedentary, monotonous work under the supervision of men, and are treated unequally with regard to pay, promotion, and responsibility. With the exceptions of teaching, nursing, social service, and library work, in which they do not hold a proportionate number of supervisory positions and are often occupationally segregated from men, they make a poor showing in the professions. . . . Even when they are admitted to the apparatus of political parties, they are subordinated to men. Socially, women have less freedom of movement, and are permitted fewer deviations in the proprieties of dress, speech, manners. In social intercourse they are confined to a narrower range of personality expression.

In the specially ascribed status of wife, a women—in several States—has no exclusive right to her earnings, is discriminated against in employment, must take the domicile of her husband, and in general must meet the social expectation of subordination to her husband's interests. As a mother, she may not have the guardianship of her children, bears the chief stigma in the case of an illegitimate child, is rarely given leave of absence for pregnancy. As a sister, she frequently suffers unequal distribution of domestic duties between herself and her brother, must yield preference to him in obtaining an education, and in such other psychic and material gratifications as cars, trips, and living away from home. . . .

Minority Comparisons

The relation between women and Negroes is historical, as well as analogical. In the seventeenth century the legal status of Negro servants was borrowed from that of women and children, who were under the patria potestas, and until the Civil War there was considerable cooperation between the Abolitionist and woman suffrage movements. According to [Gunnar] Myrdal, the problems of both groups are resultants of the transition from a pre-industrial, paternalistic scheme of life to individualistic, industrial capitalism. Obvious similarities in the status of women and Negroes are indicated in Chart 1.

CHART 1. Castelike Status of Women and Negroes

Negroes	Women

1. High Social Visibility

a. Skin color, other "racial" characteristics	a. Secondary sex characteristics
b. (Sometimes) distinctive dress—bandana, flashy clothes	b. Distinctive dress, skirts, etc.

2. Ascribed Attributes

a. Inferior intelligence, smaller brain, less convoluted, scarcity of geniuses	a. ditto
b. More free in instinctual gratifications. More emotional, "primitive" and childlike. Imagined sexual prowess envied.	b. Irresponsible, inconsistent, emotionally unstable. Lack strong super-ego. Women as "temptresses."
c. Common stereotype "inferior"	c. "Weaker"

3. Rationalizations of Status

a. Thought all right in his place	a. Woman's place is in the home
b. Myth of contented Negro	b. Myth of contented woman— "feminine" woman is happy in subordinate role

4. Accommodation Attitudes

a. Supplicatory whining intonation of voice	a. Rising inflection, smiles, laughs, downward glances
b. Deferential manner	b. Flattering manner
c. Concealment of real feelings	c. "Feminine wiles"
d. Outwit "white folks"	d. Outwit "men-folk"
e. Careful study of points at which dominant group is susceptible to influence	e. ditto
f. Fake appeals for directives; show of ignorance	f. Appearance of helplessness

5. Discriminations

a. Limitations on education— should fit "place" in society	a. ditto
b. Confined to traditional jobs—barred from supervisory positions. Their competition feared. No family precedents for new aspirations.	b. ditto
c. Deprived of political importance	c. ditto
d. Social and professional segregation	d. ditto
e. More vulnerable to criticism	e. e.g. conduct in bars

While these similarities in the situation of women and Negroes may lead to increased understanding of their social roles,
account must also be taken of differences which impose qualifications on the comparison of the two groups. Most importantly, the influence of marriage as a social elevator for women,
but not for Negroes, must be considered. Obvious, too, is the

greater importance of women to the dominant group, despite the economic, sexual, and prestige gains which Negroes afford the white South. Ambivalence is probably more marked in the attitude of white males toward women than toward Negroes. The "war of the sexes" is only an expression of men's and women's vital need of each other. Again, there is greater polarization in the relationship between men and women. Negroes, although they have borne the brunt of anti-minority group feeling in this country, do not constitute the only racial or ethnic minority, but there are only two sexes. And, although we have seen that social distance exists between men and women, it is not to be compared with the social segregation of Negroes.

At the present time, of course, Negroes suffer far greater discrimination than women, but since the latter's problems are rooted in a biological reality less susceptible to cultural manipulation, they prove more lasting. Women's privileges exceed those of Negroes. Protective attitudes toward Negroes have faded into abeyance, even in the South, but most boys are still taught to take care of girls, and many evidences of male chivalry remain. The factor of class introduces variations here. The middle class Negro endures frustrations largely without the rewards of his white class peer, but the lower class Negro is still absolved from many responsibilities. The reverse holds true for women. Notwithstanding these and other differences between the position of women and Negroes, the similarities are sufficient to render research on either group applicable in some fashion to the other. . . .

Since the days of the suffragettes there has been no overt conflict between men and women on a group basis. Rather than conflict, the dissociative process between the sexes is that of contravention, a type of opposition intermediate between competition and conflict. It includes rebuffing, repulsing, working against, hindering, protesting, obstructing, restraining, and upsetting another's plans.

The present contravention of the sexes, arising from women's competition with men, is manifested in the discriminations against women, as well as in the doubts and uncertainties expressed concerning women's character, abilities, motives. The excesses of competition and contravention are continually giving way to accommodation in the relationships between men and women. Like other minority groups, women have sought a protected position, a niche in the economy which they could occupy, and, like other minority groups, they have found these positions in new occupations in which dominant group members had not yet established themselves and in old occupations which they no longer wanted. When women entered fields which represented an extension of services in the home (except medicine!), they encountered least opposition. Evidence is accumulating, however, that women are becoming dissatisfied with the employment conditions of the great women-employing occupations and present accommodations are threatened.

VIEWPOINT

6

Inequality Is Perpetuated by Attitudes and Actions

ROBERT K. MERTON

Although Talcott Parsons was the foremost structural functional theorist, his student Robert Merton wrote *"the single most important statement on structural functionalism in sociology"* (Ritzer 1988:217). In that statement, Merton developed the concept of applied structural functionalism: the functional analysis. Among other things, he argued that each component of society may be functional or dysfunctional for the society as a whole. On a second dimension, each component may also be manifest—intended and acknowledged—or latent—unintended and unanticipated. This viewpoint contains another of Merton's important contributions to sociology, the distinction between "prejudice" and "discrimination."

Several viewpoints in this chapter used the terms "prejudice" and "discrimination" as though a clear and common understanding of them exists. Merton does not take this for granted. He describes both and argues that prejudiced people may or may not discriminate and people who discriminate may or may not have prejudice.

From "Discrimination and the American Creed" by Robert K. Merton, in *Discrimination and the National Welfare*, Robert M. MacIver, ed. Copyright 1949 by the Institute for Religious and Social Studies. Reprinted by permission of HarperCollins Publishers, Inc.

QUESTIONS

1. How does Merton describe the "American creed"?
2. What attitudes do each of the four types have toward the creed? How does each of the four types behave with respect to the creed?
3. In what ways does Merton suggest prejudice and discrimination can be decreased?

■ ■ ■

Set forth in the Declaration of Independence, the preamble of the Constitution, and the Bill of Rights, the American creed has since often been misstated. This part of the cultural heritage does *not* include the patently false assertion that all human beings are created equal in capacity or endowment. It does *not* imply that an Einstein and a moron are equal in intellectual capacity or that Joe Louis and a small, frail Columbia professor (or a Mississippian Congressman) are equally endowed with brawny arms harboring muscles as strong as iron bands. It does *not* proclaim universal equality of innate intellectual or physical endowment.

Instead, the creed asserts the indefeasible principle of the human right to full equity—the right of equitable access to justice, freedom, and opportunity, irrespective of race or religion or ethnic origin. It proclaims further the universalist doctrine of the dignity of the individual, irrespective of the groups of which he is a part. It is a creed announcing full moral equities for all, not an absurd myth affirming the equality of intellectual and physical capacity of all people everywhere. And it goes on to say that although individuals differ in innate endowment, they do so as individuals, not by virtue of their group memberships.

Viewed sociologically, the creed is a set of values and precepts embedded in American culture to which Americans are expected to conform. It is a complex of affirmations, rooted in the historical past and ceremonially celebrated in the present, partly enacted in the laws of the land and partly not. Like all creeds, it is a profession of faith, a part of cultural tradition sanctified by the larger traditions of which it is a part.

It would be a mistaken sociological assertion, however, to suggest that the creed is a fixed and static cultural constant, unmodified in the course of time, just as it would be an error to imply that as an integral part of the culture, it evenly blankets all subcultures of the national society. It is indeed dynamic, subject to change and in turn promoting change in other spheres of culture and society. It is, moreover, unevenly distributed throughout the society, being institutionalized as an integral part of local culture in some regions of the society and rejected in others. . . .

With respect to actual practices: conduct may or may not conform to the creed. And further, this being the salient consideration: *conduct may or may not conform with individuals' own belief concerning the moral claims of all people to equal opportunity.*

Stated in formal sociological terms, this asserts that attitudes and overt behavior vary independently. *Prejudicial attitudes need not coincide with discriminatory behavior.* The implications of this statement can be drawn out in terms of a logical syntax whereby the variables are diversely combined, as can be seen in the following typology.

A Typology of Ethnic Prejudice and Discrimination

		Attitude Dimension:* Prejudice and Non-Prejudice	Behavior Dimension:* Discrimination and Non-Discrimination
Type I:	Unprejudiced Non-Discriminator	+	+
Type II:	Unprejudiced Discriminator	+	−
Type III:	Prejudiced Non-Discriminator	−	+
Type IV:	Prejudiced Discriminator	−	−

* Where (+) = conformity to the creed and (−) = deviation from the creed.

By exploring the interrelations between prejudice and discrimination, we can identify four major types in terms of their attitudes toward the creed and their behavior with respect to it. Each type is found in every region and social class, although in varying numbers. By examining each type, we shall be better prepared to understand their interdependence and the appropriate types of action for curbing ethnic discrimination. The folk-labels for each type are intended to aid in their prompt recognition.

Type I: The Unprejudiced Non-Discriminator or All-Weather Liberal

These are the racial and ethnic liberals who adhere to the creed in both belief and practice. They are neither prejudiced nor given to discrimination. Their orientation toward the creed is fixed and stable. Whatever the environing situation, they are likely to abide by their beliefs; hence, the *all-weather* liberal.

These make up the strategic group that *can* act as the spearhead for the progressive extension of the creed into effective practice. They represent the solid foundation both for the measure of ethnic equities that now exist and for the future enlargement of these equities. Integrated with the creed in both belief and practice, they would seem most motivated to influence others toward the same democratic outlook. They represent a reservoir of culturally legitimatized goodwill that can be channeled into an active program for extending belief in the creed and conformity with it in practice.

Most important, as we shall see presently, the all-weather liberals comprise the group that can so reward others for conforming with the creed as to transform deviants into conformers. They alone can provide the positive social environment for the other types who will no longer find it expedient or rewarding to retain their prejudices or discriminatory practices.

Although ethnic liberals are a *potential* force for the successive extension of the American creed, they do not fully realize this potentiality in actual fact, for a variety of reasons. Among the limitations on effective action are several fallacies to which the ethnic liberal seems peculiarly subject. First among these is the *fallacy of group soliloquies*. Ethnic liberals are busily engaged in talking to themselves. Repeatedly, the same groups of likeminded liberals seek each other out, hold periodic meetings in which they engage in mutual exhortation, and thus lend social and psychological support to one another. But however much these unwittingly self-selected audiences may reinforce the creed among themselves, they do not thus appreciably diffuse the creed in belief or practice to groups that depart from it in one respect or the other.

More, these group soliloquies in which there is typically wholehearted agreement among fellow-liberals tend to promote another fallacy limiting effective action. This is the *fallacy of unanimity*. Continued association with like-minded individuals tends to produce the illusion that a large measure of consensus has been achieved in the community at large. The unanimity regarding essential cultural axioms that obtains in these small groups provokes an overestimation of the strength of the movement and of its effective inroads upon the larger population, which does not necessarily share these creedal axioms. Many also mistake participation in the groups of like-minded individuals for effective action. Discussion accordingly takes the place of action. The reinforcement of the creed for oneself is mistaken for the extension of the creed among those outside the limited circle of ethnic liberals. . . .

Type II: The Unprejudiced Discriminator or Fair-Weather Liberal

The fair-weather liberal is the man of expediency who, despite his own freedom from prejudice, supports discriminatory practices when it is the easier or more profitable course. Expediency may take the form of holding his silence and thus implicitly acquiescing in expressions of ethnic prejudice by others or in the practice of discrimination by others. This is the expediency of the timid: the liberal who hesitates to speak up against discrimination for fear he might lose esteem or be otherwise penalized by his prejudiced associates. Or his expediency may take the form of grasping at advantages in social and economic competition deriving solely from the ethnic status of competitors. Thus the expediency of the self-assertive: the employer, himself not an anti-Semite or Negrophobe, who refuses to hire Jewish or Negro workers because "it might hurt business"; the trade union leader who expediently advocates racial discrimination in order not to lose the support of powerful Negrophobes in his union.

In varying degrees, fair-weather liberals suffer from guilt and shame for departing from their own effective beliefs in the American creed. Each deviation through which they derive a limited reward from passively acquiescing in or actively supporting discrimination contributes cumulatively to this fund of guilt. They are, therefore, peculiarly vulnerable to the efforts of the all-weather liberals who would help them bring conduct into accord with beliefs, thus removing this source of guilt. They are the most amenable to cure, because basically they want to be cured. Theirs is a split conscience that motivates them to cooperate actively with people who will help remove the source of internal conflict. They thus represent the strategic group promising the largest returns for the least effort. Persistent reaffirmation of the creed will only intensify their conflict but a long regimen in a favorable social climate can be expected to transform fair-weather liberals into all-weather liberals.

Type III: The Prejudiced Non-Discriminator or Fair-Weather Illiberal

The fair-weather illiberal is the reluctant conformist to the creed, the man of prejudice who does not believe in the creed but conforms to it in practice through fear of sanctions that might otherwise be visited upon him. You know him well: the prejudiced employer who discriminates against racial or ethnic groups until a Fair Employment Practice Commission, able and willing to enforce the law, puts the fear of punishment into him; the trade union leader, himself deeply prejudiced, who does away with Jim Crow in his union because the rank-and-file demands that it be done away with; the businessman who forgoes his own prejudices when he finds a profitable market among the very people he hates, fears, or despises; the timid bigot who will not express his prejudices when he is in the presence of powerful men who vigorously and effectively affirm their belief in the American creed.

It should be clear that the fair-weather illiberal is the precise counterpart of the fair-weather liberal. Both are men of expediency, to be sure, but expediency dictates different courses of behavior in the two cases. The timid bigot conforms to the creed only when there is danger or loss in deviations, just as the timid liberal deviates from the creed only when there is danger or loss in conforming. *Superficial similarity in behavior of the two in the same situation should not be permitted to cloak a basic difference in the meaning of this outwardly similar behavior*, a difference that is as important for social policy as it is for social science. Whereas the timid bigot is under strain when he conforms to the creed, the timid liberal is under strain when he deviates. For ethnic prejudice has deep roots in the character structure of the fair-weather bigot, and this will find overt expression unless there are powerful countervailing forces—institutional, legal, and interpersonal. He does not accept the moral legitimacy of the creed; he conforms because he must, and will cease to conform when the pressure is removed. The fair-weather liberal, on the other hand, is effectively committed to the creed and does not require strong institutional pressure to conform; continuing interpersonal relations with all-weather liberals may be sufficient.

This is one critical point at which the traditional formulation of the problem of ethnic discrimination as a departure from the creed can lead to serious errors of theory and practice. *Overt behavioral deviation (or conformity) may signify importantly different situations, depending upon the underlying motivations.* Knowing simply that ethnic discrimination is rife in a community does not therefore point to appropriate lines of social policy. It is necessary to know also the distribution of ethnic prejudices and basic motivations for these prejudices as well. Communities with the same amount of overt discrimination may represent vastly different types of problems, dependent on whether the population is comprised of a large nucleus of fair-weather liberals ready to abandon their discriminatory practices under slight interpersonal pressure or a large nucleus of fair-weather illiberals who will abandon discrimination only if major changes in the local institutional setting can be effected. Any statement of the problem as a gulf between creedal ideals and prevailing practice is thus seen to be overly simplified in the precise sense of masking this decisive difference between the type of discrimination exhibited by the fair-weather liberal and by the fair-weather illiberal. . . .

Type IV: The Prejudiced Discriminator or the All-Weather Illiberal

This type, too, is not unknown to you. He is the confirmed illiberal, the bigot pure and unashamed, the man of prejudice consistent in his departures from the American creed. In some measure, he is found everywhere in the land, though in varying numbers. He derives large social and psychological gains from his conviction that "any white man (including the village idiot) is 'better' than any nigger (including George Washington Carver)." He considers differential treatment of Negro and white not as "discrimination," in the sense of unfair treatment, but as "discriminating," in the sense of showing acute discernment. For him, it is as clear that one "ought" to accord a Negro and a white different treatment in a wide diversity of situations as it is clear to the population at large that one "ought" to accord a child and an adult different treatment in many situations.

This illustrates anew my reason for questioning the applicability of the usual formula of the American dilemma as a gap between lofty creed and low conduct. For the confirmed illiberal, ethnic discrimination does *not* represent a discrepancy between *his* ideals and *his* behavior. His ideals proclaim the right, even the duty, of discrimination. Accordingly, his behavior does not entail a sense of social deviation, with the resultant strains that this would involve. The ethnic illiberal is as much a conformist as the ethnic liberal. He is merely conforming to a different cultural and institutional pattern that is centered, not on the creed, but on a doctrine of essential inequality of status ascribed to those of diverse ethnic and racial origins. To overlook this is to overlook the well-known *fact* that our national culture is divided into a number of local subcultures that are not consistent among themselves in all respects. And again, to fail to take this fact of different subcultures into account is to open the door for all manner of errors of social policy in attempting to control the problems of racial and ethnic discrimination.

This view of the all-weather illiberal has one immediate implication with wide bearing upon social policies and sociological theory oriented toward the problem of discrimination. The extreme importance of the social surroundings of the confirmed illiberal at once becomes apparent. For as these surroundings vary, so, in some measure, does the problem of the consistent illiberal. The illiberal, living in those cultural regions where the American creed is widely repudiated and is no effective part of the subculture, has his private ethnic attitudes and practices supported by the local mores, the local institutions, and the local power structure. The illiberal in cultural areas dominated by a large measure of adherence to the American creed is in a social environment where he is isolated and receives small social support for his beliefs and practices. In both instances, the *individual* is an illiberal, to be sure, but he represents two significantly different *sociological types*. In the first instance, he is a *social conformist*, with strong moral and institutional reinforcement, whereas in the second, he is a *social deviant*, lacking strong social corroboration. In the one case, his discrimination involves him in further integration with his network of social relations; in the other, it threatens to cut him off from sustaining interpersonal ties. In the first cultural context, personal change in his ethnic behavior involves alienating himself from people significant to him; in the second context, this change of personal outlook may mean fuller incorporation in groups significant to him. In the first situation, modification of his ethnic views requires him to take the path of greatest resistance whereas in the second, it may mean the path of least resistance. From all this, we may surmise that any social policy aimed at changing the behavior and perhaps the attitudes of the all-weather illiberal will have to take into systematic account the cultural and social structure of the area in which he lives.

CHAPTER

4

How Do Institutions Work?

CHAPTER PREFACE

Social institutions are organized and patterned ways of responding to ongoing social needs. Societies contain many institutions. During the 1990s, for example, the military, medicine, sports, the criminal justice system, newspapers, television, and popular music in the United States could all be considered institutions. However, five institutions most basically define the way society operates: family, religion, the economy, the polity (government), and education. This chapter contains conflicting viewpoints that focus on the first four of these institutions. Education reinforces ideas about every other institution by helping to socialize members of society concerning each of the others.

Early in U.S. history, the five institutions were nearly inseparable. From their European heritage, settlers viewed church and government as having identical interests. Early colonists made as much effort to establish correct religious beliefs as they intended to secure economic advantage. Establishment of a single publicly supported church within each colony achieved religious conformity, and all families belonged to the single church. The economy was based on agriculture and family members—men, women, and the average seven children—working together to provide food, clothing, and shelter. Parents provided the training and education children needed. Women taught their small children, fathers educated the older ones, and children were apprenticed to other families from about the age of eight to learn additional skills.

Around 1800, the beginning of industrialization meant that families could purchase manufactured goods for some essentials. It was no longer necessary for each family to produce their own cloth, since this manufacturing could be done more efficiently in factories. By the traditional division of labor, men had primary responsibility for agricultural work and women for cloth production, although both contributed to each activity. Because the earliest factories automated cloth production, popular sentiment first specified women and children as the main labor resource available to the new textile industry. As a result, women and children entered the factories and worked for low wages doing the work formerly done at home.

By about 1830, men began to work in factories during the

day and in the fields in the evenings. At the same time, the separation of church from government support, mandated in the Constitution, was finally completed. For the first time, denominations long accustomed to official support needed to compete for members. As church and state separated, competition among denominations promoted a religious revival that encouraged separation of family and economic production as well. It was about this time that modern ideals of family life as private and separate from work, church, and government emerged. Religious leaders joined factory owners in encouraging women to leave the factories and concentrate on family matters. Women who could afford to do so stayed at home with their children, who were no longer viewed as miniature adult workers but rather as needing "mother love." The colonial view of women as the strong, sturdy goodwife helping to produce household necessities began to change. The emerging view described women as delicate and in need of protection from the harsh world, but also as moral guardians.

In 1850, the average middle-income family had only five children, reducing family work and allowing older daughters to seek employment. Although some women entered the workforce, the prevailing ethic demanded that they leave the factories when they married and only half of all women ever worked outside the home. Religious denominations held diverse positions on matters such as slavery, but church officials consistently resisted women's participation in public affairs, such as speaking in public or holding office in abolitionist organizations. After the Civil War, government officials confirmed popular and religious belief about family by awarding the vote to black men, but it would take another fifty years for women to achieve the same right.

Because the industrialized workplace required literate workers, every state instituted mandatory education laws in the early 1900s. With a depressed economy, a declining birthrate, and children in school, married women began entering the workforce in larger numbers. During World War I, millions of women entered the workforce, and many more women went to the factories during World War II. After WWII, U.S. birthrates increased for the first time in the twentieth century in a decade-long "baby boom" supported by the healthy economy. Despite the larger family size, women's workforce participation continued to increase especially as the declining economy required more than one income per family. By 1975 about half of all women received paychecks at about the same time as divorce rates exceeded previous highs.

Religious and political institutions also experienced change in the second half of the twentieth century. Religious fundamentalists allied with the Republican Party. Major third-party candidates entered the 1968 and 1980 presidential election campaigns (George Wallace and John Anderson respectively), and Geraldine Ferraro was the first woman to become a major party candidate in 1980. In the economic institution, the transition from an industrial to an information and service economy, transfer of manufacturing to other countries, and global competition changed the kinds of jobs available. Layoffs, plant closings, and technological change increased unemployment at the same time that inflation and job insecurity encouraged multiple-job families.

This brief history illustrates the ways family, religion, the economy, government, and education combine to influence everyday life. Values and norms that originate in each of these institutions strongly color people's ideas about everything else. Operation of each institution governs the daily behavior of individuals, groups, organizations, and political units. Even when individuals complete their education, leave their families, reject religious beliefs, retire from their jobs, or argue against government practices, operation of these institutions still determines the course of events. For these reasons, more insight into how the institutions operate increases our understanding of society. Viewpoints in this chapter provide the beginning of such insight.

VIEWPOINT

1

Fixed Family Roles Benefit Society

TALCOTT PARSONS AND ROBERT F. BALES

As you read in Chapter 1, Parsons established the functionalist definition of a social system as a set of interrelated and complementary parts that work together to assure perpetuation of the system. Social psychologist Robert F. Bales's small group research found that in experimental groups, a task-oriented (instrumental) leader and a socio-emotional (expressive) leader each emerge as the group interacts. From many small group experiments, Bales developed a way to analyze communication patterns in small groups called interaction process analysis (IPA). He used IPA to analyze discussions among such groups as college students, enlisted military personnel, therapy patients, and juries. One finding from this research was that about two-thirds of each group discussion was task-oriented and one-third socio-emotional (Bales and Hare 1965).

The following viewpoint combines Parsons's definition of

a social system with Bales's concepts of instrumental and ex-pressive leaders and applies the combination to the family. They argue that the stable distribution of roles—males as task-oriented and females as socio-emotional—benefits family members because each member knows and performs the ap-propriate role. When marriage partners deviate from these expectations, family instability results. Stable arrangements assure perpetuation of both the family and the society.

QUESTIONS

1. What are the instrumental and expressive roles?
2. How do the authors support their argument that these roles should be sex specific?
3. How does society benefit from fixed family roles?

■ ■ ■

Among the conditions of a system's existence is at least a certain degree of differentiation along lines imposed by the orbits of the system's movement. Consider first the general pattern of differentiation which in broad outline appears from the experimental small group. There is a tendency for a *task leader* and a *sociometric star* to appear. Although there is some problem in clearly isolating the complex factors defining the task leader he seems to be associated with certain *behaviors* (in general terms, "task" behaviors; more specifically in giving suggestions, directions, opinions), and certain *attitudes* (in-volving, apparently, an inhibition of emotions and the ability to accept hostile reactions from others in the process of press-ing a point, etc.). There are also, of course, reciprocal behaviors and attitudes on the part of other system-members towards the task leader. The sociometric star, although the term originally derives from attitudes taken toward ego by alters, also tends to show a certain pattern of behaviors and attitudes; namely, the *expression* of emotions, supportive behavior to others, the de-sire to please and be liked, and a more generalized liking for other members. The star may, of course, express negative reac-tions as well as positive supports; typically these are signifi-cant in releasing negative reactions (often through humor) of the group as a whole, reducing, in consequence, the general tension level. (The difference between a "leader," here, and one who fails to become a leader may very well lie, in part, in the capacity to express reactions felt by the group as a *whole*.)

From a general theoretical point of view this is *not* a fortuitous pattern of differentiation; it defines, in fact, the two basic conditions of the existence of a social system. In order to clarify and illustrate what we mean by this, we may take the nuclear family as a specific case; and it may be useful at the same time to begin with a differentiation logically prior to role differentiation itself.

Directions of Differentiation in the Nuclear Family

Assume a time T_1 in which members of the nuclear family are dispersed somewhere in the external situation involved in devotion to the "task," or what we call "instrumental" activities. By either of these terms we mean here the manipulation of the object-world in order to provide facilities for the achievement of goals defined within the system. In our society, for instance, the husband typically goes to work in the morning, the mother shops or cleans up, the children go to school if they are old enough. In many other societies a similar dispersal, involving a departure of at least the husband-father (out hunting, or farming), often occurs. Now clearly, if there is no second occasion, T_2, during which the members of the system are *reunited*, the system will tend to disappear. It will no longer be identifiable as a system.

There is then, a most primitive level of differentiation here in the simple presence or absence of members on two different occasions. From this it is clear that one imperative of all social systems is integration, a coming together, which of course Durkheim emphasized a considerable time ago.

The other side of the coin, involving here a dispersal of members, introduces a more complex level of analysis. Although dispersal of system members is common during instrumental activities, it is not necessary to define what we are talking about. We merely suggest this as a first point of purchase on the type of analysis involved. Typically, in fact, the mother and children remain at some location symbolically associated with the system's existence—the home is the crucial symbol, of course—and there is always a *latent* existence to the system (*if* it is to reappear). This function of symbols, in giving latent existence to systems, is of obvious importance as a basis for their physical reintegration.

What is significant in the differentiation of these two occasions, however, is not the states of spatial dispersion and integration, physically, but the difference in behavior and attitudes involved. The system may in fact always act in concert from the present point of view, and still show the differentiation we are here concerned with.

Reverting to our time period T_1, then, assume that all members are physically adjacent but devoted to instrumental or task activities. The entire family, say, is out farming in the fields. These instrumental activities involve, in gross terms, the manipulation of objects (plows, or hoes, etc.), and an attitude composed of Parsons' pattern variables "specific, affectively neutral, universalistic, achievement-oriented," or in more gross terms a "rational" attitude towards the external situation, and an *inhibition* of emotions toward other members of the system. *In order for the system to continue as a system,* we now say, there must at some point be a *change* in attitude and behavior to integrative-expressive activities—to laughing, playing, release of inhibited emotions, the expression of affection for each other, a warmth and a symbolization of common membership through supportive, accepting behavior.

If we reverse our assumptions, we arrive at the same basic conclusion, something we were not able to do when we considered only physical presence or absence (we were not, that is, able to show why dispersion *had* to occur). Assume the time period T_2 in which all members are affectionate, responsive, emotionally warm and attached to each other, often symbolized in the meal-time break. The system *cannot* continue in this state forever. It must, at some point, change to the necessary activities—and the associated attitudes—involved in manipulating the facilities of the object world so that the family has the food, shelter, fire, etc., which the external situation can provide. The family then becomes reinvolved in the *task*, which, no matter how much integrative behavior there was before or will be after—and perhaps also at breaks during the task—must concentrate on *getting the job done*. It must, that is, at least for the time being, devote its attention to instrumental acts.

Family Roles

A considerable refinement is involved in the further differentiation of the structure of *roles* in the system. One clue, perhaps, is suggested by the earlier peripheral comment that while husband-father is away at work or in the fields, the mother very often stays at home symbolizing the integrative focus of the system (even though her activities may be primarily instrumental during this phase of family activity). The fact that it is the mother who stays home is not, for the present, significant although shortly it will become so. What *is* significant, is that *someone* stayed, and that someone is in fact *more* responsible for integrative-expressive behavior than the person who went off to work.

Why after all, are *two* parents necessary? For one thing, to be a stable focus of integration, the integrative-expressive "leader" can't be off on adaptive-instrumental errands all the time. For another, a stable, secure attitude of members depends, it can be assumed, on a *clear* structure being given to the situation so that an *uncertain* responsibility for emotional warmth, for instance, raises significant problems for the stability of the system. And an uncertain managerial responsibility, an unclear definition of authority for decisions and for getting things done, is also clearly a threat to the stability of the system.

We can say, then, that the system must differentiate behaviors and attitudes in order to continue to exist as a system; and that a further condition of stability is also that some specialization occur in responsibility for the attitudes and behaviors involved. . . .

Age and Sex in the Nuclear Family

At least one fundamental feature of the external situation of social systems—here a feature of the physiological organism—is a crucial reference point for differentiation in the family. This lies in the division of organisms into lactating and nonlactating classes. Only in our own society (so far as I know, that is) have we managed to invent successful bottle-feeding, and this is undoubtedly of importance for our social structure. In other societies necessarily—and in our own for structural reasons

201

which have *not* disappeared with the advent of the bottle—the initial core relation of a family with children is the mother-child attachment. And it follows from the principles of learning that the gradient of generalization should establish "mother" as the focus of gratification in a diffuse sense, as the source of "security" and "comfort." She is the focus of warmth and stability. Thus, because of her special initial relation to the child, "mother" is the more likely expressive focus of the system as a whole.

The allocation of the instrumental leadership to the husband-father rests on two aspects of this role. The role involves, first, a manipulation of the external environment, and consequently a good deal of physical mobility. The concentration of the mother on the child precludes a *primacy* of her attention in this direction although she always performs *some* instrumental tasks. In addition to the managerial aspects of the role there are certain discipline and control functions of the father role. Consider, again, why *two* parents are necessary at all. The initial mother-child subsystem can do without the father (except that he provides food, shelter, etc., for this subsystem so that it need not split up to perform many of its own instrumental tasks). But *some* significant member of the nuclear family must "pry the child loose" from the mother-dependency so that it may "grow up" and accept its responsibilities as an "adult." There is necessarily a coalition of father and mother in this, or no stable socialization pattern develops. But the mother, by her special initial relation to the child is relatively more susceptible to *seduction* out of the coalition. We may note, for instance, that one of the pathologies of family dynamics may arise because the father tends to be susceptible to seduction by daughters; and the very fact of his relative power in the coalition makes this *more* of a threat to the family as a system. The problem of the "weak, ineffectual" father is more significant than that of the "weak, ineffectual" mother. (Conversely, of course, and quite as significant, the problem of the "cold, unyielding" mother is more of a problem than the "cold, unyielding" father.) If, therefore, the female is allocated the integrative-supportive role, there must necessarily be an allocation of authority for discipline and relatively "neutral" judgment to the husband-father.

We may summarize the hypothesis we have stated then, in

this way. Because the nuclear family is a special case of the more general class of social systems, and because it must meet certain conditions of existence common to all social systems, we suggest that:

1. If the nuclear family constitutes a social system stable over time, it will differentiate roles such that instrumental leadership and expressive leadership of the system are discriminated.

Because the nuclear family, on the other hand, has certain peculiar features not common to all systems, we are further able to state a certain hypothesis about the *allocation* of these roles to system-members. This peculiar feature is the age-sex matrix of the nuclear family and the differential distribution of facilities for the performance of the fundamental roles. We suggest that:

2. If the nuclear family consists in a defined "normal" complement of the male adult, female adult and their immediate children, the male adult will play the role of instrumental leader and the female adult will play the role of expressive leader. . . .

The American Middle-Class Family

We may, as a matter of fact, consider the American middle-class case in reviewing the definitions we have given to instrumental and expressive leadership. From certain points of view the American middle-class family approaches most clearly to equal allocation (or "no allocation") of instrumental and expressive activities. The universalistic value schema (in which women are "just as good as" men) coupled with the general attitude toward the explicit expression of authority ("I'm agin it") apparently constitutes the limiting case of no differentiation at all. Underlying this broad value-schema, however, a rather clear differentiation occurs.

In the distribution of instrumental tasks, the American family maintains a more flexible pattern than most societies. Father helps mother with the dishes. He sets the table. He makes formula for the baby. Mother can supplement the income of the family by working outside. Nevertheless, the

American male, by definition, *must* "provide" for his family. He is *responsible* for the support of his wife and children. His primary area of performance is the occupational role, in which his status fundamentally inheres; and his *primary* function in the family is to supply an "income," to be the "breadwinner." There is simply something wrong with the American adult male who doesn't have a "job." American women, on the other hand, tend to hold jobs *before* they are married and to quit when "the day" comes; or to continue in jobs of a lower status than their husbands. And not only is the mother the focus of emotional support for the American middle-class child, but much more exclusively so than in most societies (as Margaret Mead has pointed out in her treatment of adolescent problems). The cult of the warm, giving "Mom" stands in contrast to the "capable," "competent," "go-getting" male. The more expressive type of male, as a matter of fact, is regarded as "effeminate," and has too much fat on the inner side of his thigh.

The distribution of authority is legitimized on a different basis in the "democratic" family than in the so-called "traditional" one; but the father is "supposed" to remain the primary executive member. The image of the "henpecked" husband makes sense only on this premise. His "commands" are validated on the basis of "good judgment," rather than *general* obedience due a person in authority. But when the mother's efforts at "disciplining" fail, she traditionally tells the errant child, "Wait till daddy gets home.". . .

On the whole, therefore, when the nuclear family can be clearly distinguished from incorporating solidarities, it differentiates in the direction expected and allocates the relevant roles to the persons expected.

VIEWPOINT

2

Traditional Family Roles Benefit Husbands

JESSIE BERNARD

The first viewpoint on family examined the institution from a macro perspective as Parsons and Bales concluded that traditional family roles benefit society. This viewpoint contains a micro analysis of our modern family institution, particularly as focused on the institution of marriage. Our culture clearly values task-oriented behavior more highly than socio-emotional behavior, as illustrated by more job opportunities and higher salaries for engineers and marketing analysts than for teachers and social workers. Bales's finding that two-thirds of his experimental discussions were task oriented seems to imply that the task leader has power over the group.

In this viewpoint, sociologist Jessie Bernard builds evidence for "his" and "her" marriage discrepancies by examining previous research findings. A substantial number of prior studies reported that wives and husbands give different answers to the same questions about their marriage. Partners answer questions about sex, the household division of labor,

Excerpted from *The Future of Marriage*, 2nd ed., by Jessie Bernard. New Haven: Yale University Press, 1982. Copyright 1972, 1982 by Jessie Bernard. Reprinted by permission of the publisher.

decision-making processes, companionship, and even length of engagement quite differently. One explanation may be differing perspectives, but Bernard concludes that an objective (measurable) reality does exist within marriages that allows research on the differences. Our institutionalized bias for male superiority and authority assigns men actual power over women and this distinguishes "his" marriage from "hers." Research such as Bernard's enlightens other researchers in addition to the reader and helps shape the course of subsequent research.

QUESTIONS

1. What research evidence leads Bernard to conclude "his" marriage is different from "hers"?
2. What can be measured that would distinguish between the two?
3. How does Bernard support her argument that we have an institutionalized bias for male superiority and authority?

■ ■ ■

Under the jargon "discrepant responses," the differences in the marriages of husbands and wives have come under the careful scrutiny of a score of researchers. They have found that when they ask husbands and wives identical questions about the union, they often get quite different replies. There is usually agreement on the number of children they have and a few other such verifiable items, although not, for example, on length of premarital acquaintance and of engagement, on age at marriage and interval between marriage and birth of first child. Indeed, with respect to even such basic components of the marriage as frequency of sexual relations, social interaction, household tasks, and decision making, they seem to be reporting on different marriages. As, I think, they are.

In the area of sexual relations, for example, Kinsey and his associates found different responses in from one- to two-thirds of the couples they studied. Kinsey interpreted these differences in terms of selective perception. In the generation he was studying, husbands wanted sexual relations oftener than the wives did, thus "the females may be overestimating the actual frequencies" and "the husbands . . . are probably underestimating the frequencies." The differences might also have been vestiges of the probable situation earlier in the marriage when the desired frequency of sexual relations was about six to seven times greater among husbands than among wives. This difference may have become so impressed on the spouses that it remained in their minds even after the difference itself had disappeared or even been reversed. In a sample of happily married, middle-class couples a generation later, Harold Feldman found that both spouses attributed to their mates more influence in the area of sex than they did to themselves.

Companionship, as reflected in talking together, he found, was another area where differences showed up. Replies differed on three-fourths of all the items studied, including the topics talked about, the amount of time spent talking with each other, and which partner initiated conversation. Both partners claimed that whereas they talked more about topics of interest to their mates, their mates initiated conversations about topics primarily of interest to themselves. Harold Feldman concluded that projection in terms of needs was distorting even simple, everyday events, and lack of communication was permitting the distortions to continue. It seemed to him that "if these sex differences can occur so often among these generally well satisfied couples, it would not be surprising to find even less consensus and more distortion in other less satisfied couples."

Although, by and large, husbands and wives tend to become more alike with age, in this study of middle-class couples, differences increased with length of marriage rather than decreased, as one might logically have expected. More couples in the later than in the earlier years, for example, had differing pictures in their heads about how often they laughed together, discussed together, exchanged ideas, or worked together on projects, and about how well things were going between them.

The special nature of sex and the amorphousness of social interaction help to explain why differences in response might occur. But household tasks? They are fairly objective and clear-cut and not all that emotion-laden. Yet even here there are his-and-her versions. Since the division of labor in the household is becoming increasingly an issue in marriage, the uncovering of differing replies in this area is especially relevant. Hard as it is to believe, Granbois and Willett tell us that more than half of the partners in one sample disagreed on who kept track of money and bills. On the question, who mows the lawn? more than a fourth disagreed. Even family income was not universally agreed on.

Inconsistent Marriages

These differences about sexual relations, companionship, and domestic duties tell us a great deal about the two marriages. But power or decision making can cover all aspects of a relationship. The question of who makes decisions or who exercises power has therefore attracted a great deal of research attention. If we were interested in who really had the power or who really made the decisions, the research would be hopeless. Would it be possible to draw any conclusion from a situation in which both partners agree that the husband ordered the wife to make all the decisions? Still, an enormous literature documents the quest of researchers for answers to the question of marital power. The major contribution it has made has been to reveal the existence of differences in replies between husbands and wives.

The presence of such inconsistent replies did not at first cause much concern. The researchers apologized for them but interpreted them as due to methodological inadequacies; if only they could find a better way to approach the problem, the differences would disappear. Alternatively, the use of only the wife's responses, which were more easily available, was justified on the grounds that differences in one direction between the partners in one marriage compensated for differences in another direction between the partners in another marriage and thus canceled them out. As, indeed, they did. For when Granbois and Willett, two market researchers, analyzed the replies of husbands and wives separately, the overall picture was in fact the same for both wives and husbands. Such canceling out of differences in the total sample, however, concealed almost as much as it revealed about the individual couples who composed it. Granbois and Willett concluded, as Kinsey had earlier, that the "discrepancies . . . reflect differing perceptions on the part of responding partners." And this was the heart of the matter.

Why "His" and "Hers"?

Differing reactions to common situations, it should be noted, are not at all uncommon. They are recognized in the folk wisdom embedded in the story of the blind men all giving different replies to questions on the nature of the elephant. One of the oldest experiments in juridical psychology demonstrates how different the statements of witnesses of the same act can be. Even in laboratory studies, it takes intensive training of raters to make it possible for them to arrive at agreement on the behavior they observe.

It has long been known that people with different backgrounds see things differently. We know, for example, that poor children perceive coins as larger than do children from more affluent homes. Boys and girls perceive differently. A good deal of the foundation for projective tests rests on the different ways in which individuals see identical stimuli. And this perception—or, as the sociologists put it, definition of the situation—is reality for them. In this sense, the realities of the husband's marriage are different from those of the wife's.

Finally, one of the most perceptive of the researchers, Constantina Safilios-Rothschild, asked the crucial question: Was what they were getting, even with the best research techniques, family sociology or wives' family sociology? She answered her own question: What the researchers who relied on wives' replies exclusively were reporting on was the wife's marriage. The husband's was not necessarily the same. There were, in fact, two marriages present:

> One explanation of discrepancies between the responses of husbands and wives may be the possibility of two "realities," the husband's subjective reality and the wife's subjective reality—two perspectives which do not always coincide. Each spouse perceives "facts" and situations differently according to his own needs, values, attitudes, and beliefs. An "objective" reality could possibly exist only in the trained observer's evaluation, if it does exist at all.

Interpreting the different replies of husbands and wives in terms of selective perception, projection of needs, values, attitudes, and beliefs, or different definitions of the situation, by no means renders them trivial or incidental or justifies dismissing or ignoring them. They are, rather, fundamental for an understanding of the two marriages, his and hers, and we ignore them at the peril of serious misunderstanding of marriage, present as well as future.

Is There an Objective Reality in Marriage?

Whether or not husbands and wives perceive differently or define situations differently, still sexual relations are taking place, companionship is or is not occurring, tasks about the house are being performed, and decisions are being made every day by someone. In this sense, some sort of "reality" does exist. David Olson went to the laboratory to see if he could uncover it.

He first asked young couples expecting babies such questions as these: Which one of them would decide whether to buy insurance for the newborn child? Which one would decide the husband's part in diaper changing? Which one would decide whether the new mother would return to work or to school? When there were differences in the answers each gave individually on the questionnaire, he set up a situation in which together they had to arrive at a decision in his laboratory. He could then compare the results of the questionnaire with the results in the simulated situation. He found neither spouse's questionnaire response any more accurate than the other's; that is, neither conformed better to the behavioral "reality" of the laboratory than the other did.

The most interesting thing, however, was that husbands, as shown on their questionnaire response, perceived themselves as having more power than they actually did have in the laboratory "reality," and wives perceived that they had less. Thus, whereas three-fourths (73 percent) of the husbands overestimated their power in decision making, 70 percent of the wives underestimated theirs. Turk and Bell found similar results in Canada. Both spouses tend to attribute decision-making power to the one who has the "right" to make the decision. Their replies, that is, conform to the model of marriage that has characterized civilized mankind for millennia. It is this model rather than their own actual behavior that husbands and wives tend to perceive.

We are now zeroing in on the basic reality. We can remove the quotation marks. For there is, in fact, an objective reality in marriage. It is a reality that resides in the cultural—legal, moral, and conventional—prescriptions and proscriptions and, hence, expectations that constitute marriage. It is the reality that is reflected in the minds of the spouses themselves. The differences between the marriages of husbands and of wives are structural realities, and it is these structural differences that constitute the basis for the different psychological realities.

The Authority Structure of Marriage

Authority is an institutional phenomenon; it is strongly bound up with faith. It must be believed in; it cannot be enforced unless it also has power. Authority resides not in the person on whom it is conferred by the group or society, but in the recognition and acceptance it elicits in others. Power, on the other hand, may dispense with the prop of authority. It may take the form of the ability to coerce or to veto; it is often personal, charismatic, not institutional. This kind of personal power is self-enforcing. It does not require shoring up by access to force. In fact, it may even operate subversively. A woman with this kind of power may or may not know that she possesses it. If she does know she has it, she will probably disguise her exercise of it.

In the West, the institutional structure of marriage has invested the husband with authority and backed it by the power of church and state. The marriages of wives have thus been officially dominated by the husband. Hebrew, Christian, and Islamic versions of deity were in complete accord on this matter. The laws, written or unwritten, religious or civil, which have defined the marital union have been based on male conceptions, and they have undergirded male authority.

Adam came first. Eve was created to supply him with companionship, not vice versa. And God himself had told her that Adam would rule over her; her wishes had to conform to his. The New Testament authors agreed. Women were created for men, not men for women; women were therefore commanded to be obedient. If they wanted to learn anything, let them ask their husbands in private, for it was shameful for them to talk in the church. They should submit themselves to their husbands, because husbands were superior to wives; and wives should be as subject to their husbands as the church was to Christ. Timothy wrapped it all up: "Let the woman learn in silence with all subjection. But I suffer not a woman to teach, nor to usurp authority over the man, but to be in silence." Male Jews continued for millennia to thank God three times a day that they were not women. And the Koran teaches women that men are naturally their superiors because God made them that way; naturally, their own status is one of subordination. . . .

The Subversiveness of Nature

The rationale for male authority rested not only on biblical grounds but also on nature or natural law, on the generally accepted natural superiority of men. For nothing could be more self-evident than that the patriarchal conception of marriage, in which the husband was unequivocally the boss, was natural, resting as it did on the unchallenged superiority of males.

Actually, nature, if not deity, is subversive. Power, or the ability to coerce or to veto, is widely distributed in both sexes, among women as well as among men. And whatever the theoretical or conceptual picture may have been, the actual, day-by-day relationships between husbands and wives have been determined by the men and women themselves. All that the institutional machinery could do was to confer authority; it could not create personal power, for such power cannot be conferred, and women can generate it as well as men. Thus, keeping women in their place has been a universal problem, in spite of the fact that almost without exception institutional patterns give men positions of superiority over them.

If the sexes were, in fact, categorically distinct, with no overlapping, so that no man was inferior to any woman or any woman superior to any man, or vice versa, marriage would have been a great deal simpler. But there is no such sharp cleavage between the sexes except with respect to the presence or absence of certain organs. With all the other characteristics of each sex, there is greater or less overlapping, some men being more "feminine" than the average woman and some women more "masculine" than the average man. The structure of families and societies reflects the positions assigned to men and women. The bottom stratum includes children, slaves, servants, and outcasts of all kinds, males as well as females. As one ascends the structural hierarchy, the proportion of males increases, so that at the apex there are only males.

When societies fall back on the lazy expedient—as all societies everywhere have done—of allocating the rewards and punishments of life on the basis of sex, they are bound to create a host of anomalies, square pegs in round holes, societal misfits. Roles have been allocated on the basis of sex which did not fit a sizable number of both sexes—women, for example, who chafed at subordinate status and men who could not master superordinate status. The history of the relations of the sexes is replete with examples of such misfits. Unless a modus vivendi is arrived at, unhappy marriages are the result.

There is, though, a difference between the exercise of power by husbands and by wives. When women exert power, they are not rewarded; they may even be punished. They are "deviant." Turk and Bell note that "wives who . . . have the greater influence in decision making may experience guilt over this fact." They must therefore dissemble to maintain the illusion, even to themselves, that they are subservient. They tend to feel less powerful than they are because they *ought* to be.

When men exert power, on the other hand, they are rewarded; it is the natural expression of authority. They feel no guilt about it. The prestige of authority goes to the husband whether or not he is actually the one who exercises it. It is not often even noticed when the wife does so. She sees to it that it is not.

There are two marriages, then, in every marital union, his and hers. And his is better than hers. The questions, therefore, are these: In what direction will they change in the future? Will one change more than the other? Will they tend to converge or to diverge? Will the future continue to favor the husband's marriage? And if the wife's marriage is improved, will it cost the husband's anything, or will his benefit along with hers?

VIEWPOINT

3

Traditional Religion Divides Society

BRYAN WILSON

Many past social thinkers have described religion as a unifying social force, but this appears only to hold within groups
with similar religious beliefs. From an historical perspective,
religion has motivated much social conflict and change and is
often divisive rather than unifying. This viewpoint presents
sociologist Bryan Wilson's depiction of religious sects as "catalysts in history" that have shaped the course of social events.
Acknowledging the ongoing importance of religion as an institution, Wilson points out that Christianity originated as a
sect in opposition to both the established church and the
Roman Empire. As the Christian church gained legitimacy
and became established, the church also gained an early association with the governmental institution. This association enabled the church to impose membership on large numbers of
people and more effectively counter formation of more sects.
Although Wilson does not make the connection explicit, notice the similarity between the ideas in this viewpoint and
Karl Marx's famous characterization of religion as a bourgeoisie tool and the "opiate of the masses."

Excerpted from *Religious Sects: A Sociological Study* by Bryan Wilson. New York:
McGraw-Hill, 1970. Copyright 1970 by Bryan Wilson. Reprinted by permission
of McGraw-Hill, Inc.

QUESTIONS

1. How does Wilson distinguish between a church and a sect?
2. How and why do new sects arise?
3. What relationships between religion and the other institutions can you extract from this viewpoint?

Sects are movements of religious protest. Their members separate themselves from other men in respect of their religious beliefs, practices and institutions, and often in many other departments of their lives. They reject the authority of orthodox religious leaders, and often, also, of the secular government. Allegiance to a sect is voluntary, but individuals are admitted only on proof of conviction, or by some other test of merit: continuing affiliation rests on sustained evidence of commitment to sect beliefs and practices. Sectarians put their faith first: they order their lives in accordance with it. The orthodox, in contrast, compromise faith with other interests, and their religion accommodates the demands of the secular culture.

At first glance, sects may appear to be marginal and incidental phenomena in history—odd groups of alienated men with outlandish ideas. Yet, at times, sects have had an immense significance for the course of history. After all, Christianity itself was only a Jewish sect at the beginning. The Mahdi movement in the Sudan in the 1880s, or the Tai-ping movement in China a couple of decades earlier, each significantly affected the history of their own peoples and that of people far from the places where these sects arose. Sects sometimes act as catalysts in history, crystallising in acute form social discontents and aspirations, and marking the moments of social structural collapse, and sometimes heralding, or even promoting, social reintegration. . . .

In a loose sense of the word, sects, as separated groups, exist within or at the fringe of all the major religions: but the concept of the sect differs according to the organisational structure of different parent religions. In Hinduism, which is diffuse, uncentralised and pluralist, sectarianism exists only in a much more limited sense than in Christendom. Diverse traditions of worship and divergent philosophical schools have existed side by side in Hinduism over centuries, and devotees of particular cults have not felt the need for separation from other people in order to practise the rituals that they have regarded as especially beneficial. Yet the term *sect* is widely if loosely used for such groups as the Lingayat movements among the Brahmins, even though these were merely movements cultivating particular styles of devotion. It is clear then that the specific connotations of the word, when used of Christian movements, are not all relevant for those outside the Christian tradition.

The early association of church and empire, and the early development of agencies of political control in the Christian church, enhanced when the church inherited the Roman Empire's administrative structure and something of its civilising mission, all conferred on Christianity a degree of centralisation and coherence lacking in Hinduism and Buddhism. The church authorities were enabled more effectively both to impose Christianity on pagan populations, and to systematise and bring into general conformity the beliefs and practices of Christians. Clearly, neither the elimination of pagan magic nor the establishment of uniformity in Christian usage was ever completely achieved. Before ancient magic had been rooted out in the rural areas of Europe, the church itself had been broken asunder at the Reformation. True as this is, the co-ordinated hierarchy and effectiveness of control of the Roman church was quite unequalled in the older world religions.

Because of this degree of religious cohesion, dissenters who deliberately departed from the accepted beliefs and practices of the faith were more emphatically distinguishable in Christianity. Sects were regarded as opposed to the church, even though sectarians saw themselves as reformers or restorers of the faith itself. Their real sin was to reject sacerdotalism, church organisation and to believe that they alone possessed the truth about God. With such ideas went distinctive conceptions of social relationships and ethics. . . .

The Christian Concept of the Sect

To Christian theologians a sect was expected to manifest distinctiveness both in doctrine and in its conception of authority. The Christian church, whilst concerned with uniformity in religious practice, always made doctrine the central criterion of orthodoxy. The power struggles of the early church were fought, if not always about belief, at least always in terms of it. There emerged in Christendom, often in finely-stated formulae, a distinct idea that only those who held the same beliefs belonged to the true faith and the true church. Whilst variations in liturgy, social practice, local tradition (especially in the celebration of local saints) might be tolerated, all must proceed under the rubric of the same doctrines. This intellectual orientation came in consequence to colour the character of sectarianism in Christendom. Sectaries were those who voluntarily professed beliefs different from those of the church, and associated together in common faith outside the church's control. New sects thus took the same criterion for the identification of the in-group as the early church had taken when it spread to include Greek and Jew, bond and free—shared common belief. Nominally, this idea of voluntary subscription was still claimed by the church, but in practice subscription to its tenets and obedience to its clergy were enforced wherever its political writ, or that of faithful princes, ran. This principle contrasts sharply with the criteria of ethnicity and the fulfilment of ritual demands associated with ethnicity which were typical of Judaism (once it ceased to proselytise) and of Hinduism.

Thus divergent belief, separation and rejection of church authority were the defining characteristics of Christian sects. Heresy and schism, together with denial of sacerdotal claims, were the essence of sectarianism as the Christian church saw it. Sects challenged the monopoly of churchly access to the supernatural and to salvation which the church had claimed for itself in suppressing earlier paganism. Since sects were enemies of the clergy, the clergy defined them as enemies of God, of his church, and of all legitimate princes. . . .

Religions may begin as sects, and in the Christian case the sect preceded the church. But once established, the church anathematised all new sects. Precisely because of its tighter organisational structure and its claim to monopoly of religious concerns, official Christianity has been more conscious and more intolerant of sects than have other world religions. Sectarians have been regarded not only as heretics but as revolutionaries, and church anathema has been used to justify political oppression. These charges have not always been warranted. Although sects do envisage some transformation of man's con-

217

dition and do represent a breach of the institutional social order, they do not always consciously intend to disrupt society, much less to mobilise men for its overthrow. That some sects believe that God intends to overturn the world must not obscure the fact that other sects expect salvation in quite different ways. Church pronouncements about sects have often been misleading and have little relevance to dispassionate sociological study.

The other common error that persists about sects, even among Christian theologians, is an inherited idea that had rather more validity in the past than it does today. This is to suppose that all sects arise around a charismatic leader, a man who claims divinity or at least strong divine inspiration. Prophets have always been the enemies of priests. Institutionalised religion is challenged by those who claim new inspiration which threatens the monopoly of access to divine knowledge that priests claim for themselves. It has often been easier to blame a leader as a false prophet for misleading men, than to accept the idea that some men conscientiously and sincerely disagreed with orthodoxy. The church had ready-made enemies in the figures of devils and Anti-Christ, who could clearly be made to symbolise sectaries. Again, when little was known about the social structural causes of tensions in society, or about the divergence of social perspective among different social groups, it was easier to blame a particular man for disturbances from the norm than to look for social causes. But the central fact in explaining this misconception is that pre-industrial societies relied considerably on at least a diluted form of charisma, on exceptional men (found in such concepts as men of high birth, nobility, genius, saintliness). And since all these mystical qualities appeared to have their distorted forms, there were prophets and there were scapegoats.

Before the nineteenth century many sects did arise around a charismatic leader. Men more readily believed in inspired or messianic personages, around whom movements sometimes came into being. The movements were often ephemeral, the leaders deluded, and sometimes demented. But they drew on a persisting element in the Christian tradition, without which Christianity itself might not have captured so readily the imaginations of its early followers—the belief in the second coming and the inauguration of a new social dispensation in the millennium. Such messianic hopes recrudesced frequently, and churchmen became used to the misguided ideas of charismatic figures, and tended to attribute all sectarianism to them. Sects in industrial societies, however, are less frequently attributable to charismatic leaders, and it is perhaps important to understand why this should be so.

Sects and Charismatic Leadership

To its members the traditional society appears to be a sacred order: customs, *mores*, relationships and authority are seen as a continuation of the divine order that embraces both nature and society. (Even the sophisticated classical societies of antiquity, where the man-made quality of the state was apparent, believed social *mores* and values to be divinely natural.) Where challenge to the existing order occurs in such societies—and in the most primitive it follows only from disturbances arising from external sources—it is necessarily a religious challenge based on a new apprehension of the divine: hence the importance of the charismatic leader. In primitive societies such a figure is almost always the source of new religious movements, and is often so in feudal societies. Occasionally such charisma has become the basis for the re-structuring of the social order; more usually it has led to the emergence of a sect. Sects facilitate the crystallisation of new social groupings, and provide social cohesion within a self-selected community, but it is not always the case that sects are charismatically inspired, particularly in industrial societies.

Advanced societies are marked by increasing division of labour, in which men are increasingly related according to their roles. In most social relationships the total personalities of individuals are not engaged; they are involved only in role obligations and role expectations. Consequently, *personal* trust is not invoked in the way in which it is essential to primary relationships. 'Put not your trust in persons' might be the motto of advanced societies—but only in specialists performing their roles, in routine procedures and technical facilities. It follows that in these societies there tends to be disbelief of the special powers of any individual. But personal trust of course is crucial to the concept of the charismatic.

Advanced societies leave little room for the manifestation of charisma, except perhaps in extreme conditions of social strain when whole societies feel their way of life threatened. When a charismatic figure does arise, it becomes evident to all that the trust he wins itself depends on the manipulation of highly technical facilities, particularly in the mass-media, and these things are in themselves profoundly anti-charismatic. Charismatic claims are found only at the fringe of the social system, in the least routinised activities of society—at the very top level in politics (and there decreasingly), in entertainment and in marginal religious groups.

Religion is that social institution in which non-rational dispositions and super-rational claims are stock-in-trade. Supernatural power is expected to operate in religious gatherings, even if, as among Quakers and Pentecostalists, the expectation is for a highly diffused charismatic experience. There are modern sects that arise in response to charismatic claims of a more traditional type, such as the followers of the Dutch fisherman, Lou, and the group that accepts the messianic claims of George Roux in France. But these sects become more marginal and less typical of sects in general. The extent to which charismatic claims have become tempered by rational considerations is also evident. Thus Mrs Eddy, founder of Christian Science, who was regarded by many of her followers as 'the woman clothed with the sun' and who did not discourage these ideas, evolved a religion that claimed to be a science and, as well as churches, instituted teachers and courses of instruction in imitation of the rational, educational every-day world. The religious prophet now acquired new appeal by adopting the model of the scientist and educationalist. These are indications of the waning of the credibility of charismatic claims in the modern world. Modern sects cannot be regarded as simply new examples of the type of sectarianism that was common in the medieval world. . . .

The importance of sects to sociologists is that they provide by far the most numerous examples of self-conscious attempts by men to construct their own societies, not merely as political entities with constitutions, but as groups with a firm set of values and *mores*, of which they are conscious. Such groups have a carefully ordered structure of social relationships and clearly established patterns of social behaviour and control. As persisting social entities, they exhibit mechanisms of socialisation of the young and identifiable processes of social change.

220

Civil Religion
Unites Society

W. LLOYD WARNER

Sociologists have debated for more than a century over an adequate definition of religion. Durkheim studied world religions and concluded that all share three elements: a distinction between the sacred and the profane, a set of shared spiritual beliefs, and a set of rituals. Events and things that people do not understand and cannot explain are taken on faith and considered sacred; things known, familiar, and directly experienced are profane. All religions include a set of shared beliefs to explain the sacred and search for meaning in birth, death, success, failure, or crisis. A set of rituals, or ceremonies, constitutes the practice of religion.

Organized religions—such as Buddhism, Catholicism, and Methodism—clearly meet these criteria. Sociologists argue, however, that another kind of religion also fulfills these requirements and must be recognized. Civil religion is the set of patriotic beliefs that accumulate and take on at least the force of any other religion. In the United States, the sacred includes the belief that God favors this country and that we

Excerpted from *American Life: Dream and Reality* by W. Lloyd Warner. Chicago: University of Chicago Press, 1953. Copyright 1953, 1962 by The University of Chicago. Reprinted with permission of the publisher.

have a divine mandate to protect and propagate the "American way" worldwide. References to "God" in the founding documents, in the Pledge of Allegiance, and printed on money; slogans such as "my country, love it or leave it"; and prosecution of a citizen for displaying a dissenting sign during the recent Persian Gulf conflict all provide evidence of widely shared spiritual beliefs. Political party affiliations and elections are the profane element, and we may legitimately disagree on these, but we have a sacred obligation to vote. Much has been made of the sacred status of "born in the U.S.A.," and dying for one's country has long been honorable. While traditional religious doctrine has bitterly divided individuals, groups, and populations in the past, civil religion produces solidarity within communities, states, and nations.

In this viewpoint, social anthropologist W. Lloyd Warner describes the "ceremonial calendar" that sets occasions for celebration of rituals associated with the civil religion. He also describes ways that wars increase a solidaristic community spirit and makes explicit connections between national symbols and Christian religious concepts. Although the nation's founders specified separation of church and state, the connection endures through civil religion as evidenced by Warner's detailed description.

QUESTIONS

1. Which holidays does Warner identify as sacred?
2. What sacred symbols does Warner mention and how are they similar to Christian symbols?
3. How does war increase citizens' satisfaction with their society?

Memorial Day is an important occasion in the American ceremonial calendar and as such is a unit of this larger ceremonial system of symbols. Close examination discloses that it, too, is a symbol system in its own right, existing within the complexities of the larger one.

Symbols include such familiar things as written and spoken words, religious beliefs and practices, including creeds and ceremonies, the several arts, such familiar signs as the cross and the flag, and countless other objects and acts which stand for something more than that which they are. The red, white, and blue cloth and the crossed sticks in themselves and as objects mean very little, but the sacred meanings which they evoke are of such deep significance to some that millions of men have sacrificed their lives for the first as the Stars and Stripes and for the second as the Christian Cross.

Symbols are substitutes for all known real and imaginary actions, things, and the relations among them. They stand for and express feelings and beliefs about men and what they do, about the world and what happens in it. What they stand for may or may not exist. What they stand for may or may not be true, for what they express may be no more than a feeling, an illusion, a myth, or a vague sensation falsely interpreted. On the other hand, that for which they stand may be as real and objectively verifiable as the Rock of Gibraltar.

The ceremonial calendar of American society, this yearly round of holidays and holy days, partly sacred and partly secular, but more sacred than secular, is a symbol system used by all Americans. Christmas and Thanksgiving, Memorial Day and the Fourth of July, are days in our ceremonial calendar which allow Americans to express common sentiments about themselves and share their feelings with others on set days pre-established by the society for this very purpose. This calendar functions to draw all people together to emphasize their similarities and common heritage; to minimize their differences; and to contribute to their thinking, feeling, and acting alike. All societies, simple or complex, possess some form of ceremonial calendar, if it be no more than the seasonal alternation of secular and ceremonial periods, such as that used by the Australian aborigines in their yearly cycle.

The integration and smooth functioning of the social life of a modern community are very difficult because of its complexity. American communities are filled with churches, each claiming great authority and each with its separate sacred symbol system. Many of them are in conflict, and all of them in opposition to one another. Many associations, such as the Masons, the Odd Fellows, and the like, have sacred symbol systems which partly separate them from the whole community. The traditions of foreign-born groups contribute to the diversity of symbolic life. The evidence is clear for the conflict among these systems.

It is the thesis of this viewpoint that the Memorial Day ceremonies and subsidiary rites (such as those of Armistice or Veterans' Day) of today, yesterday, and tomorrow are rituals of a sacred symbol system which functions periodically to unify the whole community, with its conflicting symbols and its opposing, autonomous churches and associations. It is contended here that in the Memorial Day ceremonies the anxieties which man has about death are confronted with a system of sacred beliefs about death which gives the individuals involved and the collectivity of individuals a feeling of well-being. Further, the feeling of triumph over death by collective action in the Memorial Day parade is made possible by recreating the feeling of well-being and the sense of group strength and individual strength in the group power, which is felt so intensely during the wars, when the veterans' associations are created and when the feeling so necessary for the Memorial Day's symbol system is originally experienced.

Memorial Day is a cult of the dead which organizes and integrates the various faiths and national and class groups into a sacred unity. It is a cult of the dead organized around the community cemeteries. The principal themes are those of the sacrifice of the soldier dead for the living and the obligation of the living to sacrifice their individual purposes for the good of the group, so that they, too, can perform their spiritual obligations. . . .

How Such Ceremonies Function in the Community

Memorial Day and similar ceremonies are one of the several forms of collective representations which [Émile] Durkheim so brilliantly defined and interpreted in *The Elementary Forms of the Religious Life*. He said: "Religious representations are collective representations which express collective realities." Religious collective representations are symbol systems which are composed of beliefs and rites which relate men to sacred beings. Beliefs are "states of opinion and consist in representations"; rites are "determined modes of action" which are expressions of, and refer to, religious belief. They are *visible* signs (symbols) of the invisible belief. The visible rite of baptism, for example, may express invisible beliefs about cleansing the newborn infant of sin and relating him to the Christian community.

Ceremonies, periodically held, serve to impress on men their social nature and make them aware of something beyond themselves which they feel and believe to be sacred. This intense feeling of belonging to something larger and more powerful than themselves and of having part of this within them as part of them is symbolized by the belief in sacred beings, which is given a visual symbol by use of designs which are the emblems of the sacred entities, e.g., the Cross of the Christian churches.

That which is beyond, yet part of, a person is no more than the awareness on the part of individuals and the collectivity of individuals of their participation in a social group. *The religious symbols, as well as the secular ones, must express the nature of the social structure of the group of which they are a part and which they represent.* The beliefs in the gods and the symbolic rites which celebrate their divinity are no more than men collectively worshiping their own images—their own, since they were made by themselves and fashioned from their experiences among themselves.

We said earlier that the Memorial Day rites of American towns are sacred collective representations and a modern cult of the dead. They are a cult because they consist of a system of sacred beliefs and dramatic rituals held by a group of people who, when they congregate, represent the whole community. They are sacred because they ritually relate the living to sacred things. They are a cult because the members have not been formally organized into an institutionalized church with a defined theology but depend on informal organization to bring into order their sacred activities. They are called a "cult" here, because this term most accurately places them in a class of social phenomena which can be clearly identified in the sacred behavior of non-European societies.

The cult system of sacred belief puts into the organized form of concepts those sentiments about death which are common to everyone in the community. These sentiments are composed of fears of death, which conflict with the social reassurances that our culture provides us to combat such anxieties. These assurances, usually acquired in childhood and thereby carrying some of the authority of the adults who provided them, are a composite of theology and folk belief. The deep anxieties to which we refer include anticipation of our deaths, of the deaths or possible deaths of loved ones, and, less powerfully, of the deaths or possible deaths of those we know and of men in general.

Each man's church provides him and those of his faith with a set of beliefs and a way of acting to face these problems; but his church and those of other men do not equip him with a common set of social beliefs and rituals which permit him to unite with all his fellows to confront this common and most feared of all his enemies. The Memorial Day rite and other subsidiary rituals connected with it form a cult which partially satisfies this need for common action on a common problem. It dramatically expresses the sentiments of unity of all the living among themselves, of all the living to all the dead, and of all the living and dead as a group to the gods. The gods—Catholic, Protestant, and Jewish—lose their sectarian definitions, limitations, and foreignness among themselves and become objects of worship for the whole group and the protectors of everyone.

The unifying and integrating symbols of this cult are the dead. The graves of the dead are the most powerful of the visible emblems which unify all the activities of the separate groups of the community. The cemetery and its graves become the objects of sacred rituals which permit opposing organizations, often in conflict, to subordinate their ordinary opposition and to co-operate in expressing jointly the larger unity of the total community through the use of common rites for their collective dead. The rites show extraordinary respect for all the dead, but they pay particular honor to those who were killed in battle "fighting for their country." The death of a soldier in battle is believed to be a "voluntary sacrifice" by him on the altar of his country. To be understood, this belief in the sacrifice of a man's life for his country must be judged first with our general scientific knowledge of the nature of all forms of sacrifice. It must then be subjected to the principles which explain human sacrifice whenever and wherever found. More particularly, this belief must be examined with the realization that these sacrifices occur in a society whose deity was a man who sacrificed his life for all men.

The principle of the gift is involved. In simple terms, when something valuable is given, an equally valuable thing must be returned. The speaker who quoted Scripture in his Memorial

Day speech, "Whosoever shall save his life shall lose it and whosoever shall lose his life in My name shall save it," almost explicitly stated the feelings and principles involved. Finally, as we interpret it, the belief in "the sacrifice of American citizens killed in battle" is a social logic which states in ultimate terms the subordinate relation of the citizen to his country and its collective moral principles.

This discussion has shown that the Memorial Day ceremony consists of a series of separate rituals performed by autonomous groups which culminate in a procession *of all of them as one group* to the consecrated area set aside by the living for their dead. In such a place the dead are classed as individuals, for their graves are separate; as members of separate social situations, for they are found in family plots and formal ritual respect is paid them by church and association; and as a collectivity, since they are thought of as "our dead" in most of the ceremonies. The fences surrounding the cemetery place all the dead together and separate all the living from them.

The Memorial Day rite is a cult of the dead, but not just of the dead as such, since by symbolically elaborating sacrifice of human life for the country through, or identifying it with, the Christian church's sacred sacrifice of their god, the deaths of such men also become powerful sacred symbols which organize, direct, and constantly revive the collective ideals of the community and the nation.

A Few Control the Many

ROBERT MICHELS

Sociologist Robert Michels, writing early in the twentieth century, develops the concept of "oligarchy"—rule by a few. While Michels applies oligarchy to all organizations, he uses democracy as an example in this viewpoint. Contrary to the democratic ideal, Michels argues that it is impossible for vast numbers of people to reach agreement on what should be done. Delegates must be selected to undertake the actual tasks that carry out national mandates. Over time, the process of transforming "the led into a leader" comes to include education that makes leaders into experts. The required education sets leaders apart from the rest of the population and creates a set of elites not directly subject to popular control. Through this process, oligarchy replaces democracy. As organizations develop, increasing task specialization leads inevitably to this process, leading Michels to conclude that "organization implies the tendency to oligarchy."

To study political and economic institutions, sociologists offer three competing explanations: the pluralist model, the

Excerpted from *Political Parties: A Sociological Study of the Oligarchical Tendencies of Modern Democracy* by Robert Michels, translated by Eden and Cedar Paul, 1915.

class model, and the elite model. Basic tenets of the pluralist model are that power is decentralized in society and leaders are accountable to the masses. We all receive substantial socialization into the pluralist model from parents, schools, the media, and especially the political institution itself. Each citizen has the right and obligation to participate in the political process: one person, one vote, each vote as important as any other. States are represented equally in the Senate, and according to population size in the House of Representatives. Checks and balances in government assure fair representation and prevent undue exercise of authority by any one branch. The pluralist model applies in the economic arena via competition. Serious students of the pluralist model recognize that, in fact, each citizen does not have equal political or economic power, so descriptions of the status quo often include the concept of oligarchy used to explain representative government. Descriptions of the class and elite models follow in the next two viewpoints.

QUESTIONS

1. How does Michels define "oligarchy"?
2. By what steps does Michels reach the conclusion that "organization implies the tendency to oligarchy"?
3. How can you reconcile our democratic ideal with the inevitability of oligarchy?

■ ■ ■

The practical ideal of democracy consists in the self-government of the masses in conformity with the decisions of popular assemblies. But while this system limits the extension of the principle of delegation, it fails to provide any guarantee against the formation of an oligarchical camarilla [political power faction]. Undoubtedly it deprives the natural leaders of their quality as functionaries, for this quality is transferred to the people themselves. The crowd, however, is always subject to suggestion, being readily influenced by the eloquence of great popular orators; moreover, direct government by the people, admitting of no serious discussions or thoughtful deliberations, greatly facilitates *coups de main* [sleight of hand] of all kinds by men who are exceptionally bold, energetic, and adroit.

It is easier to dominate a large crowd than a small audience. The adhesion of the crowd is tumultuous, summary, and unconditional. Once the suggestions have taken effect, the crowd does not readily tolerate contradiction from a small minority, and still less from isolated individuals. A great multitude assembled within a small area is unquestionably more accessible to panic alarms, to unreflective enthusiasm, and the like, than is a small meeting, whose members can quietly discuss matters among themselves.

It is a fact of everyday experience that enormous public meetings commonly carry resolutions by acclamation or by general assent, whilst these same assemblies, if divided into small sections, say of fifty persons each, would be much more guarded in their assent. Great party congresses, in which are present the *élite* of the membership, usually act in this way. Words and actions are far less deliberately weighed by the crowd than by the individuals or the little groups of which this crowd is composed. The fact is incontestable—a manifestation of the pathology of the crowd. The individual disappears in the multitude, and therewith disappears also personality and sense of responsibility.

The most formidable argument against the sovereignty of the masses is, however, derived from the mechanical and technical impossibility of its realization.

The sovereign masses are altogether incapable of undertaking the most necessary resolutions. The impotence of direct democracy, like the power of indirect democracy, is a direct outcome of the influence of number. In a polemic against Pierre Proudhon (1849), Louis Blanc asks whether it is possible for thirty-four millions of human beings (the population of France at that time) to carry on their affairs without accepting what the pettiest man of business finds necessary, the intermediation of representatives. He answers his own question by saying that one who declares direct action on this scale to be possible is a fool, and that one who denies its possibility need not be an absolute opponent of the idea of the state. The same question and the same answer could be repeated to-day in respect of party organization. Above all in the great industrial centres, where the labour party sometimes numbers its adherents by tens of thousands, it is impossible to carry on the affairs of this gigantic body without a system of representation. The great socialist organization of Berlin, which embraces the six constituencies of the city, as well as the two outlying areas of Niederbarnim and Teltow-Beeskow-Charlottenburg, has a member-roll of more than ninety thousand.

Responsibility Must Be Delegated

It is obvious that such a gigantic number of persons belonging to a unitary organization cannot do any practical work upon a system of direct discussion. The regular holding of deliberative assemblies of a thousand members encounters the gravest difficulties in respect of room and distance; while from the topographical point of view such an assembly would become altogether impossible if the members numbered ten thousand. Even if we imagined the means of communication to become much better than those which now exist, how would it be possible to assemble such a multitude in a given place, at a stated time, and with the frequency demanded by the exigencies of party life? In addition must be considered the physiological impossibility even for the most powerful orator of making himself heard by a crowd of ten thousand persons. There are, however, other reasons of a technical and administrative character which render impossible the direct self-government of large groups. If Peter wrongs Paul, it is out of the question that all the other citizens should hasten to the spot to undertake a personal examination of the matter in dispute, and to take the part of Paul against Peter. By parity of reasoning, in the modern democratic party, it is impossible for the collectivity to undertake the direct settlement of all the controversies that may arise.

Hence the need for delegation, for the system in which delegates represent the mass and carry out its will. Even in groups sincerely animated with the democratic spirit, current business, the preparation and the carrying out of the most important actions, is necessarily left in the hands of individuals. It is well known that the impossibility for the people to exercise a legislative power directly in popular assemblies led the democratic idealists of Spain to demand, as the least of evils, a system of popular representation and a parliamentary state.

Originally the chief is merely the servant of the mass. The organization is based upon the absolute equality of all its members. Equality is here understood in its most general sense, as an equality of like men. In many countries, as in idealist Italy (and in certain regions in Germany where the socialist movement is still in its infancy), this equality is manifested, among other ways, by the mutual use of the familiar "thou," which is employed by the most poorly paid wage-labourer in addressing the most distinguished intellectual. This generic conception of equality is, however, gradually replaced by the idea of equality among comrades belonging to the same organization, all of whose members enjoy the same rights. The democratic principle aims at guaranteeing to all an equal influence and an equal participation in the regulation of the common interests. All are electors, and all are eligible for office. The fundamental postulate of the *Déclaration des Droits de l'Homme* [Declaration of Human Rights] finds here its theoretical application. All the offices are filled by election. The officials, executive organs of the general will, play a merely subordinate part, are always dependent upon the collectivity, and can be deprived of their office at any moment. The mass of the party is omnipotent.

At the outset, the attempt is made to depart as little as possible from pure democracy by subordinating the delegates altogether to the will of the mass, by tying them hand and foot. In the early days of the movement of the Italian agricultural workers, the chief of the league required a majority of four-fifths of the votes to secure election. When disputes arose with the employers about wages, the representative of the organization, before undertaking any negotiations, had to be furnished with a written authority, authorized by the signature of every member of the corporation. All the accounts of the body were open to the examination of the members, at any time. There were two reasons for this. First of all, the desire was to avoid the spread of mistrust through the mass, "this poison which gradually destroys even the strongest organism." In the second place, this usage allowed each one of the members to learn bookkeeping, and to acquire such a general knowledge of the working of the corporation as to enable him at any time to take over its leadership. It is obvious that democracy in this sense is applicable only on a very small scale. In the infancy of the English labour movement, in many of the trade-unions, the delegates were either appointed in rotation from among all the members, or were chosen by lot. Gradually, however, the delegates' duties become more complicated; some individual ability becomes essential, a certain oratorical gift, and a considerable amount of objective knowledge. It thus becomes impossible to trust to blind chance, to the fortune of alphabetic succession, or to the order of priority, in the choice of a delegation whose members must possess certain peculiar personal aptitudes if they are to discharge their mission to the general advantage.

Such were the methods which prevailed in the early days of the labour movement to enable the masses to participate in party and trade-union administration. To-day they are falling into disuse, and in the development of the modern political aggregate there is a tendency to shorten and stereotype the process which transforms the led into a leader—a process which has hitherto developed by the natural course of events. . . .

It is undeniable that educational institutions for the officials of the party and of the labour organizations tend, above all, towards the artificial creation of an *élite* of the working-class, of a caste of cadets composed of persons who aspire to the command of the proletarian rank and file. Without wishing it, there is thus effected a continuous enlargement of the gulf which divides the leaders from the masses.

The technical specialization that inevitably results from all extensive organization renders necessary what is called expert leadership. Consequently the power of determination comes to be considered one of the specific attributes of leadership, and is gradually withdrawn from the masses to be concentrated in the hands of the leaders alone. Thus the leaders, who were at first no more than the executive organs of the collective will, soon emancipate themselves from the mass and become independent of its control.

Oligarchy Replaces Democracy

Organization implies the tendency to oligarchy. In every organization, whether it be a political party, a professional union, or any other association of the kind, the aristocratic tendency manifests itself very clearly. The mechanism of the organization, while conferring a solidity of structure, induces serious changes in the organized mass, completely inverting the respective position of the leaders and the led. As a result of organization, every party or professional union becomes divided into a minority of directors and a majority of directed.

It has been remarked that in the lower stages of civilization tyranny is dominant. Democracy cannot come into existence until there is attained a subsequent and more highly developed stage of social life. Freedoms and privileges, and among these latter the privilege of taking part in the direction of public affairs, are at first restricted to the few. Recent times have been characterized by the gradual extension of these privileges to a widening circle. This is what we know as the era of democracy. But if we pass from the sphere of the state to the sphere of party, we may observe that as democracy continues to develop, a backwash sets in. With the advance of organization, democracy tends to decline. Democratic evolution has a parabolic course. At the present time, at any rate as far as party life is concerned, democracy is in the descending phase. It may be enunciated as a general rule that the increase in the power of the leaders is directly proportional with the extension of the organization. In the various parties and labour organizations of different countries the influence of the leaders is mainly determined (apart from racial and individual grounds) by the varying development of organization. Where organization is stronger, we find that there is a lesser degree of applied democracy.

Every solidly constructed organization, whether it be a democratic state, a political party, or a league of proletarians for the resistance of economic oppression, presents a soil eminently favourable for the differentiation of organs and of functions. The more extended and the more ramified the official apparatus of the organization, the greater the number of its members, the fuller its treasury, and the more widely circulated its press, the less efficient becomes the direct control exercised by the rank and file, and the more is this control replaced by the increasing power of committees. Into all parties there insinuates itself that indirect electoral system which in public life the democratic parties fight against with all possible vigour. Yet in party life the influence of this system must be more disastrous than in the far more extensive life of the state. Even in the party congresses, which represent the party-life seven times sifted, we find that it becomes more and more general to refer all important questions to committees which debate in camera.

As organization develops, not only do the tasks of the administration become more difficult and more complicated, but, further, its duties become enlarged and specialized to such a degree that it is no longer possible to take them all in at a single glance. In a rapidly progressive movement, it is not only the growth in the number of duties, but also the higher quality of these, which imposes a more extensive differentiation of function. Nominally, and according to the letter of the rules, all the acts of the leaders are subject to the ever vigilant criticism of the rank and file. In theory the leader is merely an employee bound by the instructions he receives. He has to carry out the orders of the mass, of which he is no more than the executive organ. But in actual fact, as the organization increases in size, this control becomes purely fictitious. The members have to give up the idea of themselves conducting or even supervising the whole administration, and are compelled to hand these tasks over to trustworthy persons specially nominated for the purpose, to salaried officials. The rank and file must content themselves with summary reports, and with the appointment of occasional special committees of inquiry. Yet this does not derive from any special change in the rules of the organization. It is by very necessity that a simple employee gradually becomes a "leader," acquiring a freedom of action which he ought not to possess. The chief then becomes accustomed to despatch important business on his own responsibility, and to decide various questions relating to the life of the party without any attempt to consult the rank and file. It is obvious that democratic control thus undergoes a progressive diminution, and is ultimately reduced to an infinitesimal minimum. In all the socialist parties there is a continual increase in the number of functions withdrawn from the electoral assemblies and transferred to the executive committees. In this way there is constructed a powerful and complicated edifice. The principle of division of labour coming more and more into operation, executive authority undergoes division and subdivision. There is thus constituted a rigorously defined and hierarchical bureaucracy. In the catechism of party duties, the strict observance of hierarchical rules becomes the first article. This hierarchy comes into existence as the outcome of technical conditions, and its constitution is an essential postulate of the regular functioning of the party machine.

Elites Control Society

C. Wright Mills

Although he would clearly agree with Michels' concept of oligarchy and Edwards' description of control in the workplace, Mills extends the idea of oligarchy by analyzing who holds real power in this country. In a convergence of the political, economic, and military institutions, Mills argues that elites who have power in each area collectively determine the course of national events according to their own interests. However, interests of each component may not precisely correspond, leading elites to compete in what Mills calls "the often uneasy coincidence of economic, military, and political power." Even though all elites tend to have similar backgrounds, interlocking corporate directorates exert more pressure toward common interests. Elites from each institution hold positions on (perhaps more than one) corporate board of directors, causing a tendency toward similar views and policy decisions. Since current elites usually select those who replace them, this perpetuates the system of an elite with the power to determine the course of history.

Mills' viewpoint describes the elite model of power. Basic principles of the elite model are that (1) elites control the key institutions without accountability to the masses; (2) elites set the values by which society operates, so they are not susceptible to overthrow by revolution; and (3) elites control the mass perception of legitimate authority, so people believe the elites have a right to their privileged positions. Mills identifies the polity, the economy, and the military as the key institutions and describes how elites within these institutions maintain control.

QUESTIONS

1. How are the three key institutions related?
2. In what ways are the "instituted elite . . . frequently in some tension"?
3. What are the common demographic characteristics of the power elite?

The shape and meaning of the power elite today can be understood only when three sets of structural trends are seen at their point of coincidence: the military capitalism of private corporations exists in a weakened and formal democratic system containing a military order already quite political in outlook and demeanor. Accordingly, at the top of this structure, the power elite has been shaped by the coincidence of interest between those who control the major means of production and those who control the newly enlarged means of violence; from the decline of the professional politician and the rise to explicit political command of the corporate chieftains and the professional warlords; from the absence of any genuine civil service of skill and integrity, independent of vested interests.

The power elite is composed of political, economic, and military men, but this instituted elite is frequently in some tension: it comes together only on certain coinciding points and only on certain occasions of 'crisis.' In the long peace of the nineteenth century, the military were not in the high councils of state, not of the political directorate, and neither were the economic men—they made raids upon the state but they did not join its directorate. During the 'thirties, the political man was ascendant. Now the military and the corporate men are in top positions.

Of the three types of circle that compose the power elite today, it is the military that has benefited the most in its enhanced power, although the corporate circles have also become more explicitly intrenched in the more public decision-making circles. It is the professional politician that has lost the most, so much that in examining the events and decisions, one is tempted to speak of a political vacuum in which the corporate rich and the high warlord, in their coinciding interests, rule.

It should not be said that the three 'take turns' in carrying the initiative, for the mechanics of the power elite are not often as deliberate as that would imply. At times, of course, it is—as when political men, thinking they can borrow the prestige of generals, find that they must pay for it, or, as when during big slumps, economic men feel the need of a politician at once safe and possessing vote appeal. Today all three are involved in virtually all widely ramifying decisions. Which of the three types seems to lead depends upon 'the tasks of the period' as they, the elite, define them. Just now, these tasks center upon 'defense' and international affairs. Accordingly, as we have seen, the military are ascendant in two senses: as personnel and as justifying ideology. That is why, just now, we can most easily specify the unity and the shape of the power elite in terms of the military ascendancy.

But we must always be historically specific and open to complexities. The simple Marxian view makes the big economic man the *real* holder of power; the simple liberal view makes the big political man the chief of the power system; and there are some who would view the warlords as virtual dictators. Each of these is an oversimplified view. It is to avoid them that we use the term 'power elite' rather than, for example, 'ruling class.'

In so far as the power elite has come to wide public attention, it has done so in terms of the 'military clique.' The power elite does, in fact, take its current shape from the decisive entrance into it of the military. Their presence and their ideology are its major legitimations, whenever the power elite feels the need to provide any. But what is called the 'Washington military clique' is not composed merely of military men, and it does not prevail merely in Washington. Its members exist all over the country, and it is a coalition of generals in the roles of corporation executives, of politicians masquerading as admirals, of corporation executives acting like politicians, of civil servants who become majors, of vice-admirals who are also the assistants to a cabinet officer, who is himself, by the way, really a member of the managerial elite.

Neither the idea of a 'ruling class' nor of a simple monolithic rise of 'bureaucratic politicians' nor of a 'military clique' is adequate. The power elite today involves the often uneasy coincidence of economic, military, and political power.

Personal and Social Unity Among the Power Elite

Even if our understanding were limited to these structural trends, we should have grounds for believing the power elite a useful, indeed indispensable, concept for the interpretation of what is going on at the topside of modern American society. But we are not, of course, so limited: our conception of the power elite does not need to rest only upon the correspondence of the institutional hierarchies involved, or upon the many points at which their shifting interests coincide. The power elite, as we conceive it, also rests upon the similarity of its personnel, and their personal and official relations with one another, upon their social and psychological affinities. In order to grasp the personal and social basis of the power elite's unity, we have first to remind ourselves of the facts of origin, career, and style of life of each of the types of circle whose members compose the power elite.

The power elite is *not* an aristocracy, which is to say that it is not a political ruling group based upon a nobility of hereditary origin. It has no compact basis in a small circle of great families whose members can and do consistently occupy the top positions in the several higher circles which overlap as the power elite. But such nobility is only one possible basis of common origin. That it does not exist for the American elite does not mean that members of this elite derive socially from the full range of strata composing American society. They derive in substantial proportions from the upper classes, both new and old, of local society and the metropolitan 400. The bulk of the very rich, the corporate executives, the political outsiders, the high military, derive from, at most, the upper third of the income and occupational pyramids. Their fathers were at least of the professional and business strata, and very frequently higher than that. They are native-born Americans of native parents, primarily from urban areas, and, with the exceptions of the politicians among them, overwhelmingly from the East. They are mainly Protestants, especially Episcopalian or Presbyterian. In general, the higher the position, the greater the proportion of men within it who have derived from and who maintain connections with the upper classes. The generally similar origins of the members of the power elite are underlined and carried further by the fact of their increasingly common educational routine. Overwhelmingly college graduates, substantial proportions have attended Ivy League colleges, although the education of the higher military, of course, differs from that of other members of the power elite.

But what do these apparently simple facts about the social composition of the higher circles really mean? In particular, what do they mean for any attempt to understand the degree of unity, and the direction of policy and interest that may prevail among these several circles? Perhaps it is best to put this question in a deceptively simple way: in terms of origin and career, who or what do these men at the top represent?

Of course, if they are elected politicians, they are supposed to represent those who elected them; and, if they are appointed, they are supposed to represent, indirectly, those who elected their appointers. But this is recognized as something of an abstraction, as a rhetorical formula by which all men of power in almost all systems of government nowadays justify their power of decision. At times it may be true, both in the sense of their motives and in the sense of who benefits from their decisions. Yet it would not be wise in any power system merely to assume it.

The fact that members of the power elite come from near the top of the nation's class and status levels does not mean that they are necessarily 'representative' of the top levels only. And if they were, as social types, representative of a cross-section of the population, that would not mean that a balanced democracy of interest and power would automatically be the going political fact.

Power Elite Policy Influence

We cannot infer the direction of policy merely from the social origins and careers of the policy-makers. The social and economic backgrounds of the men of power do not tell us all that we need to know in order to understand the distribution of social power. For: (1) Men from high places may be ideological representatives of the poor and humble. (2) Men of humble origin, brightly self-made, may energetically serve the most vested and inherited interests. Moreover (3), not all men who effectively represent the interests of a stratum need in any way belong to it or personally benefit by policies that further its interests. Among the politicians, in short, there are sympathetic *agents* of given groups, conscious and unconscious, paid and unpaid. Finally (4), among the top decision-makers we find men who have been chosen for their positions because of their 'expert knowledge.' These are some of the obvious reasons why the social origins and careers of the power elite do not enable us to infer the class interests and policy directions of a modern system of power.

Do the high social origin and careers of the top mean nothing, then, about the distribution of power? By no means. They simply remind us that we must be careful of any simple and direct inference from origin and career to political character and policy, not that we must ignore them in our attempt at political understanding. They simply mean that we must analyze the political psychology and the actual decisions of the political directorate as well as its social composition. And they mean, above all, that we should control, as we have done here, any inference we make from the origin and careers of the political actors by close understanding of the institutional landscape in which they act out their drama. Otherwise we should be guilty of a rather simple-minded biographical theory of society and history.

Just as we cannot rest the notion of the power of the elite solely upon the institutional mechanics that lead to its formation, so we cannot rest the notion solely upon the facts of the origin and career of its personnel. We need both, and we have both—as well as other bases, among them that of the status intermingling.

But it is not only the similarities of social origin, religious affiliation, nativity, and education that are important to the psychological and social affinities of the members of the power elite. Even if their recruitment and formal training were more heterogeneous than they are, these men would still be of quite homogeneous social type. For the most important set of facts about a circle of men is the criteria of admission, of praise, of honor, of promotion that prevails among them; if these are similar within a circle, then they will tend as personalities to become similar. The circles that compose the power elite do tend to have such codes and criteria in common. The co-optation of the social types to which these common values lead is often more important than any statistics of common origin and career that we might have at hand. . . .

The key organizations, perhaps, are the major corporations themselves, for on the boards of directors we find a heavy overlapping among the members of these several elites. On the lighter side, again in the summer and winter resorts, we find that, in an intricate series of overlapping circles; in the course of time, each meets each or knows somebody who knows somebody who knows that one.

The higher members of the military, economic, and political orders are able readily to take over one another's point of view, always in a sympathetic way, and often in a knowledgeable way as well. They define one another as among those who count, and who, accordingly, must be taken into account. Each of them as a member of the power elite comes to incorporate into his own integrity, his own honor, his own conscience, the viewpoint, the expectations, the values of the others. If there are no common ideals and standards among them that are based upon an explicitly aristocratic culture, that does not mean that they do not feel responsibility to one another.

All the structural coincidence of their interests as well as the intricate, psychological facts of their origins and their education, their careers and their associations make possible the psychological affinities that prevail among them, affinities that make it possible for them to say of one another: He is, of course, one of us. And all this points to the basic, psychological meaning of class consciousness. Nowhere in America is there as great a 'class consciousness' as among the elite; nowhere is it organized as effectively as among the power elite. For by class consciousness, as a psychological fact, one means that the individual member of a 'class' accepts only those accepted by his circle as among those who are significant to his own image of self.

Within the higher circles of the power elite, factions do exist; there are conflicts of policy; individual ambitions do clash. There are still enough divisions of importance within the Republican party, and even between Republicans and Democrats, to make for different methods of operation. But more powerful than these divisions are the internal discipline and the community of interests that bind the power elite together, even across the boundaries of nations at war. . . .

Despite their social similarity and psychological affinities, the members of the power elite do not constitute a club having a permanent membership with fixed and formal boundaries. It is of the nature of the power elite that within it there is a good deal of shifting about, and that it thus does not consist of one small set of the same men in the same positions in the same hierarchies. Because men know each other personally does not mean that among them there is a unity of policy; and because they do not know each other personally does not mean that among them there is a disunity. The conception of the power elite does not rest, as I have repeatedly said, primarily upon personal friendship.

As the requirements of the top places in each of the major hierarchies become similar, the types of men occupying these roles at the top—by selection and by training in the jobs—become similar. This is no mere deduction from structure to personnel. That it is a fact is revealed by the heavy traffic that has been going on between the three structures, often in very intricate patterns. The chief executives, the warlords, and selected politicians came into contact with one another in an intimate, working way during World War II; after that war ended, they continued their associations, out of common beliefs, social congeniality, and coinciding interests. Noticeable proportions of top men from the military, the economic, and the political worlds have during the last fifteen years occupied positions in one or both of the other worlds: between these higher circles there is an interchangeability of position, based formally upon the supposed transferability of 'executive ability,' based in substance upon the co-optation by cliques of insiders. As members of a power elite, many of those busy in this traffic have come to look upon 'the government' as an umbrella under whose authority they do their work.

As the business between the big three increases in volume and importance, so does the traffic in personnel. The very criteria for selecting men who will rise come to embody this fact. The corporate commissar, dealing with the state and its military, is wiser to choose a young man who has experienced the state and its military than one who has not. The political director, often dependent for his own political success upon corporate decisions and corporations, is also wiser to choose a man with corporate experience. Thus, by virtue of the very criterion of success, the interchange of personnel and the unity of the power elite is increased.

Given the formal similarity of the three hierarchies in which the several members of the elite spend their working lives, given the ramifications of the decisions made in each upon the others, given the coincidence of interest that prevails among them at many points, and given the administrative vacuum of the American civilian state along with its enlargement of tasks—given these trends of structure, and adding to them the psychological affinities we have noted—we should indeed be surprised were we to find that men said to be skilled in administrative contacts and full of organizing ability would fail to do more than get in touch with one another. They have, of course, done much more than that: increasingly, they assume positions in one another's domains.

The unity revealed by the interchangeability of top roles rests upon the parallel development of the top jobs in each of the big three domains. The interchange occurs most frequently at the points of their coinciding interest, as between regulatory agency and the regulated industry; contracting agency and contractor. And it leads to co-ordinations that are more explicit, and even formal. . . . We must remember that these men of the power elite now occupy the strategic places in the structure of American society; that they command the dominant institutions of a dominant nation; that, as a set of men, they are in a position to make decisions with terrible consequences for the underlying populations of the world.

Capitalists Control
the Workers

RICHARD EDWARDS

In the first chapter, you read Marx's description of the conflict between the bourgeoisie and the proletariat. Based on that description and carrying Michels's concept of oligarchy a step further, Edwards describes the evolution of capitalist control over workers. Employers purchase labor when they hire workers, but they face the ongoing problem of turning the potential labor into actual work. Workers defend their own interests by resisting employers' efforts to continually increase profits through greater productivity without increasing worker rewards. Individual and collective wage negotiation is one routine indication that this process takes place. While capitalists always do business to increase capital accumulation, worker resistance comes in cycles. When workers resist most, employers try to make workers believe that increased production is to their own benefit.

By his description of ways capitalists control the workers, Edwards's viewpoint represents the class model of economic and political power. In the class model, control is distributed unequally by class, or ownership of the means of production. Those with enough resources own the means of production (factories, machines, transportation, communication) and have complete power over those without such resources, not only economically but over all aspects of their lives and thoughts. Edwards translates this "ownership of the means of production" into modern terms. In modern times, those with authority in corporations usually do not actually own the means of production, but they still have the same degree of control over the workers. The class model applies to the political institution in the same way: those with economic power control the workers politically.

QUESTIONS

1. How does Edwards distinguish between "labor" and "labor power" and why is this distinction important?
2. Why do capitalists usually not rely on detailed employment contracts or piece-rate pay?
3. In what ways do workers' interests oppose capitalist interests?

■ ■ ■

Capitalism itself came into being when labor power (as opposed to merely labor's products) became a commodity, that is, a thing bought and sold in the market. Employers, in business to make profits, begin by investing their funds (money capital) in the raw materials, labor power, machinery, and other commodities needed for production; they then organize the labor process itself, whereby the constituents of production are set in motion to produce useful products or services; and finally, by selling the products of labor, capitalists reconvert their property back to money. If the money capital obtained at the end of this cycle exceeds that invested initially, the capitalists have earned a profit.

Focusing on the central role of the labor process in this sequence, Karl Marx noted that:

The money-owner buys everything necessary for [production], such as raw material [and labor power], in the market, and pays for it at its full value. . . . The consumption of labor power is completed, as in the case of every other commodity, outside the limits of the market. . . . Accompanied by Mr. Moneybags and by the possessor of labor power, we therefore take leave for a time of this noisy sphere, where everything takes place on the surface and in view of all men, and follow them both into the hidden abode of production, on whose threshold there stares us in the face, "No admittance except on business." Here we shall see, not only how capital produces, but how capital is produced. We shall at last force the secret of profit making.

On leaving this sphere of [the market], . . . we think we can perceive a change in the physiognomy of our dramatis personae. He, who before was the money-owner, now strides in front as capitalist; the possessor of labor power follows as his laborer. The one with an air of importance, smirking, intent on business; the other, timid and holding back, like one who is bringing his own hide to market and has nothing to expect but—a hiding.

The market equality between buyer and seller of the commodity labor power disappears in this "hidden abode," and the capitalist takes charge. No wonder the capitalist strides ahead, "intent on business," for it turns out that the commodity he has purchased is not what is useful to him. What the capitalist buys in the labor market is the right to a certain quantity of what Marx has called *labor power*, that is, the worker's capacity to do work. Labor power can be thought of as being measured in time units (hours, days) and it may be improved or expanded by any skills, education, or other attributes that make it more productive than "simple" labor power. Thus, the capitalist, in hiring a carpenter for a day, buys one day's quantity of carpenter labor power.

But the capacity to do work is useful to the capitalist only if the work actually gets done. Work, or what Marx called *labor*, is the actual human effort in the process of production. If labor power remains merely a potentiality or capacity, no goods get produced and the capitalist has no products to sell for profit. Once the wages-for-time exchange has been made, the capitalist cannot rest content. He has purchased a given quantity of labor power, but he must now "stride ahead" and strive to extract actual labor from the labor power he now legally owns.

Workers must provide labor power in order to receive their wages, that is, they must show up for work; but they need not necessarily provide labor, much less the amount of labor that the capitalist desires to extract from the labor power they have sold. In a situation where workers do not control their own labor process and cannot make their work a creative experience, any exertion beyond the minimum needed to avert boredom will not be in the workers' interest. On the other side, for the capitalist it is true *without limit* that the more work he can wring out of the labor power he has purchased, the more goods will be produced; and they will be produced without any increased wage costs. It is this discrepancy between what the capitalist can buy in the market and what he needs for production that makes it imperative for him to control the labor process and the workers' activities. The capitalist need not be motivated to control things by an obsession for power; a simple desire for profit will do.

These basic relationships in production reveal both the basis for conflict and the problem of control at the workplace. Of course, this conflict is only superficially confronted with regard to an individual worker. Any worker who, once on the job, refuses to work or who even works less than the most eager job-seeking unemployed person will simply be fired. Individual resistance by a worker, if it is detected, is easily dealt with, so long as a replacement is standing by in the unemployment line. Meaningful conflict arises, then, with regard to groups of workers or an employer's or an entire industry's workforce. The amount of labor that can be extracted from the purchased labor power depends on the workforce's willingness to perform useful work and the enterprise's ability to compel or evoke such work. Conflict exists because the interests of workers and those of employers collide, and what is good for one is frequently costly for the other. Control is rendered problematic because, unlike the other commodities involved in production, labor power is always embodied in people, who have their own interests and needs and who retain their power to resist being treated like a commodity. Indeed, today's most important employers, the large corporations, have so many employees that to keep them working diligently is itself a major task, employing a vast workforce of its own. From the capitalist's perspective, this is seen as the problem of management, and it is often analyzed simply in terms of the techniques of administration and business "leadership." But employment creates a two-sided relationship, with workers contributing as much to its final form as managers or capitalists.

In some cases, the management task may be trivial. Employers may, for example, contract for particular labor services when workers are hired; if the exact nature of the duties can be spelled out beforehand, competition among job applicants— i.e., the labor market—effectively enforces the contract. Similarly, employers may pay only for work actually done; if each worker's output is independent, piece-rate pay compels adequate production. Other workplace schemes may be directed toward the same end.

In general, however, capitalists have found it neither practical nor profitable to rely on such devices. Complete market contracting (by exhaustively specifying the worker's duties before hire) is usually impossible and almost always too expensive. Piece-rate pay has limited application and frequently engenders conflict over the rates themselves. In both cases evaluation of the contracted work raises further problems. Other schemes—profit sharing, the distributing of company stock to workers, and more elaborate incentive schemes—also fail. Most importantly, all these devices founder because their targets, the workers, retain their ability to resist. Typically, then, the task of extracting labor from workers who have no direct stake in profits remains to be carried out in the workplace itself. Conflict arises over how work shall be organized, what work pace shall be established, what conditions producers must labor under, what rights workers shall enjoy, and how the various employees of the enterprise shall relate to each other. The workplace becomes a battleground, as employers attempt to extract the maximum effort from workers and workers necessarily resist their bosses' impositions.

Conflict on the Assembly Line

An academic observer at the beginning of the 1930s, S.B. Mathewson, gives us a glimpse of this workplace conflict in his account of one worker's experience:

> "Red," a beginner in industry, was working on an assembly line
> in a phonograph factory, producing small motors, on hourly rate.
> The line was turning out an average of only 30 motors a day.

"Red" found it so easy to keep up his part of the work that he would pile up parts ahead of the next worker in the line. He would then move over and help perform the next operation until the other worker caught up. This went on until "Red" was shifted by the foreman to the final operation in the assembly line. Here he was in a position to work as fast as he liked so far as passing on his completed work was concerned, but he was constantly waiting for the man behind. In order not to appear slow this man had to put through a few more parts, which had its effect all along the assembly line. The process of speeding up developed slowly until the gang, which formerly put through about 30 motors a day, was turning out an average of 120 a day. To "Red's" surprise, the men objected strenuously to this increase, argued with him and even threatened to "meet him in the alley" unless he slowed down his production. "Red" said that when production got up above 100 motors a day the threats became so insistent he began to fear "they might really mean something."

When he placed "Red" at the end of the line, the foreman initiated the conflict by forcing a speed-up on all workers, and in self-defense they responded. In this case, our observer tells us, the workers won and "'Red's' problem was 'solved' by his transfer to another department."

Stanley Aronowitz (1973) describes a similar situation, more recent, concerning a General Motors plant in 1971:

At Lordstown, efficiency became the watchword. At 60 cars an hour, the pace of work had not been exactly leisurely, but after [new managers] came in the number of cars produced almost doubled. Making one car a minute had been no picnic, especially on a constantly moving line. Assembly work fits the worker to the pace of the machine. Each work station is no more than 6 to 8 feet long. For example, within a minute on the line, a worker in the trim department had to walk about 20 feet to a conveyor belt transporting parts to the line, pick up a front seat weighing 30 pounds, carry it back to his work station, place the seat on the chassis, and put in four bolts to fasten it down by first hand-starting the bolts and then using an air gun to tighten them according to standard. It was steady work when the line moved at 60 cars an hour. When it increased to more than 100 cars an hour, the number of operations on this job were not reduced and the pace became almost maddening. In 36 seconds the worker had to perform at least eight different operations, including walking, lifting, hauling, lifting the carpet, bending to fasten the bolts by hand, fastening them by air gun, replacing the carpet, and putting a sticker on the hood. Sometimes the bolts fail to fit into the holes; the gun refuses to function at the required torque; the seats are defective or the threads are bare on the bolt. But the line does not stop.

These illustrations involve assembly-line production, but the basic relations exist in all workplaces; indeed, the shop-floor, the office, the drafting room, the warehouse, the hospital ward, the construction site, and the hotel kitchen all become places of continuing conflict. Workers resist the discipline and the pace that employers try to impose. At most times the workers' efforts are solitary and hidden; individual workers find relief from oppressive work schedules by doing what their bosses perceive as slacking off or intentionally sabotaging work. At other times resistance is more conspiratorial; informal work groups agree on how fast they will work and combine to discipline rate-busters; or technicians work to rules, sticking to the letter of the production manual and thereby slowing work to a fraction of normal efficiency. More openly, workers or even union locals (often against the commands of their leaders) walk off the job to protest firings, arbitrary discipline, unsafe working conditions, or other grievances. More public still, established unions or groups seeking to achieve bargaining rights strike in order to shut down production entirely. . . .

The Workplace Is a Contested Terrain

Conflict in the labor process occurs under definite historical circumstances, or, what is the same, within a specific economic and social context. Most importantly, production is part of the larger process of capital accumulation, that is, the cycle of investment of prior profits, organization of production, sale of produced commodities, realization of profits (or loss), and reinvestment of new profits. This process constitutes the fundamental dynamic of a capitalist economy. But capital accumulation, while it remains the basic theme, is played out with substantial variations, and a whole set of factors—the degree of competition among capitalists, the size of corporations, the extent of trade union organization, the level of class consciousness among workers, the impact of governmental policies, the speed of technological change, and so on—influence the nature and shape and pace of accumulation. Taken together, these various forces provide both possibilities for and constraints on what can occur within the workplace. What was possible or successful in one era may be impossible or disastrous in another. Conflict at work, then, must be understood as a product of both the strategies or wills of the combatants and definite conditions not wholly within the grasp of either workers or capitalists. As Marx put it,

> People make their own history, but they do not make it just as they please; they do not make it under circumstances chosen by themselves, but under circumstances directly found, given, and transmitted from the past.

Conflict occurs within definite limits imposed by a social and historical context, yet this context rarely determines everything about work organization. After technological constraints, the discipline of the market, and other forces have been taken into account, there remains a certain indeterminacy to the labor process. This space for the working out of workplace conflict is particularly evident within the large corporation, where external constraints have been reduced to a minimum. Here especially, the essential question remains: how shall work be organized?

The labor process becomes an arena of class conflict, and the workplace becomes a contested terrain. Faced with chronic resistance to their effort to compel production, employers over the years have attempted to resolve the matter by reorganizing, indeed revolutionizing, the labor process itself. Their goal remains profits; their strategies aim at establishing structures of control at work. That is, capitalists have attempted to organize production in such a way as to minimize workers' opportunities for resistance and even alter workers' perceptions of the desirability of opposition. Work has been organized, then, to contain conflict. In this endeavor employers have sometimes been successful.

5

How Do Societies Change?

CHAPTER PREFACE

Society has changed considerably over the history of the United States (as described in the preface for Chapter 4). The earliest colonists came to the New World seeking both economic opportunity and a chance to establish their own religious beliefs. Some came as slaves, indentured servants, or as criminals seeking a new life. Colonists found relative economic freedom but failed to establish a new state religion when country founders separated church and state. This separation forced denominations to compete for members, leading to change in the religious institution. Industrialization shaped the early course of events as the agricultural economy declined to be replaced by manufacturing. The modern family took form as transformations in the economy separated the workplace from the family. Increases in the division of labor followed from industrialization and required formerly self-sustaining people to depend on an hourly wage. Dramatic population increases resulted from advances in technology and immigration. Intermittent wars, economic fluctuations, and collective action also influenced the course of events.

Some preindustrial societies also experienced change, but most remained the same for thousands of years. Social scientists generally classify preindustrial societies by the ways they acquire food. For nearly all of human history, societies survived by hunting and gathering. Depending on their location, later societies became horticulturalists who grew their own food or pastoral societies that domesticated animals as a food source. Later, the Agricultural Revolution that preceded the Industrial Revolution enabled societies to use domestic animals and the plow to more efficiently cultivate land and produce food. Times of transition between these major societal forms changed everything about life in the societies.

People in hunting and gathering societies lived by foraging for edible plants, fishing, and hunting animals. Labor was divided by age and sex, with men doing most hunting and women doing the gathering. Because such food supplies in any geographic area are limited, these people must move to another area when supplies diminish. Hunter-gatherer societies had only about fifty members because of limited food supplies, and traveling made food storage impractical. Nevertheless, scientists estimate that hunter-gatherers worked only a few hours a day to provide for their needs. Since no food surplus accumulated and members had few other possessions in the interest of transportability, hunter-gatherers valued sharing of resources.

Beginning about nine thousand years ago, horticultural societies used a "digging stick" and later the hoe to cultivate plants for food. Since these societies domesticated plants rather than foraging, they could remain in one location for two or three years, then move on as the soil became exhausted. This allowed larger populations of up to 1,000 members and permitted the production of surplus goods and services (greater than those necessary for survival). It was not necessary for all members to work growing crops, since a few growers could support those not directly engaged in agriculture. Other members could specialize in various economic, political, and religious roles. Land and other private property (such as wives) became resources to be defended and warfare grew in importance.

At about the same time, some societies in areas not suitable for crops became pastoral and depended mainly on herds of domesticated animals for survival. These were societies of nomads who moved with their herds to new grazing pastures when necessary. Pastoral societies could trade their surplus animal products with horticulturists. They traded milk and milk products, fur, and hides, but usually not meat in order to avoid depleting the herd beyond the level required to feed their own members. Pastoralists domesticated horses and camels to help them manage the herds, and this capability increased their ability to attack other societies. Based on physical strength, powerful leaders emerged and passed the power to their descendants.

Agrarian societies used the wheel, the plow, and domestic animals to develop more efficient crop management beginning 5,000 to 6,000 years ago. For the first time, people did not need to relocate regularly and this allowed larger population size and accumulation of highly concentrated wealth. Most people in agrarian societies were peasants who had to produce enough for their own needs and fulfill the requirements of landowners and church and state officials. These elites also required the peasants to pay rent and taxes. Cities formed as population increased because fewer farmers could support the increased occupational specialization. Governments developed along with police to control the population and a military with which to pursue highly profitable warfare. Political boundaries changed frequently through military action, and rigid stratification developed based on age, sex, family background, strength, race, ethnicity, or caste. Victors often used conquered people as slaves, and strict stratification by nationality maintained the hierarchy.

Industrial societies evolved about 250 years ago with the invention of machines. With the Industrial Revolution, a large complex division of labor and broad market relationships replaced economic self-sufficiency and local market systems. Increasing urbanization transformed peasants into propertyless workers. With the rise of the capitalist economy, "big business" developed and bureaucracy became the standard organizational form for unions, universities, hospitals, and increasingly larger government. The rigid stratification of agrarian societies eased somewhat as income and wealth replaced strict inheritance. Work specialization increased and few people performed or knew about all stages of a production process. Because of this, skill monopolies developed (for example, plumbers and electricians), allowing the emergence of a new "middle class."

Some social scientists argue that a "postindustrial" society emerges when the size of the service economy increases. Capitalist economies emphasize economic growth, and that incentive produces technological advancement often using automation. Just as improvements in agriculture led to the need for fewer farmers, automation means that fewer workers perform production processes. In a postindustrial economy, businesses such as information processing, restaurants, banks, medical facilities, and schools are the main sources of employment. As Marx predicted, advanced capitalism also led to a concentration of corporate power and a few firms dominate many markets. Some large multinational corporations now have incomes greater than the gross national products of many countries.

Sociologists theorize about social change in an ongoing effort to explain changes such as those described above, and one basic idea is that societies evolve from less to more complex forms. Viewpoints in this chapter offer outlines of some social change theories sociologists have developed. As you read the competing viewpoints, think about the social change documented above and in the Chapter 4 preface. Think whether and how well the authors account for social change. A single explanation need not address all kinds of change, but think whether each viewpoint can be applied to social change that the author does not specifically address. After you read this chapter, take time to consider what each viewpoint predicts about future change in your society.

VIEWPOINT

1

Social Change Arises Through Natural Selection

HERBERT SPENCER

One of the earliest sociologists, Herbert Spencer, observes in
this viewpoint that, just as animals evolve by natural selection (survival of the fittest), human societies evolve and war
is one important factor in that evolution. Stronger and more
skilled tribes eliminate or assimilate those less so and population size increases from small to large tribes and nations. Advances in weapons technology combine with larger population size to produce advancement in other technology and
industrialization. All these effects follow from warfare as long
as all adult males participate and the strongest and most
skilled survive. When societies conscript only the best to
fight, war causes societies to regress rather than advance. At
this stage, war interferes with industrial progress as well by
diverting the focus of the society. In advanced societies, industrial competition replaces war as a force of evolution.

From *The Study of Sociology* by Herbert Spencer. London: Williams & Norgate,
1873, and *Life and Letters of Herbert Spencer* by D. Duncan. London: Williams &
Norgate, 1908.

1. How does Spencer apply evolutionary theory to humans?
2. In early societies, how does war encourage progress in other areas of society?
3. When societies are more advanced, in what ways does war cause societies to regress?

■ ■ ■

Natural Selection

One of the facts difficult to reconcile with current theories of the Universe, is that high organizations throughout the animal kingdom habitually serve to aid destruction or to aid escape from destruction. If we hold to the ancient view, we must say that high organization has been deliberately devised for such purposes. If we accept the modern view, we must say that high organization has been evolved by the exercise of destructive activities during immeasurable periods of the past. Here we choose the latter alternative. To the never-ceasing efforts to catch and eat, and the never-ceasing endeavours to avoid being caught and eaten, is to be ascribed the development of the various senses and the various motor organs directed by them. The bird of prey with the keenest vision, has, other things equal, survived when members of its species that did not see so far, died from want of food; and by such survivals, keenness of vision has been made greater in course of generations. The fleetest members of a herbivorous herd, escaping when the slower fell victims to a carnivore, left posterity; among which, again, those with the most perfectly-adapted limbs survived: the carnivores themselves being at the same time similarly disciplined and their speed increased. So, too, with intelligence. Sagacity that detected a danger which stupidity did not perceive, lived and propagated; and the cunning which hit upon a new deception, and so secured prey not otherwise to be caught, left posterity where a smaller endowment of cunning failed. This mutual perfecting of pursuer and pursued, acting upon their entire organizations, has been going on throughout all time; and human beings have been subject to it just as much as other beings.

War as Natural Selection

Warfare among men, like warfare among animals, has had a large share in raising their organizations to a higher stage. The following are some of the various ways in which it has worked.

In the first place, it has had the effect of continually extirpating races which, for some reason or other, were least fitted to cope with the conditions of existence they were subject to. The killing-off of relatively-feeble tribes, or tribes relatively wanting in endurance, or courage, or sagacity, or power of co-operation, must have tended ever to maintain, and occasionally to increase, the amounts of life-preserving powers possessed by men.

Beyond this average advance caused by destruction of the least-developed races and the least-developed individuals, there has been an average advance caused by inheritance of those further developments due to functional activity. Remember the skill of the Indian in following a trail, and remember that under kindred stimuli many of his perceptions and feelings and bodily powers have been habitually taxed to the uttermost, and it becomes clear that the struggle for existence between neighbouring tribes has had an important effect in cultivating faculties of various kinds. Just as, to take an illustration from among ourselves, the skill of the police cultivates cunning among burglars, which, again, leading to further precautions generates further devices to evade them; so, by the unceasing antagonisms between human societies, small and large, there has been a mutual culture of an adapted intelligence, a mutual culture of certain traits of character not to be undervalued, and a mutual culture of bodily powers.

A large effect, too, has been produced upon the development of the arts. In responding to the imperative demands of war, industry made important advances and gained much of its skill. Indeed, it may be questioned whether, in the absence of that exercise of manipulative faculty which the making of weapons originally gave, there would ever have been produced the tools required for developed industry. If we go back to the Stone-Age, we see that implements of the chase and implements of war are those showing most labour and dexterity. If we take still-existing human races which were without metals when we found them, we see in their skilfully-wrought stone clubs, as well as in their large war-canoes, that the needs of defence and attack were the chief stimuli to the cultivation of arts afterwards available for productive purposes. Passing over intermediate stages, we may note a comparatively-recent stages the same relation. Observe a coat of mail, or one of the more highly-finished suits of armour—compare it with articles of iron and steel of the same date; and there is evidence that these desires to kill enemies and escape being killed, more extreme than any other, have had great effects on those arts of working in metal to which most other arts owe their progress. The like relation is shown us in the uses made of gunpowder. At first a destructive agent, it has become an agent of immense service in quarrying, mining, railway-making, &c.

War Increases Population Size

A no less important benefit bequeathed by war, has been the formation of large societies. By force alone were small nomadic hordes welded into large tribes; by force alone were large tribes welded into small nations; by force alone have small nations been welded into large nations. While the fighting of societies usually maintains separateness, or by conquest produces only temporary unions, it produces, from time to time, permanent unions; and as fast as there are formed permanent unions of small into large, and then of large into still larger, industrial progress is furthered in three ways. Hostilities, instead of being perpetual, are broken by intervals of peace. When they occur, hostilities do not so profoundly derange the industrial activities. And there arises the possibility of carrying out the division of labour much more effectually. War, in short, in the slow course of things, brings about a social aggregation which furthers that industrial state at variance with war; and yet nothing but war could bring about this social aggregation.

These truths, that without war large aggregates of men cannot be formed, and that without large aggregates of men there cannot be a developed industrial state, are illustrated in all places and times among existing uncivilized and semi-civilized races, we everywhere find that union of small societies by a conquering society is a step in civilization. The records of peoples now extinct show us this with equal clearness. On looking back into our own history, and into the histories of neighbouring nations, we similarly see that only by coercion were the smaller feudal governments so subordinated as to secure internal peace. And even lately, the long-desired consolidation of Germany, if not directly effected by "blood and iron," as Bismarck said it must be, has been indirectly effected by them.

Larger Populations Industrialize

The furtherance of industrial development by aggregation is no less manifest. If we compare a small society with a large one, we get clear proof that those processes of co-operation by which social life is made possible, assume high forms only when the numbers of the co-operating citizens are great. Ask of what use a cloth-factory, supposing they could have one, would be to the members of a small tribe, and it becomes manifest that, producing as it would in a single day a year's supply of cloth, the vast cost of making it and keeping it in order could never be compensated by the advantage gained. Ask what would happen were a shop like Shoolbred's, supplying all textile products, set up in a village, and you see that the absence of a sufficiently-extensive distributing function would negative its continuance. Ask what sphere a bank would have had in the Old-English period, when nearly all people grew their own food and spun their own wool, and it is at once seen that the various appliances for facilitating exchange can grow up only when a community becomes so large that the amount of exchange to be facilitated is great. Hence, unquestionably, that integration of societies effected by war, has been a needful preliminary to industrial development, and consequently to developments of other kinds—Science, the Fine Arts, &c.

Industrial habits too, and habits of subordination to social requirements, are indirectly brought about by the same cause. The truth that the power of working continuously, wanting in the aboriginal man, could be established only by that persistent coercion to which conquered and enslaved tribes are subject, has become trite. An allied truth is, that only by a discipline of submission, first to an owner, then to a personal governor, presently to government less personal, then to the embodied law proceeding from government, could there eventually be reached submission to that code of moral law by which the civilized man is more and more restrained in his dealings with his fellows. . . .

Modern Wars Reduce Societal Fitness

Though, during barbarism and the earlier stages of civilization, war has the effect of exterminating the weaker societies, and of weeding out the weaker members of the stronger societies, and thus in both ways furthering the development of those valuable powers, bodily and mental, which war brings into play; yet during the later stages of civilization, the second of these actions is reversed. So long as all adult males have to bear arms, the average result is that those of most strength and quickness survive, while the feebler and slower are slain; but when the industrial development has become such that only some of the adult males are drafted into the army, the tendency is to pick out and expose to slaughter the best-grown and healthiest: leaving behind the physically-inferior to propagate the race. The fact that among ourselves, though the number of soldiers raised is not relatively large, many recruits are rejected by the examining surgeons, shows that the process inevitably works towards deterioration. Where, as in France, conscriptions have gone on taking away the finest men, generation after generation, the needful lowering of the standard proves how disastrous is the effect on those animal qualities of a race which form a necessary basis for all higher qualities. If the depletion is indirect also—if there is such an overdraw on the energies of the industrial population that a large share of heavy labour is thrown on the women, whose systems are taxed simultaneously by hard work and child-bearing, a further cause of physical degeneracy comes into play: France again supplying an example. War, therefore, after a certain stage of progress, instead of furthering bodily development and the development of certain mental powers, becomes a cause of retrogression.

In like manner, though war, by bringing about social consolidations, indirectly favours industrial progress and all its civilizing consequences, yet the direct effect of war on industrial progress is repressive. It is repressive as necessitating the abstraction of men and materials that would otherwise go to industrial growth; it is repressive as deranging the complex inter-dependencies among the many productive and distributive agencies; it is repressive as drafting off much administrative and constructive ability, which would else have gone to improve the industrial arts and the industrial organization. And if we contrast the absolutely-military Spartans with the partially-military Athenians, in their respective attitudes towards culture of every kind, or call to mind the contempt shown for the pursuit of knowledge in purely-military times like those of feudalism; we cannot fail to see that persistent war is at variance not only with industrial development, but also with the higher intellectual developments that aid industry and are aided by it.

Modern Wars Reduce Moral Fitness

So, too, with the effects wrought on the moral nature. While war, by the discipline it gives soldiers, directly cultivates the habit of subordination, and does the like indirectly by establishing strong and permanent governments; and while in so far it cultivates attributes that are not only temporarily essential, but are steps towards attributes that are permanently essential; yet it does this at the cost of maintaining, and sometimes increasing, detrimental attributes—attributes intrinsically anti-social. The aggressions which selfishness prompts (aggressions which, in a society, have to be restrained by some power that is strong in proportion as the selfishness is intense) can diminish only as fast as selfishness is held in check by sympathy; and perpetual warlike activities repress sympathy: nay, they do worse—they cultivate aggressiveness to the extent of making it a pleasure to inflict injury. The citizen made callous by the killing and wounding of enemies, inevitably brings his callousness home with him. Fellow-feeling, habitually trampled down in military conflicts, cannot at the same time be active in the relations of civil life. In proportion as giving pain to others is made a habit during war, it will remain a habit during peace: inevitably producing in the behaviour of citizens to one another, antagonisms, crimes of violence, and multitudinous aggressions of minor kinds, tending towards a disorder that calls for coercive government. Nothing like a high type of social life is possible without a type of human character in which the promptings of egoism are duly restrained by regard for others. The necessities of war imply absolute self-regard, and absolute disregard of certain others. Inevitably, therefore, the civilizing discipline of social life is antagonized by the uncivilizing discipline of the life war involves. So that beyond the direct mortality and miseries entailed by war, it entails other mortality and miseries by maintaining anti-social sentiments in citizens.

VIEWPOINT

2

Social Change Arises Externally

AMOS HAWLEY

Amos Hawley is a leading scholar in the field of human ecology, a sociological subfield. He analyzes the ecosystem, which is the social system in relation to environment, population, and technology. Hawley divides "the environment" into biophysical and ecumenic components. The biophysical environment includes terrain, minerals, plants, and animals. The ecumenic environment is composed of other social systems (other cities, states, or nations). Hawley's general argument is that social change occurs when new information from outside the system creates disequilibrium and openness. Once change begins, it feeds back to the external factors and can cause change in them. Since social systems tend toward equilibrium, social change can only come from factors external to the social system.

QUESTIONS

1. According to Hawley, what is "change"?
2. How does Hawley's conception of change compare with that of Marx, Sorokin, and Moore?

Excerpted from *Human Ecology: A Theoretical Essay* by Amos H. Hawley. Chicago: University of Chicago Press, 1986. Copyright 1986 by The University of Chicago. Reprinted by permission.

3. What are the two "complementary phases" of the change process?

■ ■ ■

Change is commonly regarded as an irreversible and non-repetitive alteration of an object. Irreversibility may be due to a simple improbability that elements, when moved about randomly, can be immediately returned to their original order. But it may also be due to the creation of new variables in the course of modification. For one or another of these reasons an object is changed when it cannot be restored to its initial state. If it reverts to a more primitive condition, it must follow a different path from that traversed in attaining its present form.

The object of change for purposes of this viewpoint is the ecosystem viewed as a unitary phenomenon. What constitutes change in an ecosystem is implicit in the definition of a system. That is, change occurs as a shift in the number and kinds of functions or as a rearrangement of functions in different combinations. Usually the occurrence of one involves the occurrence of the other. Simple though they may seem, such alterations have profound repercussions. They affect the number of people who are needed and who can be supported, the techniques and tools that can be used, the disposition of system parts in time and space, and the composition of the normative code.

Excluded from the conception of change as used here are internal variations that have no sequels and cyclical fluctuations that are intrinsic to the functioning of a system. A family, for example, might modify its internal routines without affecting its relations with complementing units. Or a given unit might disappear and be replaced by another similar unit without disturbing a set of relationships. Similarly, day and night alterations, the seasonal round, the life cycle, the succession of generations sow no seeds of change, though they are among the points where the visibility of change, when it occurs, is greatest.

The Origins of Change

There are two seemingly opposed views of the origins of system change. One contends that change is internally induced;

the other holds change to be the result of external influences generated in the environment. Whether change is continuous or discontinuous is also a point of some disagreement.

The classic conception of change as an internally caused process was put forth by Karl Marx. In his view, change is produced by internal contradictions that develop primarily between the "forces of production" (i.e., technology) and the "relations of production" (i.e., the organization of production). Whereas the forces of production are cumulative, the relations of production are relatively inert. The multiplication of contradictions builds an increasing pressure upon a prevailing equilibrium until the existing relations of production are dissolved and a new set of relations of production is established. Marx provided no clues as to how or by what means the forces of production accumulate. That appears to have been accepted as a given.

Pitirim Sorokin also espoused an internal causation of change. But unlike Marx, who regarded change as a discontinuous process, Sorokin thought of change as continuous. Change, he said, is immanent. It proceeds though the accretion of infinitely small alterations. Although he recognized that external influences might be facilitating, Sorokin insisted that systems change even in fixed environments. He provided no exposition, however, of how change was produced.

Wilbert Moore offers a more analytical explication of internally caused change. He finds its basis in the improbability of exact reproducibility of role behavior on the part of successive occupants of positions, in the genetic variability of successive cohorts, and in the interruptions in the staffing of roles that result from a more or less random mortality. There is therefore an inherent instability in a system that generates a creeping change leading eventually to significant cumulative effects. Moore's argument is not convincing, however. His contention that stability or continuity presupposes exact reproducibility from moment to moment begs the question, though that is a position encouraged by "functionalism." That there can be flexibility without change should need little argument. Flexibility is the guarantor of continuity. If a system were unable to tolerate minor variations in the relations among its parts, it would be threatened with destruction by every disturbance that occurred. But since disturbances are often temporary and impinge on no more than a particular relationship or sector, a system is able to return to its original state with no lasting effects. An important question concerning this as well as other aspects of structure has to do with the amount of tolerance for variation that exists in a system.

Change Originates Outside the System

The conception of change as dependent on external influences recognizes an inescapable system-environment interaction. It rests, moreover, on both logical and empirical foundations. Logically it is impossible for a thing to cause itself. On the empirical side, scholars in many disciplines have observed the critical importance of environmental inputs for system change. This is not to say that a system is a passive factor in a change process. On the contrary, it contains elements that facilitate as well as obstruct change-inducing events.

Where there is a reluctance to accept the external origins position, it rests in part on a failure to observe a distinction between what are called, in Aristotelian language, efficient and material causes. No external event A (efficient cause), let us say, can produce effect Y in the absence of certain system properties $a, a', a'', \ldots$ (material causes). On the other hand, the mere presence of properties $a, a', a'', \ldots$ will not lead to effect Y unless event A has been brought to bear on the system. That there may be feedback effects from $a, a', a'', \ldots$ to A is no contradiction of the above hypothesis; such effects merely complicate the cause-and-effect relationship.

Another source of resistance to the external origins principle of changes lies in our having lost sight of the linkages among happenings, which is easy to do when dealing with complex phenomena. A new influence usually impinges first and most forcibly on a particular segment of a system. Change in that segment is subsequently transmitted to other related segments in a concatenation of effects that might be spread over an extended period of time. Unless the whole sequence is known, it appears that change in any one segment originated within the system. The observational task posed by the sequential transmission of effects is obviously not a simple one. In instances in which a student is interested only in change in a particular segment of a system, it might not be worth the effort to trace the series of effects back to its beginnings. But that would be a decision based on expedience, not on principle. The danger of being led into an infinite regress by the external origins principle is not a serious one. How far one need retreat to earlier events to locate the exogenous factor is indicated in the definition of the unit in which change is being observed.

Perhaps the greatest difficulty encountered in applying the external origins principle rests with the inside-outside distinction that must be made. Phenomena that are amorphously bounded, as are many ecosystems, seem to lack the assumed unit character. I have minimized this difficulty by starting with an equilibrium model. But that, of course, is a heuristic fiction. Most ecosystems are open systems, and some are loose congeries of partially integrated subsystems. In such instances it is difficult to locate effective boundaries, though the issue can often be resolved by definition. As a general rule, the more closely a system approximates a unity, the greater is the necessity that change originate from external disturbances. It should be noted, however, that immanent change offers no escape from the boundary problem, for it posits an interior in which change is alleged to be generated.

Change Occurs in Two Phases

What has been presented as two opposing views of change makes much more sense if regarded as complementary phases of a single process. That is, social system change is resolvable into internal and external phases. The internal phase, which constitutes the more protracted segment, consists in drawing out the implications of accumulated information. By arranging and rearranging elements of knowledge in various combinations a series of deductions and inductions, that is, discoveries or inventions, is derived. Conceivably such a process continues until all or nearly all combinations of existing knowledge have been explored. As that point is approached, the rate of internal change subsides and equilibrium conditions begin to appear. The time required to reach such a state varies with the amount of accumulated knowledge. That, in turn, may be contingent on various other circumstances. Those will be discussed in a later section.

A resumption of the process of change requires the acquisition of new items of information, either as novel forms of behavior or as behavior abstracted to constitute information. Such acquisitions can occur only as inputs from the system's environment. Thus is added an element that can be tried in various combinations with old elements in a search for workable inferences. As those appear, an equilibrium is dissolved and a system moves through another internal phase to a new state. The latter does not happen without the input from the outside, without the external phase of change.

The interaction of internal with external phases of change is manifested in various ways. Quite often the occupance and use of a habitat by a resettled population will so modify habitat conditions that the occupying group cannot continue a given mode of life indefinitely in that location. Use might alter the soil content through repeated plantings of a single food crop without fertilization, provoke erosion by affecting the drainage pattern, or create conditions that attract new kinds of predators. Unless the group gains new information that enables it to restore habitat productivity, it will have to migrate or suffer a progressive attrition in sustenance supply with all that implies for survival. This was the outcome of cotton cultivation in the southeastern United States. Another instance of feedback effect occurs where equilibrated systems maintain themselves by expelling the surplus members of each generation. If the expelled members devise ways of surviving in the vicinity of the familiar habitat, they become a new element in the environment of the parent system. The dispossessed sons of landed families in medieval Europe, for example, became brigands, mercenary soldiers, and merchants, all potentially important bearers of novelty.

Many variations that occur in the biophysical environment, such as day-to-day temperature fluctuations, small alterations of the growing season, or rises and falls in populations of parasites, may have little or no effect. Ecosystems generally possess enough resilience to absorb the effects of small oscillations in their environments without experiencing structural changes. Even an extreme deviation from the normal, if it is of short duration, may leave no permanent mark on a system. But where one or more functions are rendered inoperative by physical or biotic shifts, the system may have to be reconstituted in a different pattern. The disappearance of a game supply, the silting of an estuary, or a volcanic eruption can force a move to a different habitat and a renewal of adaptive efforts to deal with a new set of conditions. In that event, the system reforms around a modified key function. If no new information has been acquired, the system may regress to a simpler form. But the biophysical environment is not of itself productive of information.

Exposure to an ecumenic environment has vastly greater implications. From it are transmitted influences having both additive and multiplicative effects. A site on a traveled road is directly accessible to an ecumenic environment; a location at an intersection of routes is open to a much wider ecumene. Earlier the ecumenic environment was characterized as an interaction field. In its primitive form the field is composed of a number of relatively independent systems, varying in size, resources, and accessibility of location. The origin of such a field doubtlessly lay in repeated occasions of overpopulation and group fission, followed by colonization of adjacent territories. The process is actually as old as the history of human sedentary settlement. With the spread of settlement units, a network of routes of travel develops. Travelers, moving through the network carrying ideas, artifacts, and accounts of experiences, serve inadvertently thereby as agents of change. Information piles up, as it were, in the system with a strategic location in the network and drifts outward from there to systems with less favorable locations. Ecumenes, however, can be so insular as to be sheltered from external influences. Lambert (1964) attributes the relatively static character of Indian society to extreme segmentation. While there are many intervillage networks, none is inclusive and few bridge urban and rural segments. Only where a unit in a network occupies a site on a well-traveled road is there apt to be a resumption of cumulative change.

Collective Behavior Promotes Social Change

RALPH TURNER AND LEWIS KILLIAN

In everyday life, social norms specify expected behavior in ordinary situations. Everyone knows, for example, that people wear clothes in public and eat spaghetti with a fork rather than with their fingers. Situations arise in everyday life, however, where no norms apply. For example, what behavior is appropriate for a group of Midwestern tourists witnessing a California carjacking? What position should people take on whether the last known smallpox virus should be destroyed? And how can activists accomplish their goal of banning cigarettes? In these extra-institutional situations, people look to each other for a definition of the situation and develop new (emergent) norms for behavior. This is collective behavior, which includes crowds, publics, and social movements. When innovative collective behavior becomes accepted and ordinary, this helps maintain social stability. Further, Turner and Killian argue in this viewpoint that social change is accomplished through collective behavior. Social psychologist Ralph Turner is the most prominent collective behavior scholar in

From Ralph H. Turner and Lewis M. Killian, *Collective Behavior*, 3rd ed., ©1987, pp. 395, 397, 398, 400, 401, 404, 405. Reprinted by permission of Prentice Hall, Englewood Cliffs, New Jersey.

sociology today and he and Lewis Killian published the first edition of their book on collective behavior in 1957. Since then, Turner has also published influential work on such topics as family interaction and role change.

QUESTIONS

1. According to the research Turner and Killian report, what determines the success of a social movement?
2. Turner and Killian identify the elements that bring about change in culture and in social organization. What are these two elements?
3. When does "collective behavior become the major vehicle for change?"

Has collective behavior any real effect on the course of events, or is it merely a shadow cast by significant events? Perhaps the causes for change are deeply embedded in history, and the eruptions of crowd behavior and the mobilizations of social movements are but diversionary displays. Perhaps social movements merely hamper the orderly process of change and make change more costly in lives and human happiness than need be, without materially altering long-term trends. . . .

Social Movements and Change

While collective behavior under some circumstances strengthens resistance to change in society, in other circumstances it clearly is a critical change agent. This conclusion is most obvious for social movements, such as the women's suffrage movement and ratification of the nineteenth amendment to the U.S. Constitution in 1920, the farm workers movement and enactment of legislation to guarantee collective bargaining for agricultural workers, the product safety movement and installation of seat belts and other safety devices in automobiles, and the civil rights movement and the reduction of racial segregation in the United States. What do we know of the circumstances that distinguish movements that succeed in bringing about change from movements that do not?

William Gamson selected a sample of 53 *challenging groups* that surfaced in American society between 1800 and 1945. By definition, challenging groups "are seeking the mobilization of an unmobilized constituency and their antagonist or target of influence lies outside of this constituency." Each group (or movement) was judged successful or unsuccessful by two criteria. The criterion of *acceptance* was met if the target group accepted movement leaders as valid spokespersons for a legitimate set of interests and consulted or negotiated with them. The criterion of *new advantages* was met if the group's intended beneficiaries benefitted demonstrably from movement efforts. When the two criteria are combined, 22 movements were entirely unsuccessful and 5 were accepted without being able to gain new advantages. Thus we could say that in about half of the cases the movements were unsuccessful in bringing about any of the changes they sought. Of the remaining movements, 20 were successful by both criteria and six were preempted—that is, reforms that they sought were instituted but the movement was not accorded recognition.

Comparing successful with unsuccessful movements, Gamson found that the nature of their goals was important. While most movements sought merely to change the target group's policies or organization in some way, 16 had goals requiring removal of at least some of the target group, either peacefully or by force. With one ambiguous exception, none of the latter succeeded in bringing about desired changes. Similarly, none of the nine multiple-issue groups achieved desired changes, as compared to the 44 single-issue groups. On the other hand, it didn't matter how radical the goals were, provided the movement did not seek to displace the target group.

While many of these displacing and multiple-issue movements were not revolutionary in the sense of seeking a political take-over, all revolutionary movements would be characterized by displacement goals and multiple issues. Thus Gamson's findings confirm observations by Roberta Ash Garner and others concerning the ineffectuality of revolutionary movements in American society. They also fit well with the thesis advanced by Theda Skocpol concerning the occurrence of *social revolutions*. A social revolution, as she defines it, involves "basic changes in social structure and in political structure [that] occur together in a mutually reinforcing fashion

[and] occur through intense sociopolitical conflicts in which class struggles play a key role." This definition rules out mere coups d'etats in which power changes hands without accompanying social change and historical transformations such as the industrial "revolution." Skocpol concludes that revolutions are not primarily the consequence of deliberate effort by a movement to overthrow the existing political or social order, but of a crisis of the state.

> True enough, revolutionary organizations and ideologies have helped to cement the solidarity of radical vanguards before or during revolutionary crises. And they have greatly facilitated the consolidation of new regimes. But in no sense did such vanguards—let alone vanguards with large, mobilized, and ideologically imbued mass followings—ever create the revolutionary crises they exploited. Instead . . . revolutionary situations have developed due to the emergence of politico-military crises of state and class domination.

Administrative and military power of vulnerable states broke down because of combinations of internal failures and unsuccessful economic and political competition with other states.

Skocpol's thesis suggests the importance of exploring the vulnerability of relevant social structures as well as the effectiveness of recruitment, adherent control, and other collective behavior processes in explaining whether movements succeed in bringing about change or not. Applied to other than revolutionary movements, vulnerability consists of both impairment of the agency group's ability to protect existing patterns and some ambivalence about existing practices in the movement public. For example, in the U.S. struggle for civil rights, the threat of federal intervention weakened the capacity of regional and local authorities to protect their segregation practices, the end of a plantation economy had eliminated some traditional economic advantages of segregation, and the dilution of regional cultures by an emerging national culture had rendered traditional justifications less convincing before the civil rights movements achieved its major successes in the South. Whether subsequent research supports the disproportionate emphasis that Skocpol places on the vulnerability of the state in explaining successful revolution, vulnerability to change remains a crucial consideration in explaining the success of any social movement in bringing about social change. . . .

Aside from such obvious variables as the intensity and extensiveness of disruption, we look to the public definition of the disorders and the vulnerability of relevant parts of the social system in predicting or explaining the change-effectiveness of disruptive crowds. We have discussed the public definition of disruptive crowd behavior either as social protest or as crime, mischief, or rebellion on a mass scale. With prior sensitization to the injustices suffered by the riotous class, a public may define the behavior as protest and lend support to corrective programs. When so defined the events contribute a new sense of the severity of the injustices and the urgency of the situation. Contending definitions of the disorders may also be used in community power struggles. Thus conceiving the riots as social protest was used by Democratic leaders to justify liberal social programs at a time when national enthusiasm for such programs was declining. But in the absence of a public definition of social protest, disruptive crowds are more likely to be used to justify repressive measures and to foster retrenchment rather than change.

Vulnerability, which both contributes to protest definition and is heightened by such public definition, refers as before to limitations in the ability of authorities to control such disruptions and public ambivalence about practices that publics define as issues raised by the disruptions.

But as with social movements, the effects of disruptive crowd behavior may be determined more by its effects on the participants and sympathizers than by its immediate and direct effects in the larger community. If the common-fate consciousness aroused in a riot is translated into organization so that planned strategy in support of identified goals, implemented by a disciplined body of adherents, replaces the crowds, the momentary gains from disorder can be the start of significant change. . . .

The Process of Change

In discussing the possible contributions of collective behavior to stability (rather than change) we emphasized the testing of alternatives through collective behavior. We suggest that this testing is part of a more comprehensive *tentative process* through which the major directions of change in society are crystallized. Crowd and social movement activity and response take place within the context of constantly changing publics. The process of working out a dominant major direction of change or of settling on a limited number of contending positions whose dialectic will be a continuing feature of change involves two major sets of developments.

First are the processes centering about defining issues and values. Generally accepted statements of values and issues can emerge through discussion, as affected by crowd activity and promotion by strongly valued-oriented movements. But more generally shifts in values occur obliquely. Changes in the prevalent definitions of issues permit realignments without requiring individuals to make open value reversals. Similarly, change occurs only partially through clear-cut victories by particular movements. Of more consequence for long-term change is the absorption by contending movements of important aspects of the most successful movements' values. Victories of particular movements may be ephemeral. Reactions against overly successful movements set in for a variety of reasons, often creating apparent swings between rival viewpoints. Hence, the interplay of contending movements might have little consequence for long-range directions of change were it not that the value-orientations of each of the movements undergoes change. Certain issues come to be settled, not by admitted agreement but by moving on to new issues. The value of state support for the aged was established in the United States through acceptance of this principle by the countermovements which effectively defeated the major old-age pension movements of the 1930s. The value of social security became firmly established when the movement that had unsuccessfully opposed it began concentrating its opposition on other matters.

Second, the emerging directions of change may be equally shaped by struggles and alignments to which value questions are secondary. In some movement organizations and under some circumstances, power orientations override value orientations and seizing control becomes an end in itself. Movement organizations committed to their own existence remain after issues to which their values apply have been relegated to the past. Some value-oriented movements lose out or gain more than others in the struggle among movements. Particular values gain or are discredited by being adopted for tactical purposes in such power struggles. Separatist movements may draw support away from major value orientations.

In part these two directions represent the mechanisms of change in culture and social organization respectively. Value orientations are direct proposals for alteration of the culture. Issues within publics are questions concerning the relative emphasis or the nature of application of values in the culture. Power orientations, on the other hand, concern social organization. Successful redistribution of power leads to reorganization, with implications for modification of the cultural values bound to accompany the changes.

From the preceding discussion we can summarize the relation of collective behavior to change in the following manner.

1. A certain amount of isolated and sporadic collective behavior characterizes the most stable society and has no important implications for change. It is simply a response to events that fall outside the limits with which the established order and culture are prepared to cope.
2. Widespread collective behavior over a period of time is probably not a sufficient condition to bring about social change, though it probably always makes the social order more susceptible to change when the necessary ideas and values can be supplied.
3. Widespread collective behavior becomes the major vehicle for change when contact between diverse cultures supplies novel values about which collective behavior can become focused, and when social structural changes are improving the fortunes of population segments for whom the emerging values are congenial.
4. Collective behavior then becomes the medium through which tentative directions of change are tested until one major direction prevails.
5. Thus collective behavior is an integral part of the process of social and cultural change.

Broad potential directions for change are to a considerable degree predetermined in the very developments of culture and society that give rise to the collective behavior. Hence, collective behavior is often more a process of discovery than of determination. But within the range of broadly predetermined directions, the detailed character of the changes, the rate at which change occurs, and sometimes momentous choices between important structural alternatives remain to be accomplished through collective behavior. And whether the byproduct of change is enhanced solidarity in the community and nation or a legacy of malaise and mistrust in social institutions can reflect the pattern of collective behavior and response through which new directions are established.

Capitalism Promotes Social Change

IMMANUEL WALLERSTEIN

Macro sociologist Immanuel Wallerstein argues that a capitalist economy, operating in an arena beyond the control of any one government, creates social change. Such an arena is the world-system with an occupational and geographic division of labor. Nations in more advantaged areas dominate the world-system and are called core-states. Less advantaged countries with weaker governments occupy the world-system periphery. Wallerstein also recognizes a semiperiphery composed of former core-states or countries currently gaining power. Core-states exploit the periphery in the dynamic world-system, but the periphery resists and challenges the exploitation. It is this continual economic exchange, based on capitalism, that produces social change.

QUESTIONS

1. How does Wallerstein define a "world system"? What two varieties of world systems have existed?

Excerpted from *The Modern World-System* by Immanuel Wallerstein. New York: Academic Press, 1974. Copyright ©1974 by Academic Press, Inc. Reprinted by permission of Academic Press, a division of Harcourt Brace and Company.

2. According to Wallerstein, what is the relationship between capitalism and the political system?
3. What are the components of the division of labor in the world-system?

■ ■ ■

In order to describe the origins and initial workings of a world system, I have had to argue a certain conception of a world-system. A world-system is a social system, one that has boundaries, structures, member groups, rules of legitimation, and coherence. Its life is made up of the conflicting forces which hold it together by tension, and tear it apart as each group seeks eternally to remold it to its advantage. It has the characteristics of an organism, in that it has a life-span over which its characteristics change in some respects and remain stable in others. One can define its structures as being at different times strong or weak in terms of the internal logic of its functioning.

What characterizes a social system in my view is the fact that life within it is largely self-contained, and that the dynamics of its development are largely internal. The reader may feel that the use of the term "largely" is a case of academic weaseling. I admit I cannot quantify it. Probably no one ever will be able to do so, as the definition is based on a counterfactual hypothesis: If the system, for any reason, were to be cut off from all external forces (which virtually never happens), the definition implies that the system would continue to function substantially in the same manner. Again, of course, substantially is difficult to convert into hard operational criteria. Nonetheless the point is an important one, and key to many parts of the empirical analyses of this book. Perhaps we should think of self-containment as a theoretical absolute, a sort of social vacuum, rarely visible and even more implausible to create artificially, but still and all a socially-real asymptote, the distance from which is somehow measurable.

Using such a criterion, it is contended here that most entities usually described as social systems—"tribes," communities, nation-states—are not in fact total systems. Indeed, on the contrary, we are arguing that the only real social systems are, on the one hand, those relatively small, highly autonomous subsistence economies not part of some regular tribute-demanding system and, on the other hand, world-systems. These latter are to be sure distinguished from the former because they are relatively large; that is, they are in common parlance "worlds." More precisely, however, they are defined by the fact that their self-containment as an economic-material entity is based on extensive division of labor and that they contain within them a multiplicity of cultures.

It is further argued that thus far there have only existed two varieties of such world-systems: world-empires, in which there is a single political system over most of the area, however attenuated the degree of its effective control; and those systems in which such a single political system does not exist over all, or virtually all, of the space. For convenience and for want of a better term, we are using the term "world-economy," to describe the latter.

Finally, we have argued that prior to the modern era, world-economies were highly unstable structures which tended either to be converted into empires or to disintegrate. It is the peculiarity of the modern world-system that a world-economy has survived for 500 years and yet has not come to be transformed into a world-empire—a peculiarity that is the secret of its strength.

Capitalism and the World-Economy

This peculiarity is the political side of the form of economic organization called capitalism. Capitalism has been able to flourish precisely because the world-economy has had within its bounds not one but a multiplicity of political systems.

I am not here arguing the classic case of capitalist ideology that capitalism is a system based on the noninterference of the state in economic affairs. Quite the contrary! Capitalism is based on the constant absorption of economic loss by political entities, while economic gain is distributed to "private" hands. What I am arguing rather is that capitalism as an economic mode is based on the fact that the economic factors operate within an arena larger than that which any political entity can totally control. This gives capitalists a freedom of maneuver that is structurally based. It has made possible the constant economic expansion of the world-system, albeit a very skewed distribution of its rewards. The only alternative world-system that could maintain a high level of productivity and change the system of distribution would involve the reintegration of the levels of political and economic decision-making. This would constitute a third possible form of world-system, a socialist world government. This is not a form that presently exists, and it was not even remotely conceivable in the sixteenth century.

The historical reasons why the European world-economy came into existence in the sixteenth century and resisted attempts to transform it into an empire have been expounded at length. We shall not review them here. It should however be noted that the size of a world-economy is a function of the state of technology, and in particular of the possibilities of transport and communication within its bounds. Since this is a constantly changing phenomenon, not always for the better, the boundaries of a world-economy are ever fluid.

The Division of Labor in a World-System

We have defined a world-system as one in which there is extensive division of labor. This division is not merely functional—that is, occupational—but geographical. That is to say, the range of economic tasks is not evenly distributed throughout the world-system. In part this is the consequence of ecological considerations, to be sure. But for the most part, it is a function of the social organization of work, one which magnifies and legitimizes the ability of some groups within the system to exploit the labor of others, that is, to receive a larger share of the surplus.

While, in an empire, the political structure tends to link culture with occupation, in a world-economy the political structure tends to link culture with spatial location. The reason is that in a world-economy the first point of political pressure available to groups is the local (national) state structure. Cultural homogenization tends to serve the interests of key groups and the pressures build up to create cultural-national identities.

This is particularly the case in the advantaged areas of the world-economy—what we have called the core-states. In such states, the creation of a strong state machinery coupled with a national culture, a phenomenon often referred to as integration, serves both as a mechanism to protect disparities that have arisen within the world-system, and as an ideological mask and justification for the maintenance of these disparities.

World-economies then are divided into core-states and peripheral areas. I do not say peripheral *states* because one characteristic of a peripheral area is that the indigenous state is weak, ranging from its nonexistence (that is, a colonial situation) to one with a low degree of autonomy (that is, a neocolonial situation).

There are also semiperipheral areas which are in between the core and the periphery on a series of dimensions, such as the complexity of economic activities, strength of the state machinery, cultural integrity, etc. Some of these areas had been core-areas of earlier versions of a given world-economy. Some had been peripheral areas that were later promoted, so to speak, as a result of the changing geopolitics of an expanding world-economy.

The semiperiphery, however, is not an artifice of statistical cutting points, nor is it a residual category. The semiperiphery is a necessary structural element in a world-economy. These areas play a role parallel to that played, *mutatis mutandis*, by middle trading groups in an empire. They are collection points of vital skills that are often politically unpopular. These middle areas (like middle groups in an empire) partially deflect the political pressures which groups primarily located in peripheral areas might otherwise direct against core-states and the groups which operate within and through their state machineries. On the other hand, the interests primarily located in the semiperiphery are located outside the political arena of the core-states, and find it difficult to pursue the ends in political coalitions that might be open to them were they in the same political arena.

The division of a world-economy involves a hierarchy of occupational tasks, in which tasks requiring higher levels of skill and greater capitalization are reserved for higher-ranking areas. Since a capitalist world-economy essentially rewards accumulated capital, including human capital, at a higher rate than "raw" labor power, the geographical maldistribution of these occupational skills involves a strong trend toward self-maintenance. The forces of the marketplace reinforce them rather than undermine them. And the absence of a central political mechanism for the world-economy makes it very difficult to intrude counteracting forces to the maldistribution of rewards.

Expansion of Core and Periphery Differences

Hence, the ongoing process of a world-economy tends to expand the economic and social gaps among its varying areas in the very process of its development. One factor that tends to mask this fact is that the process of development of a world-economy brings about technological advances which make it possible to expand the boundaries of a world-economy. In this case, particular regions of the world may change their structural role in the world-economy, to their advantage, even though the disparity of reward between different sectors of the world-economy as a whole may be simultaneously widening. It is in order to observe this crucial phenomenon clearly that we have insisted on the distinction between a peripheral area of a given world-economy and the external arena of the world-economy. The external arena of one century often becomes the periphery of the next—or its semiperiphery. But then too core-states can become semiperipheral and semiperipheral ones peripheral.

While the advantages of the core-states have not ceased to expand throughout the history of the modern world-system, the ability of a particular state to remain in the core sector is not beyond challenge. The hounds are ever to the hares for the position of top dog. Indeed, it may well be that in this kind of system it is not structurally possible to avoid, over a long period of historical time, a circulation of the elites in the sense that the particular country that is dominant at a given time tends to be replaced in this role sooner or later by another country.

We have insisted that the modern world-economy is, and only can be, a capitalist world-economy. It is for this reason that we have rejected the appellation of "feudalism" for the various forms of capitalist agriculture based on coerced labor which grow up in a world-economy. Furthermore, although this has not been discussed it is for this same reason that we will regard with great circumspection and prudence the claim that there exist in the twentieth century socialist national economies within the framework of the world-economy (as opposed to socialist movements controlling certain state-machineries within the world-economy).

If world-systems are the only real social systems (other than truly isolated subsistence economies), then it must follow that the emergence, consolidation, and political roles of classes and status groups must be appreciated as elements of this *world*-system. And in turn it follows that one of the key elements in analyzing a class or a status-group is not only the state of its self-consciousness but the geographical scope of its self-definition. . . .

Class in the World-System

The European world-economy of the sixteenth century tended overall to be a one-class system. It was the dynamic forces profiting from economic expansion and the capitalist system, especially those in the core-areas, who tended to be class-conscious, that is to operate within the political arena as a group defined primarily by their common role in the economy. This common role was in fact defined somewhat broadly from a twentieth-century perspective. It included persons who were farmers, merchants, and industrialists. Individual entrepreneurs often moved back and forth between these activities in any case, or combined them. The crucial distinction was between these men, whatever their occupation, principally oriented to obtaining profit in the world market, and the others not so oriented.

The "others" fought back in terms of their status privileges—those of the traditional aristocracy, those which small farmers had derived from the feudal system, those resulting from guild monopolies that were outmoded. Under the cover of cultural similarities, one can often weld strange alliances. Those strange alliances can take a very activist form and force the political centers to take account of them. . . .

The capitalist strata formed a class that survived and gained *droit de cité*, but did not yet triumph in the political arena.

The evolution of the state machineries reflected precisely this uncertainty. Strong states serve the interests of some groups and hurt those of others. From however the standpoint of the world-system as a whole, if there is to be a multitude of political entities (that is, if the system is not a world-empire), then it cannot be the case that all these entities be equally strong. For if they were, they would be in the position of blocking the effective operation of transnational economic entities whose locus were in another state. It would then follow that the world division of labor would be impeded, the world-economy decline, and eventually the world-system fall apart.

It also cannot be that *no* state machinery is strong. For in such a case, the capitalist strata would have no mechanisms to protect their interests, guaranteeing their property rights, assuring various monopolies, spreading losses among the larger population, etc.

It follows then that the world-economy develops a pattern where state structures are relatively strong in the core areas and relatively weak in the periphery. Which areas play which roles is in many ways accidental. What is necessary is that in some areas the state machinery be far stronger than in others. . . .

The mark of the modern world is the imagination of its profiteers and the counter-assertiveness of the oppressed. Exploitation and the refusal to accept exploitation as either inevitable or just constitute the continuing antinomy of the modern era, joined together in a dialectic which has far from reached its climax in the twentieth century.

Technology Promotes Social Change

GERHARD LENSKI, JEAN LENSKI, AND PATRICK NOLAN

Defining subsistence technology as information needed to produce food and energy, sociologists Jean and Gerhard Lenski and Patrick Nolan maintain that the state of this technology limits the size and development of societies. Advances in subsistence technology (the means societies use to produce food and protection from the elements) encourage other technological developments as well. Cultural beliefs and values shape and guide technological choices. This viewpoint agrees with Spencer that the fittest societies are naturally selected and particularly those with more advanced military technology, and concurs with Hawley on the importance of contact with other societies. Like Wallerstein, this viewpoint notes that more technologically advanced countries dominate the world system. Unlike the others, however, this viewpoint considers growth and development within societies and in the world system, and insists that technology is the basis for all change.

1. How do the authors define technology? Which kind of technology is most important to change and why?
2. Concerning change, how does the influence of technology compare with the influence of ideology?
3. Are wars and violence necessary to social change?

■ ■ ■

Most societies changed little during the course of their existence. Moreover, most of the changes that occurred were of little importance—gradual changes in the pronunciation of words, minor alterations in the content of rituals and legends, changes in etiquette, and so on.

Occasionally, however, more significant changes have occurred. Some societies have grown substantially. Some have shifted from a nomadic way of life to permanent settlements in villages, and some have shifted from a predominantly rural mode of life to a predominantly urban one. Such changes have usually been accompanied by important changes in social organization—substantial increases in organizational complexity, marked increases in the division of labor, and significant increases in social inequality. In short, some societies have experienced a process of substantial growth and development while others have not.

How can we explain such a profound difference in the experience of societies? . . .

Technology's Role in Societal Growth and Development

Technology is that part of a society's store of cultural information that is used to transform the resources of the biophysical environment into the material products its members need or desire. *Subsistence* technology is the most critical part of this store of information, since it is information used to produce the food and other sources of energy on which all of the activities of a society ultimately depend. Without energy, not even thinking or planning are possible. Thus, it is not surprising that *an advance in subsistence technology is a necessary precondition for a significant increase in the size and complexity of a society.*

Societies that depend on hunting and gathering as their chief means of subsistence cannot sustain populations nearly as large as those that depend on farming; and those that depend on slash-and-burn horticulture, a more primitive method of farming, cannot sustain populations as large as those that depend on plow agriculture. These differences in the limits set on the size of a society by its subsistence technology are matched by differences in the limits set on other aspects of societal development, such as the extent of the division of labor, the degree of social inequality, the size and complexity of communities, the wealth of the society and its standard of living, and the power of the society over its biophysical environment and over other societies. In short, *technology defines the limits of what is possible for a society.*

Within the range of options made possible by its technology, a society's choices are often influenced by the relative economic costs of the various alternatives. China's technology, for example, makes the production of automobiles and the construction of a highway system *possible*, but its decision makers have opted instead for less costly solutions to their society's transportation needs: mass public transport and private bicycles. In a world in which resources are never sufficient to meet all of the demands for goods and services, differences in cost can never be ignored by societies, and they are compelled to adopt one of the less expensive solutions much of the time. Thus, in addition to determining the limits of the possible for a society, *technology also affects the choices that are made by influencing the costs of various alternatives.*

Advances in a society's subsistence technology are also important because *they stimulate advances in other kinds of technology.* For example, advances in subsistence technology tend to be accompanied or followed by advances in other productive technologies and in the technologies of transportation, communication, and defense, all of which contribute to societal growth and development (see Figure 1).

Technology's critical role in societal growth and development is not surprising when we consider that a society's tools and machines are, in effect, the functional equivalent of improvements in the basic organs with which its members are endowed—eyes, ears, voice box, arms, legs, brain, nervous system, and the rest. Microscopes, telescopes, and television all

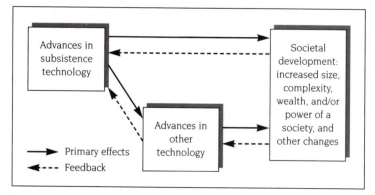

FIGURE 1 Model of the effects of advances in subsistence technology on other technologies and on societal development.

extend the range of our vision, just as telephones and radios extend the range of our hearing, and bicycles, automobiles, and airplanes increase our mobility. Where technological advances have occurred, they have enabled the members of societies to act as if they had acquired a new and improved genetic heritage—improved sight, more acute hearing, new powers of locomotion, and so forth. Thus, technological advances—especially advances in subsistence technology—are functionally equivalent to the important kinds of changes that occur in the course of biological evolution.

One important feature of the process of societal development that should not be overlooked is indicated by the feedback loops shown in Figure 1. Advances in subsistence technology stimulate advances in other technologies and lead to growth in the size and complexity of a society. But these developments, once they have occurred, usually increase the probability of further advances in subsistence technology. Population growth, for example, increases the number of potential innovators and, although few individuals ever make an invention or discovery of practical value, the greater the number of potential innovators in a society, the greater tends to be the rate at which innovations occur. Thus, as this example suggests, *once the process of societal development is set in motion, it tends to become self-sustaining.* While this is not inevitable, the probabilities of continued development clearly increase.

Societal growth and development, while advantageous to societies in many ways, are not unmixed blessings. They create new problems and these often lead to changes that many members of society would prefer not to make—changes in beliefs and values, changes in patterns of social organization, changes in institutional arrangements. Among preliterate societies, for example, technological advance often leads to population growth, and population growth necessitates changes in social organization. Such societies must choose either to split up into smaller independent groups in order to preserve their traditional kin-based system of governance, or to remain united but adopt a more authoritarian political system that is dominated by a small elite minority.

Ideology's Role in Societal Growth and Development

Whenever its technology presents it with a range of options, a society's beliefs and values—the core elements of ideology—always come into play. These often have little or no effect on societal growth and development, as when people choose one style of clothing in preference to another, one form of entertainment rather than another, or even one form of marriage over another. Sometimes, however, ideologies do have a substantial effect, as when they dispose people to accept and even welcome change or, conversely, to view it negatively. Western capitalism, for example, is far more supportive of new ideas and innovation of all kinds than is Islamic fundamentalism.

When the beliefs and values involved are felt to be sufficiently important, a society may reject the most economic solution to its needs in favor of a solution that is ideologically preferable. The United States, for example, has chosen to make private automobiles and an extensive system of superhighways a major part of its solution to its transportation needs, reflecting, at least in part, the individualism of its members and their desire for ease and freedom of movement.

Ideologically based decisions that affect a society's basic institutions may have extremely grave consequences. In eastern Europe, for example, countless decisions by Communist leaders over the years eventually led to a political and economic crisis of such proportions that the members of these societies rose up in mass revolt. And in a number of Third World societies, deeply ingrained beliefs about the value of large families have resulted in such high rates of population growth that it has been virtually impossible to improve living conditions for the majority of people.

Since one of the important consequences of technological advance is that it increases the range of options available to societies and their members, such advance leads to greater scope for the exercise of beliefs and values. Advanced societies today have far more choices available to them than societies of the past, and they are much freer to apply diverse ideologies in making their decisions. This does not guarantee happy results, of course, as the bitter experiences of Nazi Germany and the Soviet Union remind us. . . .

Change in the World System of Societies

The key to the major changes that have occurred in the world system of societies in the last 10,000 years is the process of intersocietal selection that has drastically reduced the number of societies. Were it not for this process, in which the units that survive (or become extinct) are entire societies, human life would not have changed nearly as rapidly as it has.

This process of selection presupposed the existence of differences among societies. Such differences were inevitable once the human population began to spread out geographically and occupy new and different kinds of environments. Chance also contributed to the process of societal differentiation, so that even when two societies confronted similar environmental challenges, they did not respond in exactly the same way. Differences in vocabulary provide a good example of this: even when all societies were confronted with identical experiences, such as birth and death, or the differences between males and females, they created different symbols to represent them. More important still, different beliefs developed to explain and interpret these experiences, and varied norms evolved to guide behavioral responses.

Not all the differences that have developed among societies have been equally important from the standpoint of intersocietal selection. Differences that influenced societal growth and development have been especially important, because *soci-*

eties that have grown in size and developed in complexity and military power have been much more likely to survive and transmit their cultures and institutional patterns than societies that have preserved traditional social and cultural patterns and minimized innovation (see Figure 2).

The reasons for this are obvious. To survive, societies must be able to defend their populations and territories against a variety of threats. These include the ravages of epidemics, natural disasters of other kinds, and, above all, threats from other societies. One only need consider the history of the United States, Canada, Australia, Brazil, or the Soviet Union to see what happens to smaller and less developed indigenous societies (i.e., the American Indians, the Australian aborigines, and various tribal groups in Siberia and Soviet Asia) when they compete for territory with larger and more developed societies. Larger societies have greater manpower and can more easily absorb military casualties. In addition, their more advanced technology has military applications, so that their soldiers have more deadly weapons, better logistical support, and greater mobility. Finally, their more complex patterns of social organization can easily be adapted to military needs and this, too, provides an important competitive advantage. Thus, while it would be a mistake to suppose that more developed societies always prevail over their less developed rivals, the odds are strongly in their favor.

Intersocietal selection is not always a violent process. Sometimes societies collapse simply because of insufficient support from their members. This is especially likely to occur when a less developed society comes into contact with one that is much more highly developed. Many members of the less developed society become impressed with the wealth and power of the more advanced society and either migrate to it or begin to adopt its customs. If these tendencies become widespread, the institutional fabric of the less developed society begins to fray and a process of societal disintegration begins. There are a number of well-documented cases of this in India, where primitive tribes in the hill country have simply disintegrated and their former members have been absorbed into Indian society. . . .

Because technologically advanced societies have had the advantage in this process of intersocietal selection, *their characteristics have increasingly come to be the characteristics of the world*

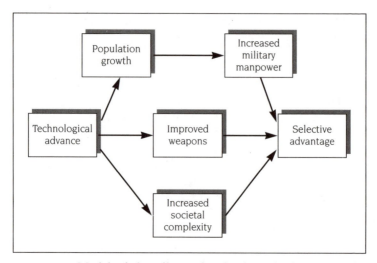

FIGURE 2 Model of the effects of technological advance on the process of intersocietal selection.

system as a whole. Thus, because technologically advanced societies tend to be larger than other societies, the average size of societies has been increasing for the last 10,000 years. Similarly, because technologically advanced societies are structurally more complex than other societies, the trend in the world system has been in the direction of increasingly complex societies. . . .

There is, of course, nothing inevitable or unalterable about these trends. A number of factors could disrupt them. For example, a deadly new disease could sweep through human societies and, in a short period of time, reverse most of the trends of the last 10,000 years. The Black Plague of the fourteenth century had this effect in a number of societies, and it is not inconceivable that something comparable could happen on a global scale. An unpredictable catastrophe involving the biophysical environment could also reverse the trends of history, as could a war fought with modern military technology. Both nuclear and biochemical warfare have the potential for producing a global catastrophe, and there is no technological antidote for either. Ecological-evolutionary theory clearly provides no grounds for complacency regarding the future.

Although we cannot predict the future, we can say that, so

far, the process of intersocietal selection has favored technologically advanced societies. Like the old game of musical chairs, it has eliminated first one, then another, of the less developed societies. The result is a world system that, with the passage of time, increasingly consists of what were once the exceptions—innovative and developing societies.

By now it is clear that *sociocultural evolution is the process of change and development in human societies that results from cumulative growth in their stores of cultural information*. Although sociocultural evolution is an extraordinarily complex phenomenon, it is easier to understand once we recognize that it includes both continuity and change.

FOR FURTHER DISCUSSION

Chapter 1

1. In what two ways does Dahrendorf's coercion theory follow Marx's ideas? How is coercion theory similar to structural-functional theory?
2. Parsons' structural-functionalism uses basic concepts from both Durkheim and Weber. Explain how Parsons uses concepts from each work and how he would differ from each.
3. Of the viewpoints in the first chapter, Mead's most closely represents the symbolic interaction perspective. Which two other viewpoints in this chapter present concepts compatible with this micro perspective? How so?

Chapter Two

1. Do you think your biological heredity or your social environment more strongly influences your own social behavior? Explain.
2. In what three ways does social structure, as illustrated by status and role, influence your social behavior today?
3. On what recent occasion have you engaged in an exchange transaction with someone? When (and how) did you last conform to group behavior? Have you managed any impressions lately? Did all these occasions involve rewards and/or punishments? Do you find exchange, conformity, or audience influence to be strongest?

Chapter Three

1. In your own experience, do people talk about social class? If so, what do they say? If inequality benefits society as Davis and Moore claim, why would people avoid discussing class (in discussions similar to those about such topics as patriotism or family values)?
2. Do minorities (including women) have a disadvantage in all three environments Warner and his colleagues mention—economic, religious, and cultural? Why or why not?

Chapter Four

1. Friedrich Engels, Karl Marx's collaborator, wrote about the traditional fixed family roles that Parsons and Bales describe. What do you suppose he said? Put another way, how would a conflict theorist approach traditional family roles?
2. What historical and current events illustrate the argument that religion divides society? Which events support the opposing argument that religion unites society?
3. What characteristics of the workplace qualify it as a democracy? In what ways is the workplace not democratic? In his article on oligarchy, Michels addresses political power. Does oligarchy apply to the workplace?

Chapter Five

1. Which of the five social change theories can account for the transition from hunter-gatherer to horticultural or pastoral society? For the transition to agrarian society?
2. Which theory or theories best explain(s) change within a society?
3. Do societies ever resist technological change? How do they resist? Does technological change always benefit a society? Explain.

Suggestions for Further Reading

Chapter 1

Works that explore Marx's and Dahrendorf's viewpoints:

Boswell, Terry and William J. Dixon. 1993. "Marx's Theory of Rebellion: A Cross-National Analysis." *American Sociological Review* 58:681-702.

Bottomore, T. B. and Maxmillien Rubel. 1963. *Karl Marx: Selected Writings in Sociology and Social Philosophy.* London: C. A. Watts.

Hazelrigg, Lawrence. 1972. "Class, Property and Authority: Dahrendorf's Critique of Marx's Theory of Class." *Social Forces* 50:473-87.

Tucker, Robert C., editor. 1972. *The Marx-Engels Reader.* New York: W. W. Norton.

Weingart, Peter. 1969. "Beyond Parsons? A Critique of Ralf Dahrendorf's Conflict Theory." *Social Forces* 48:151-65.

Works that explore Durkheim's viewpoint:

Brealt, Kevin D. 1986. "Suicide in America: A Test of Durkheim's Theory of Religious and Family Integration, 1933-1980." *American Journal of Sociology* 92:628-56.

Durkheim, Emile. 1951 [1897]. *Suicide.* New York: Free Press.

———. 1964 [1895]. *The Rules of Sociological Method.* New York: Free Press.

Jones, Robert Alun. 1985. *Emile Durkheim.* Beverly Hills: Sage.

Pope, Whitney. 1975. "Durkheim as Functionalist." *Sociological Quarterly* 16:361-79.

Works that explore Weber's viewpoint:

DiMaggio, Paul J. and Walter W. Powell. 1983. "The Iron Cage Revisited: Institutional Isomorphism and Collective Rationality in Organizational Fields." *American Sociological Review* 48:147-60.

Jackson, Elton F., William S. Fox, and Harry J. Crockett, Jr. 1970. "Religion and Occupational Achievement." *American Sociological Review* 35:48-52.

Scaff, L. A. 1981. "Max Weber and Robert Michels." *American Journal of Sociology* 86:1269-86.

Udy, Stanley H., Jr. 1959. "'Bureaucracy' and 'Rationality' in Weber's Theory." *American Sociological Review* 24:791-5.

Weber, Max. 1968 [1921]. *Economy and Society.* 3 vols. Totowa, NJ: Bedminster Press.

Works that explore Simmel's viewpoint:

Blau, Peter and Joseph E. Schwartz. 1984. *Crosscutting Social Circles: A Macrostructural Theory of Intergroup Relations.* Orlando: Academic Press.

Coser, Lewis A. 1977. "Georg Simmel's Neglected Contributions to the Sociology of Women." *Signs* 2:869-76.

Granovetter, Mark S. 1973. "The Strength of Weak Ties." *American Journal of Sociology* 78:1360-80.

McPherson, J. Miller, Pamela A. Popielarz, and Sonja Drobnic. 1992. "Social Networks and Organizational Dynamics." *American Sociological Review* 57:153-70.

Turner, Bryan S. 1983. "Simmel, Rationalization and the Sociology of Money." *The Sociological Review* 34:93-114.

Works that explore Mead's viewpoint:

Byers, Bryan, editor. 1993. *Readings in Social Psychology: Perspective and Method.* Boston: Allyn and Bacon.

Fine, Gary Alan and Sherryl Kleinman. 1986. "Interpreting the Sociological Classics: Can There Be a 'True' Meaning of Mead?" *Symbolic Interaction* 9:126-46.

Hewitt, John P. 1991. *Self and Society: A Symbolic Interactionist Social Psychology.* Fifth edition. Boston: Allyn and Bacon.

McPhail, Clark and Cynthia Rexroat. 1979. "Mead vs. Blumer." *American Sociological Review* 44:449-67.

Turner, Jonathan H. 1982. "A Note on G. H. Mead's Behavioristic Theory of Social Structure." *Journal for the Theory of Social Behavior* 12:213-22.

Works that explore Parson's viewpoint:

Alexander, Jeffrey. 1985. *Neofunctionalism.* Beverly Hills: Sage.

Coleman, James. 1986. "Social Theory, Social Research, and a Theory of Action." *American Journal of Sociology* 91:1309-35.

Colomy, Paul. 1986. "Recent Developments in the Functionalist Approach to Change." *Sociological Focus* 19:139-58.

Liska, A. E. and B. D. Warner. 1991. "Functions of Crime: A Paradoxical Process." *American Journal of Sociology* 96:1441-63.

Scuilli, D. and D. Gerstein. 1985. "Social Theory and Talcott Parsons in the 1980s." *Annual Review of Sociology* 11:369-87.

CHAPTER 2

Bandura, Albert, Dorothea Ross, and Sheila Ross. 1963. "Imitation of Film-Mediated Aggressive Models." *Journal of Abnormal and Social Psychology* 66:3-11.

Biddle, Bruce J. 1979. *Role Theory: Expectations, Identities, and Behaviors.* New York: Academic Press.

Blau, Peter. 1964. *Exchange and Power in Social Life.* New York: Wiley.

———. 1980. "A Fable About Social Structure." *American Sociological Review* 83:26-54.

Emerson, Richard. 1981. "Social Exchange Theory." Pp. 30-65 in *Social Psychology: Sociological Perspectives,* edited by Morris Rosenberg and Ralph H. Turner. New York: Basic Books.

Fausto-Sterling, Anne. 1985. *Myths of Gender: Biological Theories About Women and Men.* New York: Basic Books.

301

Fisher, A. 1992. "Sociobiology: Science or Ideology?" *Society* 29:67-79.

Gillespie, Joanna B. 1980. "The Phenomenon of the Public Wife: An Exercise in Goffman's Impression Management." *Symbolic Interaction* 3:109-25.

Haas, J. and W. Shaffir. 1982. "Taking on the Role of Doctor: A Dramaturgical Analysis of Professionalization." *Symbolic Interaction* 5: 187-203.

Homans, George C. 1964. "Bringing Men Back In." *American Sociological Review* 29:809-818.

Kelley, Harold and John Thibaut. 1978. *Interpersonal Relations: A Theory of Interdependence.* New York: Wiley.

Kollock, Peter and Jodi O'Brien. 1994. *The Production of Reality: Essays and Readings in Social Psychology.* Thousand Oaks, CA: Pine Forge Press.

Mayhew, Bruce H. 1981. "Structuralism vs. Individualism: Part II, Ideological and Other Obfuscations." *Social Forces* 59:627-48.

Mayhew, Bruce H. and Roger L. Levinger. 1976. "On the Emergence of Oligarchy in Human Interaction." *American Journal of Sociology* 81:1017-49.

Reskin, Barbara F. 1988. "Bringing the Men Back In: Sex Differentiation and the Devaluation of Women's Work." *Gender and Society* 2:58-81.

Skvoretz, John and David Willer. 1991. "Power and Exchange Networks: Setting and Structural Variations." *Social Psychology Quarterly* 3:224-38.

Snow, David A., Louis A. Zurcher, and Robert Peters. 1981. "Victory Celebrations as Theater: A Dramaturgical Approach to Crowd Behavior." *Symbolic Interaction* 4:21-42.

South, Scott J. and Steven F. Messner. 1986. "Structural Determinants of Intergroup Association: Interracial Marriage and Crime." *American Journal of Sociology* 91:1409-30.

CHAPTER 3

Beeghley, Leonard. 1989. *The Structure of Social Stratification in the United States.* Boston: Allyn and Bacon. (Section on Monopoly on pages 71-72).

Blau, Peter M. and O. D. Duncan. 1967. *The American Occupational Structure.* New York: Wiley.

Brown, J. Larry. 1987. "Hunger in the U.S." *Scientific American* 256:37-41.

Casper, Lynne M., Sara S. McLanahan, and Irwin Garfinkel. 1994. "The Gender-Poverty Gap." *American Sociological Review* 59:594-605.

Clarke, Kevin. 1993. "Growing Hunger." *Utne Reader* November/December 1993 60:63-68.

Della-Fave, Richard. 1980. "The Meek Shall Not Inherit the Earth." *American Sociological Review* 45:955-71.

Dewart, Janet, editor. 1988. *The State of Black Americans 1988.* New York: National Urban League.

Dollars & Sense. "U-Turn on Equality: The Puzzle of Middle Class Decline." May 1986:11-3.

Ellwood, David T. 1988. *Poor Support: Poverty in the American Family.* New York:

Basic Books.

Basic Books.

Ferraro, Geraldine. 1985. *Ferraro, My Story*. New York: Bantam Books.

Harrington, Michael. 1984. *The New American Poverty*. New York: Penguin Books.

Jacobs, Jerry A. 1989. *Revolving Doors: Sex Segregation and Women's Careers*. Stanford, CA: Stanford University Press.

Kerbo, Harold R. 1983. *Social Stratification and Inequality: Class Conflict in the United States*. New York: McGraw-Hill.

Piven, Frances Fox and Richard A. Cloward. 1971. *Regulating the Poor: The Functions of Public Welfare*. New York: Vintage Books.

Reich, Robert B. 1989. "Why the Rich Are Getting Richer and the Poor Poorer." *The New Republic* May 1.

Ritzer, George. 1988. *Sociological Theory*. Second edition. New York: Alfred A. Knopf.

Tumin, Melvin M. 1953. "Some Principles of Stratification: A Critical Analysis." *American Sociological Review* 18:378-94.

Wall Street Journal. "Special Report: The Corporate Woman: The Glass Ceiling." March 24, 1986.

Wilson, William Julius. 1978. *The Declining Significance of Race*. Chicago: University of Chicago Press.

———. 1987. *The Truly Disadvantaged*. Chicago: University of Chicago Press.

Wright, Eric Olin, D. Hacken, C. Costello, and J. Sprague. 1987. "The Transformation of the American Class Structure." *American Sociological Review* 47:709-26.

Wright, Richard. 1992 [1940]. *Native Son*. New York: HarperPerennial.

CHAPTER 4

Research on marriage and family

Bales, Robert F. and A. P. Hare. 1965. "Diagnostic Use of the Interaction Profile." *Journal of Social Psychology* 67:239-58.

Bielby, William T. and Denise D. Bielby. 1989. "Family Ties: Balancing Commitments to Work and Family in Dual Earner Households." *American Sociological Review* 54:776-89.

Blumstein, Philip and Pepper Schwartz. 1983. *American Couples*. New York: William Morrow.

Booth, Alan, editor. 1991. *Contemporary Families*. Minneapolis: National Council on Family Relations.

England, Paula and George Farkas. 1986. *Households, Employment, and Gender: A Social, Economic, and Demographic View*. New York: Aldine.

Gerstel, Naomi and Harriet E. Gross, editors. *Families and Work*. Philadelphia: Temple University Press, 1987.

Goldscheider, Frances K. and Linda J. Waite. 1991. *New Families, No Families? The Transformation of the American Home.* Berkeley: University of California.

Hochschild, Arlie. 1989. *The Second Shift: Working Parents and the Revolution at Home.* New York: Viking.

Shelton, Beth Anne. 1992. *Women, Men and Time.* New York: Greenwood Press.

West, Candace and Don H. Zimmerman. 1981. "Doing Gender." *Gender and Society* 1:125-51.

Research on religion

Ammerman, Nancy Tatom. 1987. *Bible Believers: Fundamentalists in the Modern World.* New Brunswick: Rutgers University Press.

Bellah, Robert N. and Phillip E. Hammond. 1980. *Varieties of Civil Religion.* New York: Harper and Row.

Durkheim, Emile. 1965 [1912]. *The Elementary Forms of Religious Life.* New York: The Free Press.

Malinowski, Bronislaw. 1948. *Magic, Science, and Religion.* New York: The Free Press.

Niebuhr, H. Richard. 1929. *The Social Sources of Denominationalism.* New York: Henry Holt.

Stark, Rodney and W. S. Bainbridge. 1987. *A Theory of Religion.* New York: Peter Lang.

Troeltsch, Ernst. 1931 [1912]. *Social Teachings of the Christian Churches.* New York: Macmillan.

Weber, Max. 1964 [1922]. *The Sociology of Religion.* Boston: Beacon Press.

Wilson, Bryan. 1982. *Religion in Sociological Perspective.* New York: Oxford University Press.

Wuthnow, Robert. 1988. *The Restructuring of American Religion.* Princeton, NJ: Princeton University Press.

Research on the polity and the economy

Barlett, Donald L. and James P. Steele. 1992. *America: What Went Wrong?* Kansas City: Andrews and McMeel.

Berger, Peter. 1992. "The Uncertain Triumph of Democratic Capitalism." *Journal of Democracy* 3:7-17.

Blauner, Robert. 1964. *Alienation and Freedom.* Chicago: University of Chicago Press.

Braverman, Harry. 1974. *Labor and Monopoly Capital.* New York: Monthly Review Press.

Dahl, Robert A. 1989. *Democracy and Its Critics.* New Haven: Yale University Press.

Domhoff, G. William. 1983. *Who Rules America Now?* Englewood Cliffs, NJ: Prentice-Hall.

Lipset, Seymour Martin. 1994. "The Social Requisites of Democracy Revisited." *American Sociological Review* 59:1-22.

Orum, Anthony. 1989. *Introduction to Political Sociology: The Social Anatomy of the Body Politic.* Third edition. Englewood Cliffs, NJ: Prentice-Hall.

Riesman, David. 1961. *The Lonely Crowd.* New Haven: Yale University Press.

Weber, Max. 1947 [1925]. *The Theory of Social and Economic Organization.* New York: Oxford University Press.

CHAPTER 5

Applebaum, Richard P. 1970. *Theories of Social Change.* Chicago: Markham.

Bell, Daniel. 1989. "The Third Technological Revolution and Its Possible Socioeconomic Consequences." *Dissent,* Spring, 164-76.

Berger, Peter. 1976. *Pyramids of Sacrifice: Political Ethics and Social Change.* Garden City, NY: Anchor Books.

Caplow, Theodore. 1991. *American Social Trends.* New York: Harcourt Brace Jovanovich.

Chirot, Daniel. 1986. *Social Change in the Modern Era.* Orlando: Harcourt Brace Jovanovich.

Dublin, Max. 1991. *Futurehype: The Tyranny of Prophecy.* New York: Dutton.

Fischer, Claudes and Glenn R. Carroll. 1988. "Telephone and Automobile Diffusion in the United States, 1902-1937." *American Journal of Sociology* 93:1153-78.

Gamson, William. 1975. *The Strategy of Social Protest.* Homewood, IL: Dorsey.

Goode, Erich. 1992. *Collective Behavior.* Fort Worth: Harcourt Brace Jovanovich.

Kornhauser, William. 1959. *The Politics of Mass Society.* New York: Free Press.

Lofland, John. 1985. *Protest: Studies of Collective Behavior and Social Movements.* New Brunswick: Transaction.

So, Alvin Y. 1990. *Social Change and Development: Modernization, Dependency, and World System Theories.* Newbury Park: Sage.

Sorokin, Pitirim. 1941. *The Crisis of Our Age.* New York: Dutton.

Tarrow, Sidney. 1988. "National Politics and Collective Action: Recent Theory and Research in Western Europe and the United States." *Annual Review of Sociology* 14:421-40.

Toennies, Ferdinand. 1963. [1887]. *Community and Society (Gemeinschaft und Gesellschaft).* New York: Harper and Row.

Toffler, Alvin. 1981. *The Third Wave.* New York: Bantam Books.

Vannoy-Hiller, Dana and William W. Philliber. 1989. *Equal Partners: Successful Women in Marriage.* Newbury Park: Sage.

Wallerstein, Immmanuel. 1991. *Geopolitics and Geoculture: Essays on the Changing World-System.* New York: Cambridge University Press.

Index

Allport's experiment on, 130, 133
Asch's experiment on, 128,
130-32, 133
distress caused by, 132
reasons for, 124-25, 133
Sherif's experiment on, 127-29,
132-33
variation within subcultures,
191-92

oligarchy, 228-35
Olson, David, 210
opinion polls, 171-72, 173-74
organization, social, 110-11
communication in, 115
structuralist vs. individualist, 113-14
see also network, social

Park, Robert, 168
Parsons, Talcott, 59, 70, 84, 153, 184, 197
politicians, 238, 240-44
politics
activism in
by African Americans, 170-71
attitudes toward, 152
ineffectual, 187-88
by proletariat, 26-27, 233
apathy toward, 148
centralized system of, 22
women's subordination in, 179
see also democracy
population
growth, technology promotes, 293
and natural selection, 259-65
structuralist study of, 111
Third World, 294
power
defined, 73, 160
held by elites, 236-44
multiple sources of, 161, 165
within marriage, 208, 211, 212, 213
see also authority
prejudice, 186-92
see also discrimination; racism
prestige, 160, 162-65
primitive societies
compared to advanced, 30-31, 33,
163, 164
sects in, 219
studies on
conformity, 125
race and culture, 170
proletariat
modern economy exploits, 24-26
political organizing of, 233
revolution against bourgeoisie, 26-27
Protestantism, 36-37
beliefs about wealth, 38
work ethic of, 37
opposes idleness, 39
and racism, 173

psychology, 119, 120
behavioral, 121, 122-23, 125
belief in shared values, 123-24
racist theories, 168, 170
social, 111, 112
Puritan beliefs, 38-42

Quakers, 38, 40, 42, 220

racism
in attitudes about intelligence,
168, 170, 171
biology's promotion of, 167-68
is no longer socially acceptable,
171-72
persistence of, 173-74
scientists' rejection of, 169-71
sociology's promotion of
stereotypes, 168
typology of, 186-92
rational-choice model, 121-22
religion, 221, 226
beliefs unite people, 224-25, 227
ceremonies' purpose, 225
civil, 221-22
sanctions male authority, 211-12
sects in, 214-20
social role of, 161-62
and status, 164-65
role
of authority, 73-74
defined, 76, 101-102
unequal, leads to conflict, 73
see also family; men; status;
women
Roman society, 19, 216
rules
children's interest in, 55
conformity to, 124-25
see also norms

schools
class distinctions in, 146-47,
149-50, 177
racial integration in, 172-73, 174
science
impact of on popular culture, 169
racist theories of, 166-68
rejection of, 169-71
Sears, David, 173, 174
sects, 215-16
charismatic leaders of, 218-20
in Christianity, 216-19
importance to sociologists, 220
segregation, 167, 172-73
sexuality
is cultural and physiological, 61
Kinsey's research on, 206-207
Puritan beliefs about, 39-40
spouses view differently,
206-207

310

312